The Cantonists

Jewish Boys in the Russian Military, 1827–1856

Touro University Press Books

Series Editors
Michael A. Shmidman, PhD (Touro University, New York)
Simcha Fishbane, PhD (Touro University, New York)

The Cantonists

Jewish Boys in the Russian Military, 1827–1856

Josef Mendelevich

Translated by Rachelle Emanuel

NEW YORK
2025

Library of Congress Cataloging-in-Publication Data

Names: Mendelevich, Iosif, author. | Emanuel, Rachelle, translator.
Title: The cantonists : Jewish boys in the Russian military, 1827–1856 /
   Josef Mendelevich ; translated by Rachelle Emanuel.
Other titles: σanṗonisḋm. English
Description: New York : Touro University Press, 2025. | Series: Touro
   University Press books | Includes bibliographical references.
Identifiers: LCCN 2024032800 (print) | LCCN 2024032801 (ebook) | ISBN
   9798887196817 (hardback) | ISBN 9798887196824 (pdf) | ISBN 9798887196831
   (epub)
Subjects: LCSH: Cantonists--Russia. | Jews--Russia--History--19th century.
   | Jewish children--Russia--History--19th century. | Child
   soldiers--Russia--History--19th century. | Russia--Armed
   Forces--Recruiting, enlistment, etc--History--19th century. |
   Russia--History--Nicholas I, 1825-1855.
Classification: LCC DS134.84 M3613 2025 (print) | LCC DS134.84 (ebook) |
   DDC 355.0083/0947--dc23/eng/20240904
LC record available at https://lccn.loc.gov/2024032800
LC ebook record available at https://lccn.loc.gov/2024032801

Copyright © Touro University Press, 2025
ISBN 9798887196838 (paperback)
ISBN 9798887196824 (pdf)
ISBN 9798887196831 (epub)

Book design by PHi Business Solutions
Cover design by Ivan Grave

Published by Touro University Press and Academic Studies Press
Typeset, printed, and distributed by Academic Studies Press

Touro University Press
Michael A. Shmidman and Simcha Fishbane, Editors
3 Times Square, Room 654,
New York, NY 10036, USA
press@touro.edu

Academic Studies Press
1007 Chestnut St.
Newton, MA 02464, USA
press@academicstudiespress.com
www.academicstudiespress.com

Acknowledgements for the help and support in publishing the Hebrew edition
of this book go to
Professor Carmi Horowitz, former Rector of Machon Lander
Rabbi Nachman Kahane, author of *Mei Menuchot*

The Hebrew edition of this book was published with the generous support of
The America-Israel Cultural Foundation
Nadav Fund
and with the help of Nathan Sharansky

In Tribute to our Rebbe

Rabbi Dr. Aaron Rakeffet-Rothkoff

for his many decades of teaching Torah
and his friendship and support of
Rabbi Josef Mendelevich

"Be of the disciples of Aaron, loving peace and pursuing peace, loving your
fellow human beings, and drawing them near to Torah"
(Avot 1:12).

Cindy and Elliott Forgash
Rachma and Gedaliah Friedenberg
Steven Gross
Jacques Semmelman
Lois and Dr. Norman Sohn

Contents

Preface to the English Edition xiii
Foreword to the Hebrew Edition xv
   Shaul Stampfer, Rabbi Edward Sandrow
Introduction xvii

Cantonists Speak for Themselves 1
   1. The Tale of a Veteran Jewish Soldier, Chaim Merimzon 1
      Part 1 1
      Part 2 5
   2. From the Memories of an Ex-Cantonist 12
   3. The Story of a Cantonist in the Town of Arkhangel'sk 16
   4. Alexander Herzen, *My Past and Thoughts* 21
   5. The Story of the Cantonist Yaakov Son of Hirsch Hermanovitz 23

Part I   Forced Conscription of Jews: The Decree and Its Implementation 27
   1 Preparatory Measures for the Legislation of Compulsory Conscription of Jews 29
      A. Social and Sociological Motives 29
      B. Administrative Considerations 31
      C. Ideological Motives 34
      D. Economic Motives 38
      E. The Jews' Influence on the Development of the Conscription Law 41
   2 Who Was Tsar Nicholas I? 46
      A. The Influence of the Tsar on the Development of the Legislation 46
      B. Hatred of Jews 50
      C. The Army as a Supreme Value 52
   3 Changes in the Tsar's Policies during the Course of His Reign, 1825–1855 53
      A. Who Influenced the Tsar's Decisions? 53
      B. The 1840s: A Turning Point in the Treatment of the Jews 57

		C. Changes in the Russian Empire—a List of Events	58
		1. A List of Main Events Connected to the Conscription of Cantonists	58
		2. A Summary of Events in Chronological Order	63

Part II Implementation of the Conscription Law 65
    1 Community Preparations for the Implementation of the Decree 67
    2 The Statute 69
        A. The Text 69
        B. Order of Recruitment Procedures for the Civil Administration of the Province 74
        C. Procedure for the Civil Authority That Carries out the Recruitment 77
        D. Who Was Fit for Conscription and Who Was Exempt 79
    3 The Positions and Activities of the Community, Its Spiritual Leadership, and Its Members 81
        A. The Legal Status of the Community Institutions in Implementing the Conscription Law 81
        B. Changes in the Position of the Community Administration (*Kahal*) and the Relations between the *Kahal* and the Community Members 81
        C. The Struggle with the Authorities over the Status of the *Kahal* 83
        D. Activities of the *Kahal* in Relation to Jewish Conscription 84
        E. Was There Any Point in Passive Resistance 86
        F. International Efforts to Abolish the Conscription Decree 88
        G. The Jews' Immediate Response to the Conscription Decree 90
        H. The Position of Jewish Spiritual Leadership 92
    4 The Implementation of the Jewish Conscription Law 97
        A. How Many Soldiers Was It Possible to Enlist from the Jewish Community in Russia? 97
        B. Changes in the Recruitment Procedures among the Jews 98
        C. The Activity of the Draft Committees (Analysis of the Gendarmes' Report on the Regularity of the Conscription) 100
        D. The Method of "Comprehensive" Conscription 104
            1. The Revolt in Mstislaw 104
            2. Conscription in Berdychiv. Conscription as a Punitive Tool 106

		E. Jewish Conscription in the Mid-1850s, and the "Tithe" Decree of 1852	108
		F. The Struggle of Groups within the Community to Receive Exemptions	110
		G. The Army's Attitude towards Jewish Conscripts—an Analysis of the Sources	113
		H. Discrimination against Jewish Soldiers Who Did Not Convert	117
		1. Promotion of Jews	117
		2. Granting Rights to Jewish Paramedics	118
		3. Jewish soldiers in St. Petersburg, March 1847	120
		4. Nicholas I's Interest in the Jewish Soldiers	120
		5. Concerning Desertion of Jewish Conscripts	122
		I. Religious Life of Jewish Soldiers	123
		1. Religious Services for Jews in the Army. Documents, Analysis, Conclusions	123
		a. Religious Routine of Jewish Soldiers	123
		b. Kosher Slaughter	124
		c. The Decision of the Ruling Senate on the Exemption from Tax Payment on Slaughter of Cattle, etc., Granted to Jewish Soldiers, according to the Tsar's Ordinance	125
		2. Rabbis in the Army	126
		3. Sabbath and Festivals in the Army	129
Part III		The Cantonists	135
	1	Review of the Establishment of the Institution for Minors in the Russian Army. Description of Service Frameworks	137
	2	Military Training Units and Military Schools for Minors	142
		A. Recruitment and Absorption Procedures	142
		B. The Activity of the Abductors	146
		1. Chaim Merimzon's Testimony	147
		2. Nikolai Leskov, "Monastyrskii sad"	148
		3. Korobkov's Article	149
		4. Beilin's Memoirs	150
		C. Life in the Cantonist Units	152
		D. Studies of the Cantonists	157
		E. Living Conditions, Food Supply, Conditions of Service	159

	3	Social Aspects of the Cantonists' Lives	161
		A. Contact with Family	161
		B. Contact with the Local Jews	163
		C. Relationships among the Boys	169
		D. The Relationship between the Boys and Their Gentile Environment	170
	4	The Cantonists' Religious Life—Documents and Certificates	171
		A. Festivals	171
		B. Cantonists in Synagogues	172
Part IV		Coercion and Conversion Processes	179
	1	The Policy of Conversion: The Concept and Its Implementation	181
	2	Punishment and Pressure as Means of Coercion	191
	3	Criminal Constitutional Law as a Means of Coercion	195
	4	Group Dynamics	197
	5	Conversion on the Way	198
	6	Incentives	200
	7	Participation in Christian Rituals	202
	8	Missionary Instructional Literature	206
	9	Supervision of Conversion Methods	208
	10	The Jewish Boys' Resistance to Conversion	211
	11	Documents of Missionary Activity	215
	12	The Extent of Conversion	219
Part V		The Revolt of the Arkhangel'sk Half-Battalion of Military Cantonists	223
	1	The Reports	225
	2	Investigation Documents; Sailors' Testimonies	233
	3	Summary and the Decisions of the Investigation Committee	247
	4	Analysis and Conclusions	250
		A. Behavior on the Way to Arkhangel'sk	250
		B. Methods of Coercion	251
		C. Behavior of the Jews on the Base	251
		D. The Age of the Cantonists and the Cirumstances of Conversion	252
		E. How Did the Young People Come to Their Decision to Deny the Validity of Their Conversion?	253
		F. Echoes of the Opposition to Conversion in Kronshtadt	256

Part VI	The Abolishment of the Cantonist Decree	259
1	The Process of the Abolishment and Its Reasons	261
2	The Process of Dismantling the Cantonist Institution	263
3	Was It Alexander II Who Initiated the Reform in the Regulations on Jewish Conscription?	265
4	Legal Procedures against Those Who Returned to Judaism	271
Part VII	Conclusions and Miscellanea	275
1	Important Documents	277
2	The Efforts of the Jewish Communities to Ease the Cantonists' Conditions	278
3	Conclusions	289
4	Topics Raised in This Book That Merit Additional Discussion	296
5	Analysis of the Material Available for the Research and the Research Methods	297
	A. The Material at Our Disposal	297
	B. Materials for Further Research	299
6	"The Small Soldiers of the Large Empire"	300
Index		305

Preface to the English Edition

It is not an easy story to relate. In addition to the history of the Cantonists, this is the author's story.

In the 1960s I studied at the University in Riga. I finished four years of studying, and suddenly I was informed by the management of the State University in Riga, Latvia, that I was expelled from my studies. They didn't write the reason, but it was clear. In 1969 I applied to leave for the State of Israel.

In 1970, I and a group of Jewish students were arrested at the airport on the charge of attempting to flee illegally to Israel. During the Soviet regime there was no freedom to leave the country. Basically, there was no freedom in any manner concerning human rights.

I remember that when I was brought to prison, I asked a policeman if they would let me read books. The jailer told me: "They will give you books. You can apply to two universities." He was right. I sat in prison for almost 11 years – enough time to complete studies in two subjects and to do a post-doctoral degree.

When I was expelled from prison and the Soviet Union, thanks to demonstrations of millions of people all over the world, I was invited to attend a university and received a PhD Honoris Causa degree. I wanted to complete my studies, but I had to continue the struggle for the liberation of all the Jews of the USSR.

After the victory and the fall of the Iron Curtain that separated the USSR from the free world, I received an invitation from Mr. Matthias Adler, of blessed memory. He invited me to head a department for Russian speakers at Touro College in Jerusalem. At the same time as my work at Touro I completed graduate studies in the history of the people of Israel. Therefore, I now publish in English the fruit of the research I first completed at Touro College.

With this book, I express my gratitude to Professor Bernard Lander, of blessed memory, founding president of Touro College (now Touro University) who opened the Touro College Israel branch, to Mr. M. Adler, who invited me to work with him, to Professor Carmi Horowitz who advised me to pursue research on the subject of the history of Russian Jews in the nineteenth century and to Professor Shaul Stampfer who served as my adviser.

The book was published in Hebrew and since then it has been utilized by many researchers and scholars who deal with this field, on which there is limited academic scholarship.

I thank Touro University Press and the entire administration of Touro University, led by President Alan Kadish, and in particular Rabbi Dr. Simcha Fishbane, Rabbi Dr. Michael Shmidman, and Rabbi Moshe Krupka for facilitating the publication of the book in English. And last, but not least, my thanks go to Rabbi Aharon Rakeffet who did everything possible to enable the publication of the book in English.

Josef Mendelevich

Foreword to the Hebrew Edition

There are topics in the history of the Jewish people that have received much attention, and yet there are topics which, despite their importance, have not received the attention they deserve. The conscription of Jews to service in the tsarist army in the nineteenth century is certainly a topic whose significance cannot be disputed. The conscription caused fractures within Jewish society, broke down the Pale of Settlement, and was a sign of substantial change in the Russian authorities' policy toward the Jews. What began as the conscription of a small minority of the Jewish public ended, in the Soviet era, in much more extreme steps that influenced every single Jew who lived under their rule.

It is therefore interesting that, after a wave of research and publications at the end of the tsarist empire, and a few significant studies in the interbellum period, this topic has hardly been touched for fifty years—from the outbreak of the Second World War until a few years ago. But recently, Yohanan Petrovsky-Shtern in America published the important book *Jews in the Russian Army, 1827–1917: Drafted into Modernity*, while in Israel David Pur and Shimon Ram published their books (*Ha-Kantonistim be-re'i ha-sifrut ha-ivrit* and *Ha-Kantonistim: Al yeladim yehudim she-guysu la-tzava ha-russi be-me'a ha-19 veha-20*, respectively.) We are now privileged to see an additional publication in Hebrew: a comprehensive, deep study regarding the entire phenomenon, authored by our friend Yosef Mendelevich.

The reader will learn of the scope of the study from just a brief glance at the table of contents. What is perhaps less prominent is one of the items that make this study unique. Yosef Mendelevich has succeeded in researching, analyzing, and reaching very interesting conclusions regarding processes and motives among the authorities, while discussing in depth what was happening within the Jewish public. Few are the researchers capable of examining both the world of the initiators and that of the public on which they attempted to implement their plan. This approach, which seems to be self-understood and even simple, is deserving of admiration, as in practice, the matter is not so simple.

In retrospect, the process of conscription into the Russian army seems to be a turning point in the Jewish history of Eastern Europe. One of the substantial insights that the reader learns from this book is that, although the Jews of the time were very disturbed by the conscription decree, and made tremendous efforts to defer it, from the moment it was implemented, these efforts decreased significantly. There was an increase in the number of those who studied in the *batei midrash*, as Azriel Shochet and Motti Zalkin have shown, but in general the Jews did not make any methodical effort to help the miserable recruits. Several explanations have been given for this, but it demands more serious treatment.

Parallel to the question of the public response to conscription, it is important to note that even those destined for conscription tended to regard it as an unalterable decree. Indeed, anyone able to, went to the *batei midrash*, as those who studied were generally protected from conscription, but we don't find many young conscription candidates trying to escape abroad, or to Poland where there was no conscription. There certainly was no massive stream of entire families who left the empire as they tried to distance themselves from the danger. Even one hundred years later, at the time of the Soviet decrees, there were not many attempts of Torah-observant Jews to leave the Soviet Union. Perhaps there were too many difficulties, or perhaps they found solutions that seemed to be better.

As every good book, Yosef Mendelevich's work not only gives answers, but also leads us to new questions. The questions of the individual's responsibility, of holding on to values instead of going along with what is accepted and maintaining the existing situation, are existential questions today just as they were one hundred years ago. In addition, we meet in this book wonderful personalities who demonstrated commitment, loyalty to their values, and sensitivity to their fellow man. This does not prove that we will be privileged to have such figures in our generation, but there is yet hope.

Professor Shaul Stampfer, professor of East European Jewry,
Hebrew University of Jerusalem (emeritus)

Rabbi Edward Sandrow

Introduction

"Cantonists?[1] Those are the Jewish children who were seized by the Russian tsar and sent to the army with the intention of being forced to convert to Christianity. The youngsters did all they could, with much self-sacrifice, so as not to convert. What else can be said?" asks the reader who once listened inattentively to a lecture on the subject. And there are many others who do not know even that much.

Indeed, as we can say concerning any topic about which we have heard with half an ear, that we actually know nothing about it, so it is with the cantonists.

Why should we learn about the subject at all?

The historical period in question was a fateful one for the Jewish people, most of whom lived in Eastern Europe during the nineteenth century. It was during this period that the Vilna Gaon, the *Baal haTanya* (Rabbi Shneur Zalman of Liadi), Rabbi Nahman of Breslov, and Rabbi Haim of Volozhin lived, as well as many other great personalities. The Jewish people underwent a great upheaval. It fell into the hands of the Russian tsars, which resulted in all the significant developments that preceded the modern era: the disintegration of the community, secularization, the revolutionary movements, Zionism . . . One could say that the topic of the cantonists with its dynamic progression allows a glimpse into unique processes within the Jewish community, giving us a better understanding of what happened to the Jewish people.

The Jewish nation does not exist in a vacuum. It is impossible to understand events without learning, even the minimum, about the Russian Empire and its leaders. By doing so we will receive the tools with which to understand processes

---

1 The word *canton* (from the Latin *canto*) means "district," and it entered the Russian language as a term for military institutions for minors from the French *cantonnement*, "military camp." There was nothing new in the existence of a framework for small children in the Russian army. Moreover, many Russian families regarded it as a privilege to have one of their children admitted into a military institution with the likelihood of promotion later on. Therefore, the decision to forcibly enlist Jewish children was anomalous within these frameworks. Even without the aim of forced conversion, it could be considered tyranny for its own sake. For the history of the cantonist institution, see M. Lialev, *Obzor uchebnykh uchrezhdenii rossiiskoi armii do vremen Aleksandra Vtorogo (1700–1880)* [Overview of educational institutions of the Russian army before the time of Alexander II (1700–1880)] (St. Petersburg: n.p., 1880).

and permutations that the Jewish people experienced during that period, from the beginning till the middle of the nineteenth century. Any imaginable reader who might possibly be able to ask that innocent question mentioned in the first lines of this introduction, as well as the erudite one who knows a chapter in Jewish history, will discover how minor and incorrect their concepts of this topic are.

One needs to just glance at the table of contents in order to see the complexity of the subject summed up in the term "cantonists." Undoubtedly, one can delve into the topic in even further detail than is done in this book, but its chapters present the main components that will help to understand and analyze the topic. Each one of the reasons for which the mandatory conscription law was enacted could have been sufficient to impose the decree. It is impossible to decide on the main motive for the enactment of the law. Therefore, we will present the whole range of known factors that were publicized or that can be considered reasonable. By doing so, the popular opinion can be negated, according to which the conscription decree of Jews in general, and Jewish children in particular, was purely an expression of antisemitism on the part of the new tsar, who enacted the law less than two years after ascending the throne.

In our approach, we will attempt to examine the point of view of the enforcers—the tsar, his ministers, advisors, and the empire officials—and not just "our" blood-soaked, tormented side. Without rejecting any research method, we have tried to follow an unconventional path, exposing the complexity of decision-making in the Russian regime, on the one hand, and the response of the entire Jewish community, on the other hand: ranging from ideological support and cooperation on the part of the first *maskilim* to active opposition and bravely upholding the faith of our forefathers to the point of great self-sacrifice on the part of observant Jews.

In the background were people's daily routine and conduct according to the accepted patterns of behavior within their society. Therefore the actions of the members of the *kahal*,[2] including the community leaders and the *khappers*,[3] must be handled objectively. We have not come to judge them, either positively or negatively. The *kahal* operated within a very complex reality. Its first interest was to uphold Jewish autonomy, but when a body was formed that represented the Jews and interceded with the authorities on their behalf, the latter immediately saw it as an address for exerting pressure, extortion purposes, and

---

2   The community's administrative committee, elected by the seniors.
3   Yiddish for "seizers"—community workers who forcibly abducted conscription candidates.

demanding cooperation. It is therefore interesting to distinguish between the corruption of those high up in the government and the genuine effort to operate for the community's benefit.

The term "positively" must also be treated critically. From the viewpoint of the population of any given town, it was preferable to conscript young children in order to allow the exemption of the breadwinners. The community leadership was interested in protecting the wealthy, because it was they who funded the deficit in the payment of the community's taxes. On the other hand, there was the horrific dilemma of sending innocent children straight into the arms of the Church in exchange for saving the breadwinners. Was that moral? And where were those who determine such questions—the Torah sages and spiritual leaders in the generation when Hasidism and the Lithuanian yeshivot flourished? Was their voice heard? And what can one expect from a thirteen-year-old boy, or one even younger, when falling into the hands of Russian gentiles? Strong resistance for the principles on which he had been raised at home, or calculated submission with the intention of returning to Judaism at the first opportunity? Such questions arise automatically when researching this topic.

It is not the researcher's job to distribute grades, but keeping an open eye for all sides may contribute to a deep discussion on all the issues, the significance of which has not decreased till today. However, the attempt to present the "other side," that of the authorities, should not be seen as defending them. One should read the correspondence of the tsar's officials with the assumption that more is concealed than revealed, but even that which is concealed must be deciphered without prejudice. Most of the researchers till now have taken a moral-national stand, basically just, but not accepted in scientific research. Therefore, a significant part of this research constitutes a fresh reading of forgotten material. Nevertheless, we have attempted to limit our discussion of issues already researched.

My hope is that this volume will serve as a reading book for the curious and especially as a textbook for high school, university, and yeshiva students. The method used is to bring the sources, analyze them, and draw conclusions, while inviting the reader to be an active partner in clarifying matters.

I believe that my "Russian" origin does not detract from the study's objectivity. To the contrary. Many things have changed in Russia during the last one hundred and fifty years, but the Russian mentality has still preserved its unique features. It seems that it is almost impossible to correctly understand the connotations of terms and events of the period without feeling matters from "within."

In short, on finishing reading this book, I presume that you will have discovered a new and surprising page in a significant chapter of our history.

Cantonists Speak for Themselves

1. The Tale of a Veteran Jewish Soldier, Chaim Merimzon[1]

The testimony of Chaim Merimzon was publicized in 1912 in the journal *Evreiskaia starina* under the title "The Tale of a Veteran Soldier," edited by Simon Dubnow.

Merimzon was born in Vilkovishki (now Vilkaviškis), a town in the province of Suvalki (now Suwałki), in present-day Lithuania. He was abducted to serve as a cantonist in 1854, two years before the abolishment of compulsory conscription of minors, and served for twenty-five years.

Part 1

> I remember myself from the age of five. My mother dressed me in *ziẓit* and gave me coins to put in the *pushke* of the *beit midrash*, and if I met beggars on the way, I should give to them, too. Of all the children, I was my mother's favorite because I was called after her father. Her father was the town rabbi, and she dreamt that I too would be a rabbi.
>
> ... My eleventh birthday was on a Friday. My father decided to buy *maftir* [the honor of reading the chapter of the Prophets] for me. He tested me in advance to ensure that I wouldn't embarrass my parents. They planned to arrange refreshments for the honorary [members of the community], to be served after my being called to the Torah. My mother baked honey cake—*lekakh*, and my father sent me to the store to buy drinks. I happily ran to the store. I said to myself, "What a wonderful Shabbat we'll have.

---

1 Chaim Merimzon, "Rasskaz starogo soldata" [The tale of a veteran soldier], *Evreiskaia starina* 3–4 (1912): 290–301.

The guests will sit and help themselves to cake and drink, and I'll sing *zemirot*." Walking to the store, I turned into Varshavskaia Street. A carriage with a pair of horses came toward me. The driver was a Lithuanian gentile, and two older Jews were sitting in the carriage. One of them asked me, "Where does the innkeeper live?" I said that it's at the end of the road and that I was going just there.

"Come on up. We'll take you."

As I sat down, they said something in Lithuanian to the driver, and he waved his whip and the horses took off in a gallop.... When we reached the inn, I told them to stop, but they continued galloping until they came to the forest. The sun was setting. The men got down from the carriage and started to recite the *minḥa* afternoon prayers. Suddenly I realized that these were the kidnappers, *khappers*, who seize people for conscription. I started crying and shouting. I tried to escape, but the gentile held me with all his strength until they finished their prayers. They got back into the carriage and restrained me hard. The carriage drove along a dirt road until we came to a lone and quite neglected house.

Shabbat candles were already burning in the house. In a corner of the room sat a child sobbing loudly. Those present tried to convince him to go and say *Kabbalat Shabbat* and to make *Kiddush*, but he refused. They sat me down by a table and gave me a *siddur*, so that I would start singing *Lekha Dodi*. I almost burst out crying, but then I remembered that my father used to say that it was forbidden to cry on Shabbat; it's a sin. I pulled myself together and started to pray as I would at home with a Shabbat tune. When I got to the chorus, *lekha dodi*, I even began to sing like a cantor, but not very successfully. The members of the household praised me saying that I was a very good boy. The lady of the house gave me a kiss, but I said to myself, "May the angel of death kiss you." The *khappers* walked around the room during the prayers, sang the *Kabbalat Shabbat* service, and even said the *Amida* prayer, standing at the eastern wall and swaying back and forth enthusiastically. Truly glorious Hasidim.

At the end of the service they all sat down at the Shabbat table. The *khappers* tried to persuade the sobbing boy to join the meal. One of them even went up to him and wanted to take him in his arms, but the child pulled at his beard like a leech.

"Leave the fellow," said those present. "We should call the driver to take him into the forest, to the wolves." They left him alone, and he remained miserable and hungry. He continuously tried to escape, but the *khappers* kept their eyes on him.

I was brought up to honor Shabbat, and I acted according to the halakha. The table was elaborately set. Next to each place were *challot*, and next to the householder's place were two large loaves with a beautiful *challa* cover on them; he made *Kiddush*. They also gave me a wine cup and I made *Kiddush* too. They then washed their hands for bread. Meanwhile the lady of the house served everyone with *gefillte fish* on flat plates. They drank vodka, ate fried goose with white noodles, and for dessert, plum compote. I had never eaten such a good meal, even in my parents' house.

At the end of the meal, the householder tried to begin to sing Shabbat songs, but the *khappers* said they were tired from their work. He honored one of them, a *kohen*, to lead Grace after Meals. After the meal, they locked us in a narrow room with one window. It was dark in the room, and the child did not stop crying.

"Sweetie, stop crying," I said to him. "It's Shabbat today, and it's forbidden to cry on Shabbat; it's a sin."

"Yes, for you it's Shabbat because you stuffed yourself together with those bandits."

"And why didn't you eat? They invited you to the table, and instead you pulled an older Jew's beard."

"You idiot! Don't you understand why they caught us and where they're going to send us? They'll take us to Russia and hand us over to Christians who'll feed us pork and baptize us. What's there to be happy about?"

"Oh, that's it! And what will crying help? Who cares if you don't eat? So long as you're alive, you have to eat and drink, and God will help. Listen, tomorrow morning you'll sit and eat."

The next morning the Lithuanian gentile opened the blinds for us, brought us water with which to wash our hands and face, and the lady of the house brought us prayer books for the Shabbat morning prayers. The kidnappers wrapped themselves in *tallitot* and we began to pray. After the service we sat down to a meal.

The householder asked the child who had cried, "What's your name?"

"Yaakov Kleizmer," he answered.

"You have such a happy name,[2] why should you cry?"

I also said in a loud voice so that the *khappers* would hear, "On Shabbat we sing 'Do not fear, my servant Jacob [Yaakov] . . .' We must rely on God, and He is everywhere. God will not forsake us even in our exile. Perhaps we'll

---

2   *Kleizmer* is a type of instrumental music that is traditional to Central and Eastern European Jews, as well as the name for musicians who play it.

meet the children of these *khappers* there, because God repays measure for measure."

Yaakov calmed down, took a cup of wine and made Kiddush. When the kidnappers heard him they left the table out of shame, saying they'd eat later. "*Oy vay*! If only we could get rid of these bastards," they said. "They're giving us a bad conscience, especially that Chaimke, with all his talk."

After the meal they again shut us in the room. The lady of the house gave us a *chumash* and a book of Psalms, telling us to ask God to give us a good week. Yaakov started crying again. Tears ran down his fat cheeks. He sighed and sobbed all the time. What would be with his poor parents who have no idea where he had disappeared to? I was also on the verge of tears, but I held myself back with all my strength and tried to calm him down.

We prayed *Minḥa*. The *khappers* brought two retired soldiers[3] to keep guard over us.

The sun set. We began to say the evening prayers. They lit a *havdala* candle and gave us a sip from the wine,[4] but I refused. Shabbat was over, and one was allowed to be sad. I called Yaakov to our room and began to say psalms: "Even when I walk in the valley of death, I shall not fear evil . . .," and then I burst out crying. Our cries rose to heaven. The guards came running and started to drag us to the wagon.

On the way the *khappers* tried to persuade us that they would try to intercede on our behalf that we would not be enlisted. During the course of the journey we stopped crying and fell asleep. When we awoke, the wagon was already standing next to a tall stone building, and a soldier with a rifle was marching back and forth next to it. The *khappers* took rags out of their pockets, wiped our tears and rubbed our cheeks so that we would look good. They then led us to the second floor. The official who sat next to a table told the *khappers* to bring us near to the table and asked us our names. I did not understand, so they translated. "My name is Chaim Merimzon," I said. He glanced at his papers and began to scream: "Incorrect! Your name is Meir, not Chaim!"

---

3   The use of retired soldiers and a private home with householders who helped the kidnappers, testifies to the existence of an organized system in which Jews and locals cooperated.

4   Offering a sip from the *havdala* wine shows that the *khappers* were particular about halakha with regard to the abducted children, even though they knew what awaited the children in the army. This is evidence of the split personality that is known from the world of crime.

That was how I understood that they had brought me to be conscripted instead of one of the boys of a wealthy family with the same name. The official continued and asked Yaakov for his name. He answered, "My name is Yaakov Kleizmer."

"You're lying!" he hollered. "Your name is Yaakov Greenblatt." That's what he wrote down on his papers, and he sent us, with an escort of soldiers to the detention center. Meanwhile, they began to cut off our sidelocks. Before they left, the *khappers* said to us, "Goodbye, children. Don't let your spirits fall. In another few days you'll be free."[5]

On hearing this I shouted at them: "And I wish you that you never see your children again; that disease devour your heads, hearts, and guts; that every possible sorrow befall your families, you cursed *khappers*!" They spat three times so that my curse would not be effective, and disappeared.

Part 2

From the recruiting office, the soldiers took us to the detention center. They led us, mocking and pushing us. There were several cells in the detention center that were designated for conscripted soldiers. In each cell were wooden boards with dirty straw mattresses. The boards were arranged as two-layered bunks, on which adult soldiers were lying. On the floor was room for the minors. We had to sleep face down, as if we slept on our backs we would swallow the straw dust that spilled out of the mattresses. When the enlistment of the adults was completed and they were taken out of the jail, it was a festival for us. We got up onto the boards and felt happy.

Before we were sent out of the town, they did not give us non-kosher food. They appointed a Jew who brought pots of food—a stew of peas and beans, or potato soup with bulgur wheat. The adult daily bread ration was three-quarters of a kilogram, and the children received half a kilogram. Jews from the town brought *challot* for Shabbat. We did have a small amount of money but the peddlers who sold all sorts of things were afraid to come near the jail.

---

5   It would seem that there was no need for the *khappers* to lie anymore. It was just a psychological urge.

When my poor father heard that I had ended up in a "room" like that, he came to see me. Later they told me that he had come too close to the guard. Because he did not know military procedure, the sentry immediately struck him with the butt of his rifle, and my father fell and fainted. Some kind Jews carried him to the clinic. Thus I did not get to see him.

After six weeks of waiting, the time came for our deportation from the prison. They dressed us in army uniform and loaded us onto wagons. They squeezed sixteen children into a wagon. We were suffocating. We were assigned to a cantonist battalion in Kiev [Kyiv]. It was a very long journey.

I became friends with a boy called Greenblatt. He said, "I heard that they are taking us somewhere where they force children to convert. Whoever refuses is beaten and tortured, but whoever submits is taught military science till the age of eighteen, and then he is trained to be an officer. I will never, in my whole life, be tempted. I won't exchange the God of my fathers for their military rank. They can cut me into pieces... kill me! What do you think, will I get *Gan Eden* for the merit of such a *Kiddush Hashem*?"

"I also want to die for *Kiddush Hashem*, but I'm afraid that the evil inclination will get the better of me and will tempt me to be an overlord, walking around in an officer's fancy uniform, giving orders to the soldiers, and going to the theater in the evening."

"What will your parents say? They'll curse you. They'll cry; and the tears of parents reach the divine throne. Officers also die eventually. Your converted soul will go up to heaven, and there a terrible angel, one that is in charge of the underworld, will ask you: 'What is your name?' 'My name is Ivan,' you'll say. The angel will retort, 'There's no such name here. Go to your Ivans.' And then your converted soul will fly all over the world like a moth at night... Just think of that, and you won't want to be an officer anymore."

Thus we tried, throughout the journey, to solve the problem of our fate in our childish minds. We talked about memories from life at home, or about meals that we used to eat in *chayder*, remembering our mischievous pranks. We sang Shabbat songs and acted as though we were jesters at weddings. In short, we encouraged each other to keep up our spirits.

It was a long journey from the town of Suvalki in Lithuania to Kiev. We traveled in wagons, and behind us walked soldiers. They kept all eyes on us as though we were dangerous criminals. Every so often we stopped on the way. In the villages we spent the night with peasants, but in the towns they would put us into military barracks or jails, so that we would not meet Jews.

We were not given the opportunity to wash ourselves for three months, so all sorts of fleas and vermin multiplied on our bodies, giving us no rest either day or night. Once, while praying, we burst into tears from the pain. The soldiers pounced on us, shouting: "Dirty Zhids![6] What are you screaming for?" The shouts shocked us, and our tears streamed down our cheeks in silence.

We arrived in Kiev. The year was 1855. We felt that the fateful day had come. The wagon stopped by the barrier at the entrance to the city. "Zhids, get out!" We took our rucksacks; they placed us in rows and marched us into the city. I tried to locate a synagogue along the way, but I did not succeed. The city made a great impression on me. The men were very tall and looked like ruffians, talking in loud voices—not like in our town. Our Jews were thin, bent over, talked quietly, constantly sighing and coughing.

They also brought the boys from Poland. The made us stand in the courtyard of the military base in three rows. The soldiers told us that soon the commanding officer would come. He would say, "Greetings, boys," and we were to reply, "Greetings, honorable commander." Meanwhile the soldiers brought several bunches of birch rods for lashing.

When I saw the rods, my heart fell. My knees trembled, and my eyes were filled with tears. I said to myself: "Mother Rachel, may your merit protect us. Arise from the dust and pray to the almighty God to hear your voice and send the redeeming angel to protect us from all evil mishaps. May He give us strength and trust to observe our holy Torah!"

The commanding officer came, got down from the carriage, looked at us with a smile and said, "Greetings, children." Then they started dividing us into battalions. My friend Greenblatt was assigned to battalion 4, whereas I—to battalion 5. They took us to the washhouse. I said to myself that it was just a trick. They were going to start beating us so that we would convert. I was wrong. We simply washed ourselves and got rid of the pests.

From there we were taken to the province of Chernigov [Chernihiv]. They brought us to a village and assigned us to houses. The village belonged to a Christian sect called Staroobriadtsy [Old Believers]. The landlady took me to a place where there was a huge oven heater and pointed that I was to sleep behind the oven on a straw mattress. She tried to explain something

---

6   A derogatory term for Jews.

to me, but I indicated that I did not understand the language. She spat on the floor in anger, and went about her business, while I lay down to sleep. I felt thirsty, so I went to a bucket of water and took a little to drink with a ladle. The woman suddenly jumped on me with horrific screams, pushing my hand away, that I would not contaminate the water. "Go away from here, you Satan, Jesus-hater!" I didn't understand the meaning of what was happening, and I went outside. There, a veteran cantonist explained to me that "they" do not allow Jews to drink from the same bucket as they do.

I lay down again behind the oven. I couldn't fall asleep. My stomach was empty, and the cockroaches didn't stop biting me. I remembered Mama, how she used to sing me songs before I went to sleep. So, crying, I finally fell asleep.

The next morning the woman acted kindlier. She gave me a slice of bread with salt and a piece of ham. I ate the bread and gave the meat to the cat.

A drummer passed through the village calling everyone to assembly. I also ran to the meeting place. They took us to the outskirts of the village, stood us in rows, and placed heaps of birch rods in front of us. The battalion officer announced: "Whoever wants to convert to Christianity, take one step forward!" There were many children who took that step. I said to myself, "I'm the son of a *melamed* and the grandson of a rabbi; I will remain faithful to my father's Torah. If necessary, I will give up my life in Sanctification of God's Name." From then on, they began to make us suffer, but I will not go into details concerning stories of this, as these things are known.[7]

After that they again divided us into groups. There were fifteen in each group. They began to abuse us in all sorts of ways. I suffered more than everyone, as other boys said that they would only listen to me and that they would do "whatever Merimzon was willing to do."

I also suffered a lot from lack of food, because I did not touch pork. Even if I was ready to eat non-kosher food out of hunger, my "kosher" stomach rejected the food. Thus, for three months I made do with bread and water, until the day when I understood that I would not be able to survive anymore on a meager diet of bread and water, and I started to get myself used to eating their disgusting stuff.

---

7 Skipping this part of the story is surprising. What is more surprising is that many researchers point to Merimzon's story as a source for narratives of forced conversions.

Then, military training and exercises began. At first, they just taught us Christian prayers and the titles of various officers, starting with our sergeant and ending with the tsar. I excelled in these exercises, as I took a teacher and paid him with sunflower seeds and rolls, which I bought with my own money. He would dictate the titles that I wrote in Hebrew and then I would learn them by heart. The next morning I would march to school in a good mood, hoping that I would know the material. After an unsuccessful test, the sergeant would give me a slap on my face with his five fingers. That's how I would get a "5," not in my notebook,[8] but on my face. All because Hebrew does not have the same sounds as Russian and I did not know how to pronounce the words correctly, and so I was beaten. The sergeant would hit the palm of any failing student with a small cane. Thus, I would return to the house at the end of each lesson with swollen hands and teary eyes.

The gentile woman's children also bullied me constantly. They chalked crosses on my army coat, mocked me, and tried to smear lard on my lips.[9]

I once returned from our studies sad and depressed. As I entered the house the woman's son fell on me, wanting to smear my lips with lard. I gave him a decent whack on the nose with a rolling pin I grabbed. His nose started bleeding profusely. The woman of the house pounced on me like a lioness. Luckily, I managed to escape. She ran after me shouting, "Help! This Zhid has murdered my son!" The drummer gathered everyone together. I was placed against the wall, holding a pickaxe. There was just one prayer in my heart: "I await Your salvation, O Lord . . ."

The master sergeant ordered me to drop the pickaxe and took me to the battalion officer, who questioned me. I did not understand well what he said in Russian, but I knew that I should answer every question with "Yes, officer." At the end he said that I should be moved to a different house, and he promised the woman that I would be beaten the next day.

I moved to a new house, which surprisingly was very good. There were no children in the house, just a man and a woman. The woman gave me a separate room with a bed and a pillow. Next to the bed stood a table covered with a tablecloth. I simply did not believe that such a paradise was meant for me. She signaled with her hand: "Come little soldier, come." I began to take off my coat, and she noticed fleas crawling all over it. She took me to the

---

8   According to the scale of Russian grades, five was a low mark.
9   A routine type of abuse of Jews on the part of Christians.

wash house, and washed me like a true mother. When we got back home, she prepared a meal for me from everything she had. When I finished eating all I could, I went up to her, knelt down, and kissed her hand.

The husband was also a good-hearted man. He sat down next to me and started asking me questions: Where I came from; who my parents were. I answered him in my broken Russian, but I did not know how to say my father's work—*melamed*. He told me that his son was serving in the army in the Caucasus Mountains. The good woman of the house noticed that I was tired and sent me to bed. I fell asleep murmuring thanks to God for the kindness He had bestowed on me.

I got up early the next morning, and the good-hearted woman prepared me breakfast and accompanied to where we studied. In those moments I imagined that she was my mother taking me to learn in *chayder*.

I lived with them for a whole year. From then on I went to my studies happily and upright. No one could recognize me as Chaimke the *melamed*'s son. I finished my year of studies and received the rank of private. I already knew how to speak Russian, I was no longer beaten, and I knew all the "tricks" a soldier has to know.[10]

All that year my parents would send me a letter once a month together with some money.[11] Suddenly, everything stopped. I was very worried that perhaps something had happened to them, and I sent a letter to Reuven "the Cossack." A letter finally arrived together with a ruble. I was really happy, but when I opened the letter and read it, my eyes grew dim with sorrow:

> Chaim, our son of the past; now Ivan or who knows what. Don't send us any more of your false letters. Take the ruble and buy yourself a rope with which to strangle yourself. We curse you harshly for putting us and your righteous grandfather, whose name you bear, to shame. All the children here bully us by shouting, "Your Chaimke is an apostate!" If this is not the case, bring us approval from the local rabbi, and then you will remain our beloved son.

---

10 This is important testimony of cantonists' adaption period. It usually lasted six months.
11 It should be noted that the distance from Suvalki to Chernihiv is close to 1,000 km, and yet the parents could locate him and make contact.

What sorrow! How could I convince my poor parents that I had not been baptized? Where would I get approval from a rabbi in a gentile village? How did this happen? I carried on corresponding with Reuven, who told me that they had abducted another boy and sent him to Kiev. But his father was a simple *melamed*. He secretly accompanied him and planned to pay ransom to have him released. In the end, when they reached Kiev, he managed to release his son. It was this man who heard in Kiev that our whole group had converted, and it was he who spread the rumor. Thus I had no contact with my parents until my release from the army.[12]

Shortly thereafter, Alexander II ascended the throne.[13] He accepted the government's advice that the army of children had no benefit, and that its maintenance was costing the state treasury many millions, paid as salary to the officers.[14] These officers did not belong to the actual military and did nothing. They just made sure to report the numbers of converts, and for that they received ranks and bonuses. The tsar then ordered the army to be dismantled. The Christian children were immediately sent home, but as we were Jewish, they took us as drafted to the army, no longer as cadets, and they kept us in the army. They sent the children who had converted to vocational schools to train as medics, clerks, etc., whereas us boys who had not converted were sent to labor battalions. I got to a private carpenter in Moscow, where I learned a trade.

Once a priest came to the carpenter and asked to speak to me. He started by saying, "You've learned Torah, haven't you? There it says that God chose you as His chosen people, but because the Jewish nation did not go in God's path, He was furious with them and scattered them to the four corners of the earth. Every nation has a state. Your people does not have any safe shelter in the world. Therefore, I would like to recommend that you deny your connection to your people and choose our Christian faith. Cling to it wholeheartedly, and you will merit joy and wealth in this world, and in the next world you will merit Paradise. Only those who believe in Jesus merit Paradise. This is the path to the great light—choose it!"

---

12   At the end of Merimzon's narrative, which is not brought here, he relates that he returned to his town at the end of his military service and proved that he had remained a faithful Jew.
13   In case it is said that as a result Merimzon was not bullied too much, it should be noted that 130 cantonists converted to Christianity in Arkhangel'sk at exactly that time.
14   This explanation reflects the opinion then popular in the army. It is interesting that the government was seen as being the initiator. See our discussion of the subject below.

I answered him: "Sir, the fact that God was angry with Israel and scattered them, that is true justice. Moreover, as He is the King of kings in the whole world, it is fitting that we too should be in the whole world. Surely you have studied the holy language. God says, "For mine is the silver, and mine is the gold" [Hagai 2:8], and whoever believes in God will merit goodness. I'm surprised at you. Why are you selling me your religion like any storekeeper in the market, promising me joy and wealth in this world? You should be persuading me with spirituality, not materialism. For example, convince me that you observe the tenet of "love your fellow as yourself" better than us."

The priest took off the way he came, and the owner of the workshop and all the tradesmen began to respect me and stopped trying to persuade me to convert...

2. From the Memories of an Ex-Cantonist[15]

This story is told by Moisy Spiegel of Irkutsk, Siberia.

1911

My name is Moisy Spiegel. I was born to wealthy parents in the region of Zaslavsky Uezd in the province of Volhynia.[16] My father died when I was six years old. In 1851, when I turned seven, I was abducted for army service, but my mother paid a lot of money to have me released. However, at the age of eight I was again abducted. This is how it happened:

There were Jewish agents who were willing, in exchange for a large amount of money, to smuggle us across the border. In fact, Moldavian gentiles actually did that. They took me and another large group of children and left us in the bushes near the border. They warned us to sit quietly, and then they disappeared. Towards evening soldiers on horseback came to our hiding place and took us to jail. They chained us with handcuffs in the middle of Shabbat...

---

15 M. Spiegel, "Zapiski kantonista" [Notes of a cantonist], *Evreiskaia starina* 6 (1911): 249–259.
16 Present-day western Ukraine.

I was sent to the town of Zhitomir [Zhytomyr] in Ukraine. It was about a week before Rosh Hashana. I was brought to the recruitment center, where I was stripped naked and presented before an officer and a doctor. They examined me from all sides, and pronounced me "fit for the military." They put me in another room, where there were other chicks like me who were crying loudly. Gentile women brought us food, saying that they would do so every day, that we should eat, and there was no reason to cry. They got us dressed in army uniform. They had gathered about two hundred children, most of them only about one or one and a half meters tall. My mother finally found me, but it was too late. Bribery did not help anymore.

We began our journey. We received uniform: a grey coat with a stand-up collar, a big ugly hat of thick material, large, bulky pants that a small child can't get dressed in alone. We also received boots of coarse leather. They gave us rucksacks; in mine was a cotton shirt, kerchiefs, socks, underwear, and other things that Mama had bought. She also gave me a little money, but the rest she gave to the captain to look after for me. Did she really think that that thief would ever return the money?

We were loaded onto wagons, and we set out on our way. A crowd of weeping adults accompanied us, as if they were taking us to the graveyard. Fathers and mothers followed their children many kilometers. Mama parted from me tearfully, saying, "My child, don't exchange our religion for any other."

We arrived in Moscow. The cold was horrific. We were billeted in the homes of Christians in the city suburbs, but these did not want us to stay, and they shouted curses at us: "Zhids, Christ-killers!" Meanwhile, the soldiers who escorted us had robbed us of all we had and began to get drunk and go berserk. They left us completely alone.

We children decided to return to Moscow. When we arrived at the barrier at the entrance of the city, policemen surrounded us. Among them was one apostate. We told him what had happened. The matter reached the Minister of Defense. We were fed, and they arranged a warm place for us to sleep. The next day they fired all the officers, appointing new ones in their stead.

We set out again on our journey; this time to the town of Nizhnii Novgorod on the Volga River. Many children became sick on the way from spoiled food, various diseases, and the cold. When we arrived in the town, we were assigned lodging. I and another Jew spent the night in the house of a Christian merchant. His wife and daughter took us to the bathhouse, after which they gave us to eat. We didn't believe it possible: They gave us white bread, eggs, and butter. All the family sat round the table, and the merchant muttered continuously, "What sorrow! May the Lord have mercy."

Before leaving the town, they assembled all of us in the central square. There were crowds of people. The rich distributed gifts to each one—white bread, shirts, towels, boots, and even money. Finally, they brought us to Tobol'sk in central Siberia. Again, it was almost the eve of Rosh Hashana. Only one hundred and ten children made it there. All the rest had become sick and remained along the way.

Immediately, all sorts of commanders, teachers, and sergeants appeared. The medic, incidentally, was a converted Jew. All the officials and teachers had been cantonists. They gave us a medical examination and found that most of us suffered from itching. They sent us to the bathhouse, gave us a change of clothes, and allowed us to rest for a whole month. At the end of the month, they began to introduce discipline. Wake-up time was six o'clock in the morning. Each class had a group leader, who was supposed to take his boys to wash, brush their teeth, and wash out their mouth. After that they made their beds in a fixed manner, and mended their clothes. Every boy had to take part in the Christian morning prayers. After prayers, we received about 100 grams of bread with salt. They were very particular that we shouldn't talk to each other during prayers and eating time. Concerning our prayers, there was absolutely nothing to talk about. There were some Jewish children from Siberia among us. We tried to find out from them about the conditions. They told us that their parents were forbidden to visit them, and they were also not allowed vacation for the festivals. All this made a harsh impression on us.

After our month's rest, they introduced us to a strict regimen. We drilled twice a day. The main part of the exercise was proper posture and walking. It was particularly difficult to learn to march. We had to raise one leg and stand on the second one. The weak boys would collapse . . . We stood in a row in statue-like posture. It was so difficult that the children cried, but the sergeants pretended not to see anything.

Whoever did not fulfill the demands was sent to work in the kitchen to peel potatoes, fetch firewood, or help bake bread. They assigned boys to run office errands to fetch all sorts of letters, to stoke the ovens in the offices, or to sweep and clean the large courtyard. In addition, whoever did not succeed in his studies or did not do homework[17] was made to polish the

---

17 Although the method of education was violent, the demand for homework should be noted. It seems that the aim of the institution was high-level vocational training.

classroom floor with sawdust. Teachers would also take children to work for them in their homes.

In addition to marching drills, there were also studies in classes. At the end of the school year of 1854, they moved me to second grade. To my bad luck, in a drawing lesson I was supposed to draw an eagle's claws. I didn't manage to do the assignment, and I received "dry rewards." The teacher hit me on my palm with the edge of a metal ruler. He beat me saying, "What, Jew boy? Don't you want to learn how to draw the icon that's in the church?"

Fortunately, my hands hurt so much from the flogging that I was hospitalized. Later, I learned from other cantonists how to redden my eyes to stay in hospital longer. The medic, an apostate, had a kind heart. He cooperated with us and did not give us [the prescribed] eyedrops, as he knew that we really had no problem.

Meanwhile, out of the 120 children, there were only thirty or forty children who refused to convert. We were constantly harassed to get us to submit to their efforts that we convert. They were interested in reporting that we had converted of our own volition.[18] They forced us to learn prayers in Russian, and on Sundays they took us as a group to church.

After having spent about a month in the hospital, I found it difficult to return to studies. I especially disliked the lessons on Christianity.[19] The priest was particular to ask me questions about religion, especially when an external inspection was being conducted at the base. He enjoyed hearing my exact answers to anything connected to Christianity. The priest Bogoliubsky would take me to his home, where I played with his son Gavriil and his daughters. The girls and his wife tried to persuade me to convert. They told me that Jesus was a Jew, and so they tried to hang a cross round my neck. But I remembered Mama's parting words to me, and I stayed firm. In the end, even the priest understood that he did not have a chance of convincing me.

In third grade I took arithmetic, grammar, and writing very seriously.

I was often appointed as head of the class, head of the dormitory, and responsible for the marching drills.

---

18   We can understand from this that they did indeed try to coax and convince the children.
19   In the instruction booklet for priests it was recommended to involve the Jews in discussion. On missionary instruction literature, see below, chapter 8 "Missionary Instructional Literature," 47.

Sometimes I was appointed to assist the brigade commander, General Dometti. Then I would stay in his house, and eat and play with his children. That was already when all the cantonists, except the Jews, were sent home.[20] Once, when I was working in the office, I glanced at some papers, and I found a letter from the commander of military educational institutions, General Annenkov, which stated that it was forbidden to force Jewish children to convert.

When the cantonists were sent to schools, I was designated to serve in the Cossack cavalry brigade, and I became close to the commander and his wife. They admired my handwriting, and often asked me to copy different documents. Later I served as adjutant to the commander of the unit's headquarters, and I traveled with him throughout the area.

3. The Story of a Cantonist in the Town of Arkhangel'sk[21]

This story is told by Eliyahu (Israel Leib) Itzkovitz.

I was born to a prosperous family in Lithuania, near the town of Druia [Druya]. My grandfather leased land from landowners. Unfortunately my grandfather died, and my father was arrested for smuggling goods across the border and sent to Siberia. In 1853, my mother and I moved to the city of Polotsk in the Vitebsk region of White Russia. I was seven years old (so my mother told me) when I was abducted by Jewish kidnappers during morning prayers.

My mother tried to scream for help, to resist, but nothing helped. They moved me to a house where I found another few dozen miserable children. I had contact with my mother and other relatives who tried to get me released.

After three weeks we were brought to the recruitment office. There we were shaved. They asked me my name, and although it is Eliyahu Leib Beilin, my relatives instructed me for some reason to change my name. I therefore, gave my name as Israel Itzkovitz. We were then moved to the cantonment,

---

20 In 1856.
21 Eliyahu Itzkovitz, "Vospominaniia evreiskogo kantonista" [Memories of a Jewish cantonist], *Evreiskaia starina* 2 (1909): 55–65.

and provided with clothes: an army coat, a sheepskin coat, boots. They also gave me a rucksack stuffed with various items.[22]

On my draft form was listed: "Israel Itzkovitz, twelve years old, drafted 23.10.53 instead of adults who escaped military service."

When we started out on our way, the whole town accompanied us. The ground shook from the screams. The loaded us onto wagons—six children in each wagon. Every day we traveled about thirty kilometers.[23] When we stopped for the night we slept in cold houses with dirt floors. We were filthy and frozen. We were so cold that we didn't even have the strength to open our pants to relieve ourselves. The sergeants just shouted at us and beat us. Several children died on the way to St. Petersburg.

We finally arrived at the capital city, St. Petersburg. They told us that Nicholas I wanted to see us. In the end some major-general or other came. I remember that a daughter of one of the officers held me affectionately by the hand and gave me hot tea to drink, and even a white roll . . .

In July 1854, we arrived at the city of Arkhangel'sk, at the unit's building. There they stood us in rows and sorted us into groups. Children between the ages of seven and fifteen were directed to battalion 1, and from fifteen and above, to battalion 2. A "tutor" was attached to every three children. Their job was to familiarize us with what was going on. They did this very willingly—beating us nonstop. The first thing they did was to snatch our *tefillin*,[24] *tzitzit*, and prayer books. I have no idea what they did with them. We were put into rooms and assigned beds—a straw mattress and a pillow.

And now for the daily schedule on the base.

Wake-up time at 6:00 am; making the beds. Whoever did not make his bed neatly was beaten by the "tutor," an eleven- or twelve-year-old boy. They usually hit us on the jaw, head, and all parts of the body. They then sent us to wash and pray. Everyone, no matter what religion, had to show up for prayers with the priest.

Breakfast: 100 grams of bread with salt.

Then we started memorizing the roles and ranks of the military, the titles, and how to address the commanders.

---

22 The description matches that of Moisy Spiegel, above.
23 In comparison, see below a document that describes the death of a cantonist while walking on foot.
24 It would seem that only boys over the age of *bar mitzva* had *tefillin*. Itzkovitz himself did not have *tefillin*.

Immediately after that—polishing boots and buttons of our coats. Whoever did not want to convert was given ragged clothes, which he had to repair on his own and at his personal expense. Whoever was unable to was punished.

From 7:00 am: marching drill. We learned to march in a unique way. First, we had to raise one foot to our thigh and to stand like that for as long as possible. Anyone who collapsed was flogged.

At 11:00 am, we went for lunch. Several dozen cantonists sat round each table. The tables were black and dirty. Every six children received one plate and a portion of sliced bread. The moment the bread was served, everyone would fall on it, trying to snatch some. The strong managed to seize a few slices, the weak were left with nothing. They served us rotten cabbage soup with crabs and other disgusting ingredients. Although we were hungry, some of us were incapable of touching this "food." At the end they gave us a barley stew, and that was all.

Then we learned reading, writing, arithmetic, and grammar in a classroom. Even a boy who did not understand had to learn everything by heart. We also learned all sorts of crafts, sewing, and carpentry.

The battalion commander, Podpolkovnik (Lieutenant) D'iakonov Vasilii Vasil'evich was the ruling master over the entire base. He gave the order to hit the boys mercilessly. We were beaten early in the morning, and also during studies. You eat—you get flogged; you go to sleep—you get flogged.

Every Saturday, the cantonists had to wash the floor. We would kneel down and start to scrub the floor with water and twigs. Whoever did not scrub with the required force was immediately beaten by the sergeant attached to our unit. Open wounds that did not heal formed on our knees. We were afraid to complain because they even hit us in the clinic. Our battalion 2 had a non-commissioned officer, Evgraf Gulevich, a converted Jew, baptized by Lieutenant D'iakonov. At the first roll call the commander announced: "No one will leave here as a Jew." He really stood by his word.

Every evening at nine o'clock, before going to bed, Gulevich would lie down on his bed and order some boys to go over to him and kneel down. He held a Bible in his hand, quoted from it, and tried to prove that Jesus was the true Messiah. Finally, in a threatening tone, he would demand that the boys convert to Christianity. Whoever agreed, could go to sleep, and the next day would receive an extra portion of bread and new clothes. Those who refused had to stay on their knees all night, would miss their bread ration, and on top of it, would be endlessly beaten. Of course, under such conditions, the little children did not have the strength to resist. The children above the age of twelve were more stubborn and so suffered more. Every so often we were informed that one of our friends was about to die. By the beginning of 1856, the whole battalion had converted....

In 1854,[25] the boys who had turned eighteen were sent to Petersburg to be assigned to units. The late Samuel Mil told me that in Peterburg an imperial review was conducted in the presence of the tsar. Many of the cantonists complained that they had been forcibly converted. All those who complained were arrested and sentenced to three thousand lashes. However, the sentence was not carried out because of the death of Nicholas I.[26] Those who complained were sent to remote army bases in Siberia.

After the complaint was raised, a general from Petersburg came to visit us. He questioned us, wanting to know whether it was true that we had been forced to convert. I do not remember what the adult cantonists replied. I just remember that our commander Podpolkovnik D'iakonov was summoned to Petersburg to explain matters, but before he left, he died. Our officer ordered us to light memorial candles next to the icon, and we did so with great joy.

Our officers used all means possible to force Christianity on us, and they achieved their goal: All converted except for one boy. Ostensibly, from then on we should have enjoyed equality with the rest of the Christians, but that was a vain hope. Whenever a quarrel broke out with a Christian friend, we would receive insults—"Dirty Zhid." Already then I decided to return to Judaism.[27]

The manifesto of Alexander II of August 26, 1856, forbade the conscription of Jewish children as cantonists. In the years 1857–1858, an order was issued to release all the children from cantonist frameworks, and to return them to their homes. However, this did not apply to the Jews. The cantonists who had turned eighteen were sent to military units, and our battalion was attached to a military academy. In 1860, we ended our studies in the academy, and were assigned by lot. Five of us were sent to units in Finland, another three were to remain in Arkhangel'sk. Another ten, myself among them, were dispatched to an elite unit in Moscow.

---

25 It was, in fact, 1855.
26 There is no verification of this section of the memoir in academic research. See below.
27 Itzkovitz does not detail his conversion and, without this comment, it would have been impossible to understand that he had indeed taken that step.

> In Moscow I was commissioned to the third artillery brigade. The commander was a very kind man, who liked me, and after a year I was already promoted to the rank of junior office. Because I had been abducted at the age of eight, but registered as though I was twelve, I was an officer at the age of fourteen.
>
> In 1872, I had already finished my mandatory military service and went on pre-retirement leave. I set out to search for my relatives. I managed to see my mother and sisters. The did not believe that I had survived; I, too, never thought that I would see them again. I also managed to find my father who was still in exile in Tomsk in Siberia for smuggling he had been involved in to support the family.
>
> When I returned from my leave, I had another ten months to serve in the army. After some time, I informed my commanding officers that I no longer wished to be a Christian. They began to persecute me. They threatened me with a trial. They even said that I would be sentenced to death. I wrote an explanatory letter to the high command, in which I claimed that although I had been abused as a child of seven, I had served the tsar faithfully. "Just as you forged my Christianity," I claimed, "and no one complained about that, similarly do not prevent me from annulling the forged conversion."
>
> Then came the order: "Send junior officer Itzkovitz, who is renouncing his Christianity, for exhortation by a priest. If he remains unconvinced, he is not to be punished, but sent to another unit." When the priest tried to speak to me, I smiled and said that I was no longer seven years old, but twenty-six. They finally decided to release me from service, as I had finished twenty years in the military. In 1873 I was finally released.

Itzkovitz's narrative demands several observations. First, the mass refusal of the cantonists in Arkhangel'sk to convert was in 1856, not 1854. As proof that the author is not referring to another, unknown, rebellion, it should be noted that, in the penalty order, the precedent of the Perm' battalion of 1846 is mentioned. Similarly, all the circumstances of the rebellion, including location, type of punishment etc., have been confused.

The circumstances of Podpolkovnik D'iakonov's death are also doubtful. The matter can be explained by the fact that Itzkovitz was still a small boy, and he heard the story later from Samuel Mil, whose name is mentioned in research documents of 1856.

It seems strange that already in the days of Alexander II, after the unit had been dismantled, fourteen-year-old Itzkovitz was thought to be nineteen years old, and promoted to the rank of officer.

Itzkovitz does not relate the circumstances of his own conversion, only that of others. This is characteristic of other memoirs. The lack of the personal narrative about this detail raises doubts concerning other events that he mentions. It is typical of adults to reconstruct memories on the basis of sources not their own. In this connection it should be noted that most of the researchers of documents concerning narratives of forced conversion rely on the memoirs of Itzkovitz and Chaim Merimzon, when these are not memories of their own experiences, but stories of what happened to others.

4. Alexander Herzen, *My Past and Thoughts*[28]

Alexander Herzen, a well-known Russian writer, was born to a wealthy family. As a result of his critical views of the state leadership, he was exiled to Perm' to work as a clerk in the governor's office. In his memoirs, published in London, Herzen tells of an unexpected encounter with Jewish children who were being taken to a cantonist school. He shows that concepts of efficiency, good citizenship, and a mechanized social structure helped the officers justify their inhumane treatment of the Jews.

Herzen's account is the testimony of someone unbiased, and therefore it is of great value. Usually only a small excerpt of the story is brought, but I have seen fit to quote more.

> **1835**
>
> On the day after we left Perm' there was a heavy, unceasing downpour of rain ever since dawn...; at about two o'clock we reached a very poor Votyak village.... I wanted to get dry and warm and to have something to eat.... A soldier came and reported that an escorting officer had sent to invite me to a cup of tea.
>
> "With the greatest pleasure. Where is your officer?"

---

28 Alexander Herzen, *My Past and Thoughts*, trans. Constance Garnett (Berkeley: University of California Press, 1973), 169–170. The spelling of the geographical names has been modified.

"In the hut near by [sic], your honor," and the soldier made the familiar left-about-turn.

I followed him.

A short, elderly officer with a face that bore traces of many anxieties... met me with all the genial hospitality of deadly boredom. He was one of those unintelligent, good-natured "old" soldiers who pull at the collar for twenty-five years in the service, and plod along without promotion and without reasoning about it, as old horses work....

"Whom are you taking, and where to?"

"They have collected a crowd of cursed little Jew boys of eight or nine years old. Whether they are taking them for the navy or what, I can't say. At first the orders were to drive them to Perm'; then there was a change and we are driving them to Kazan'. I took them over a hundred versts farther back. The officer who handed them over said, 'It's dreadful, and that's all about it; a third were left on the way' (and the officer pointed to the earth). Not half will reach their destination," he said.

"Have there been epidemics, or what?" I asked, deeply moved.

"No, not epidemics, but they just die off like flies. A Jew boy, you know, is such a frail, weakly creature, like a skinned cat; he is not used to tramping in the mud for ten hours a day and eating biscuits—then again, being among strangers, no father nor mother nor petting; well, they cough and cough until they cough themselves into their graves. And I ask you, what use is it to them? What can they do with little boys?"

I made no answer.

"When do you set off?" I asked.

"Well, we ought to have gone long ago, but it has been raining so heavily.... Hey, you there, soldier! Tell them to get the small fry together."

They brought the children and formed them into regular ranks: it was one of the most awful sights I have ever seen, those poor, poor children! Boys of twelve or thirteen might somehow have survived it, but little fellows of eight and ten... Not even a brush full of black paint could put such horror on canvas. Pale, exhausted, with frightened faces, they stood in thick, clumsy, soldiers' overcoats, with stand-up collars, fixing helpless, pitiful eyes on the garrison soldiers who were roughly getting them into ranks. The white lips, the blue rings under their eyes bore witness to fever or chill. And these sick children, without care or kindness, exposed to the icy wind that blows unobstructed from the Arctic Ocean, were going to their graves.

And note that they were being taken by a kind-hearted officer who was obviously sorry for the children. What if they had been taken by a military political economist?[29]

What monstrous crimes are obscurely buried in the archives of the wicked, immoral reign of Nicholas! We are used to them, they were committed every day, committed as though nothing was wrong, unnoticed, lost in the terrible distance, noiselessly sunk in the silent sloughs of officialdom or kept back by the censorship of the police.

Have we not seen with our own eyes seven hungry peasants from Pskov, who were being forcibly removed to the province of Tobol'sk, wandering, without food or lodging for the night, about Tverskaia Square in Moscow until Prince D. V. Golitsyn ordered them to be looked after at his own expense?[30]

5. The Story of the Cantonist Yaakov Son of Hirsch Hermanovitz

Written and brought to print by Rabbi S. Beilin, rabbi of the town of Irkutsk, Siberia.[31]

Yaakov Hermanovitz was born in 1828 in a village near Irkutsk, and was released from the military in 1869.

His father was a "prisoner-settler." At that time many prisoners were exiled to Siberia to develop the region. Their children were considered property of the military, as these new settlements belonged to the department of military colonies. In the days of Arakcheev, cantonist institutions were also attached to that department.

In 1844, Hermanovitz, aged sixteen, was conscripted to the Irkutsk half-battalion as the son of a prisoner-settler. Pressure was immediately exerted on him that he should convert to Christianity. He was seized, put into a

---

29 *Polit-ekonom*—according to Herzen, someone who places considerations of efficiency above humane values.
30 See a similar event in Moisy Spiegel's testimony above.
31 S. Beilin, "Iz rasskazov o kantonistakh" [From stories about cantonists], *Evreiskaia starina* 2, no. 3 (1909): 115–119.

mattress cover, and thrown with ropes down the stairwell from the second floor. He was then dragged back up. As a result of this "exhortation," he was hospitalized for six months.

Hermanovitz further relates that when they went to bathe in the river, the sergeant would take hold of Jewish children by their heads and dunk them up to fifteen times into the water. The children screamed, drowning, but the sergeant would continue, shouting, "Cross yourself and I'll let go." If the child persisted in his stubbornness, he would finally be found on the riverbank—unbaptized.

Hermanovitz was considered stubborn. Three of his friends had already yielded and converted. He was abused in all sorts of ways. Once, a military barber injured his head seventeen times. Another method of abuse was stealing and damaging possessions. The children kept their uniform in personal drawers. A boy would get up in the morning, go to his drawer, and suddenly discover that everything had been stolen. The commanders would come and start to threaten the boy with heavy punishment for "selling army property." The child would beg to let him go, and then the commander would give him some good advice—to convert to Christianity and thus erase his "sins."

Or they brought cabbage soup with some pork. A Jewish boy only eats bread.

"Hey, Zhid, why aren't you eating soup?" the sergeant would scream.

"I can't; the pork stinks."

"Oh, that's why? Go and kneel in front of Jesus's icon!"

They would keep him on his knees for one or two hours until he collapsed, and in the end they gave him lashes.

The commanders chose Hermanovitz and another boy, Leib Sod, to be an example. They thought that, if they succeeded in forcing these two children to convert, others would follow suit. They were sent for exhortation with the head of the local church, but the boys persisted in their refusal. They were taken up to the church belltower and kept there till six o'clock in the morning. The priests pretended to have forgotten the boys, who stood clinging to each other to somehow get warm. It was very cold. The next morning the verger arrived and was horrified. The children had almost frozen to death. The verger allowed them to warm up in the monastery kitchen and gave them hot tea to drink. That was when the harassment ended. Finally, Petukhov, the head of the priests' academy, summoned them. According to Hermanovitz's description, he looked like our patriarch Abraham with a long white beard and a kind expression on his face.

"Who are you, children?" he asked.

"We are Jews."

"Don't you want to become Christians?"

"No, no. We want to remain Jewish like our fathers and forefathers."

"Then that is what you will do—you will remain Jewish, and may the God of Israel be with you."

It was absolutely forbidden for Jewish parents to visit their cantonist children and even to speak to them. Once, Hermanovitz saw his mother walking past the cantonist school and he called to her: "Mama!" She stopped and started to talk to him from a distance in Yiddish. The commander arrested the mother and sent her to the police station where she was made to wash the floors for four days.[32]

---

32   The circumstances of this story are unclear. How could the mother, the wife of a prisoner-settler, not have been careful? As a resident of the city she had easier possibilities to make contact with her son. We should note that Hermanovitz is the only one who details how they abused him. Nevertheless, he did not convert.

Part I

FORCED CONSCRIPTION OF JEWS: THE DECREE AND ITS IMPLEMENTATION

1

Preparatory Measures for the Legislation of Compulsory Conscription of Jews

A. Social and Sociological Motives

After the occupation of Poland at the end of the eighteenth century, more than a million Jews were incorporated into the Russian Empire as a result of the partitions of Poland in 1772 and 1793 and its final annexation in 1795. The empire with all its state systems, and the Russian people in general, now encountered a people whose culture was very different from the Russian civilization that mixed Orthodox Christianity with Asian influences.

In contrast to the situation in Western Europe, the Jewish people (called the People of Israel in Russian official documents) managed to exist in the new era in Eastern Europe with national, social, and judicial autonomy as a result of the lack of central government in the region. The changes in society in Europe at the time of the French Revolution and thereafter did affect the Jewry of Eastern Europe, but did not penetrate it.

As we will learn, the Jewish public was not homogeneous and did not remain stagnant. It too experienced changes that characterized European nations in the new era, if at a slower pace. From the social point of view, the Jews who lived in Russia included well-educated people—merchants, industrialists, craftsmen in advanced trades, the first *maskilim*, or more exactly: the forerunners of Haskalah, scientists educated outside Russia, authors, philosophers, etc. Nevertheless, there were no signs of differentiation leading to community disintegration, as occurred among other populations in Russia at the beginning of the twentieth century.

For the purpose of this study, we will discuss the question of how the Russian people in general, and the monarchy in particular, viewed the Jews. The first study on this subject was conducted by Senator Derzhavin, a poet and historian, who was commissioned by Tsar Alexander I in 1800 to investigate the causes of the famine and impoverishment of the peasants in Belarus.[1] He described the financial situation in Belarus in somber colors: "The Polish estate owners are lazy; they do not develop businesses in fields other than agriculture, are not concerned for the future of their homesteads, and only look for entertainment."

To maintain such a lifestyle, Derzhavin wrote, estate owners rented out their estates to Jewish or Christian tenants, granting each tenant the status of a real landlord, to whom the farmers had to sell their produce, and from whom they had to buy their goods. This assumption, at first sight, required us to draw conclusions about the owners of the estates as being irresponsible. However, Derzhavin was aware of the mindset among the ministers, who viewed the Jews as responsible for the famine, and therefore he wrote in some of his conclusions that the Jews were not a productive factor in the economy, but were parasites. "They do not grow crops, but obtain them from the farmers." His obvious conclusion: to forbid renting out estates, "so that people will not deal in activities that do not suit their social status." When writing "people," Derzhavin meant "Zhids" and minor Polish nobles (known as *shliakhta*).

In forming his opinion of the desired ways of changing the situation, Derzhavin was assisted by Il'ia Frank, a *maskil* from Courland in present-day Latvia, who composed a memorandum for him titled "Can a Jew be a Good and Useful Citizen?" Derzhavin himself wrote in one of his letters that he "learned ideas of how to influence the Jews for the better from one scholarly Jew."[2]

Derzhavin noted the "lowly" state of the Jews from the point of view of morals and good character, and concluded that they should be made to study in public schools to bring them closer to Christians. However, until these achievements became possible, steps were to be taken to separate Jews and Christians.

Derzhavin further wrote in his conclusions that the Belarusian peasants were becoming impoverished because "the Jews control commerce here, particularly the sale of wheat."[3] Therefore their greed for money should be restrained by

---

1 See Gavrila Derzhavin, "Mnenie ob otvrashchenii v Belorussii goloda i ustroistve byta evreev" [An opinion letter regarding the prevention of famine in White Russia and the organization of the way of life of the Jews], in *Arkhiv istoricheskikh i prakticheskikh svedenii* [Archive of historical and practical information] (St. Petersburg: Imperatorskaia akademiia nauk, 1872), 286.
2 Archives of the Ministry of Justice, file 251, 1800, according to Iulii Gessen, *Istoriia evreiskogo naroda v Rossii* [History of the Jewish people in Russia] (Moscow and Jerusalem: Gesharim, 1993), 133. Frank sent his letter to Derzhavin from the town of Krāslava.
3 The truth is that the financial activity of the Jews contributed to the peasants' welfare.

their moral reformation. It is essential to invest in the re-education of the Jews. For that purpose:

- Jewish children should be sent to public schools;
- Jews should be forbidden from employing Christians;
- Jews should be made to leave the villages, thus removing their negative influence.

Thus, already in 1800, we meet the idea of forcibly educating the Jews. It remained only for the idea of enforcing non-Jewish education to be superimposed onto the framework of military schools.

Derzhavin enjoyed a senior position in the imperial court, and shortly after the publication of the report he was appointed minister of justice, a fact that gave added validation to his opinion on "curbing the Jews' greed for money."

B. Administrative Considerations

Following Derzhavin's proposal, and to implement his recommendations, Alexander I established the State Committee for the Organization of Jewish Life. The creation of this committee testifies to the authorities' serious attitude to the "Jewish problem." It was made up of significant intellectuals in Russia—Counts Pototsky and Speransky—as well as of the top ministers: minister of the interior—Count Kochubei and deputy foreign minister—the Polish Prince Chartoryski.[4]

The committee worked energetically. Among other members, it included high-ranking Jews: Abram Perets, a known tax-leaser, a very learned man who was a close friend of Count Kochubei; the wealthy Nota Notkin (Shklover); Leiba (Leib) Nevakhovich; and others. The representatives of the Jewish communities, who also sat in St. Petersburg, did not enjoy too much affinity with the Russian nobility, and therefore it is no wonder that the committee's decisions were directed at spreading European-style education among the Jews, while giving equal rights to "reformed" Jews.[5]

---

4   Prince Chartoryski served as governor general of Podillia, a region with a large Jewish population.
5   See, for example, the poem written by Nevakhovich, "Vopl' dshcheri Iudeiskoi" [The crying voice of the daughter of Judah] in the journal *Budushchnost'* 3 (1903): 136–139.

In summary of the committee's activity, already in 1804 it was proposed to legislate "regulations concerning the Jews" that were implemented immediately to evict them from the villages, as proposed by Derzhavin. From this we can learn of the tsar's haste in taking steps against the Jewish population.

I claim and prove that the corridors of power were largely populated by Jews, and a picture should not be painted of a homogeneous Jewish community, cut off from the imperial court and facing a hostile regime. Such an opinion, for example, is brought in the memoir of Tsiprinus, a senior official in the Ministry of the Interior at that time,[6] who would meet a scholar by the name of Mordechai Lipschitz and discuss esoteric matters of Kabbala (!), which the official was studying at the time.

At any rate, the functional attitude of the authorities toward the Jews did not stem from a distinctly ideological basis, but rather as a response to the socio-economic reality. It can be said that the decision to spread education among the Jews did not come from the will to assimilate the Jews as a goal in its own right, but as one of the tools with which to deal with this problem.

With the same ambition, the influential merchant, Nota Notkin (Shklover) proposed transferring the Jews to uncultivated areas on the coast of the Black Sea, and to establish factories there,[7] with the aim of reforming the Jews' social and economic structure.

In contrast, among the steps to be taken to reform the people, the governor of Lithuania, Ivan Frizel',[8] listed:

1. introduction of the Jews to the general education system;
2. granting equal rights to the Jews;
3. cessation of tax collection through the community administration.

Frizel''s proposal reached the ears of Derzhavin, who was already an elderly senator. And the latter adopted many of his ideas, particularly that of introducing modern education into the Jewish community (but not granting them equal rights!).

---

6   S. Stanislavskii, "K istorii kantonistov," *Evreiskaia starina* 4 (1909): 266–268.
7   *Voskhod* 6 (1900): 131.
8   Ivan Grigorievich Frizel' (1760—1810), Russian statesman, Lithuanian governor (1799-1801). *Voskhod* 3 (1895): 136, as quoted in Gessen, *Istoriia*, 136.

The elite of the Russian administration, and among them the governor of Novorossiia,[9] Count Vorontsov, as well as the Jewish representatives in the court, could point out the way to treat this problematic tangle at its root, as Sir Moses Montefiore proposed to Nicholas I: granting equal rights to the Jews.

It must therefore be understood that beneath the guise of attempting to "reform" the Jews in a step taken to be an expression of the authorities' modern and relative attitude toward the "Jewish problem," was the absolute refusal to grant equality—a refusal that has no economic or other explanation, other than prejudice. This solution, in fact, constituted the only relevant means of advancing the status of the Jewish population.[10]

The administration immediately implemented some of Derzhavin's recommendations, among other things, in the 1804 regulations concerning the Jews.[11] In order to "save the Belarusians from the exploitation of Jewish traders and leasers," an effort was made to evict Jews from the villages. It quickly became apparent that the task was impossible to carry out, requiring much continuous and costly effort. After the failure of "the operation of evicting Jews from rural settlements," a report of the Jewish Committee of March 17, 1812, written by Senator Vasilii Popov, was brought to the knowledge of Tsar Alexander. Its conclusion was that it was *not the Jews*, but the landowners, who were guilty of the impoverishment of the peasants, and therefore the Jews were not to be expelled. The tsar did not approve the report.[12] The Napoleonic War deferred the continuation of the committee's activity, and it was only in August 1825 that the committee was reestablished to plan its policy toward the Jews.

It should be noted that in the recommendations of Derzhavin, Frizel', and Notkin there was no mention of drafting Jews to military service. This idea stemmed from another source, and only later were "reformation of the Jews" and imposing mandatory military service combined. Mandatory service for Jews was imposed by Emperor Joseph II in Austria in 1788, and by Louis XVI in France in 1790. Soon, in Russia, too, proposals for the mandatory draft of the entire population poured into the chancellery of Tsar Alexander I. The war against France, which left a deep scar on the Russian people and remained in its

---

9 "New Russia": an extensive area on the coast of the Black Sea, which underwent occupation and was quickly populated by the empire.
10 It would certainly have accelerated the process of the disintegration of the Jewish community and assimilation.
11 For the 1804 government regulations, see *Pervoe polnoe sobranie zakonov Rossiiskoi Imperii* [The first complete collection of laws of the Russian Empire] (St. Petersburg: n.p., 1878), vol. 3, part 1, 841–842, no. 21547.
12 *Voskhod* 5 (1903), quoted in Gessen, *Istoriia*, 335–337.

national collective memory for more than a century, accelerated the initiative of enlisting the Jews. However, at that time, Tsar Alexander rejected these proposals, claiming that the time was not yet ripe for their implementation.

Examining the reasons for the delay of conscription by Alexander leads us to the question of when and how, if at all, his doubts were allayed, and the road was cleared for decision-making. We can assume that one of the reasons is the profit that entered the state coffers from tax payments in exchange for exemption from conscription. Already in 1794, close to Russia's occupation of Poland, the state imposed a ransom tax of 500 rubles per male for exemption from mandatory service. The money was collected by the community administration (the *kahal*), ensuring the security of the income. On the other hand, Russia had no lack of manpower, and the Jews were not considered to be good soldiers. This stereotype did not stem from their failure in military service, but from a negative and disparaging perception of the Jews.

Iulii Gessen[13] found a proposal written in French[14] in the archives of the Tsar's Own Chancellery, file 602 from 1811, according to which Jews were to be conscripted for labor in factories. The writer cited as a motive the rapid natural reproduction of the Jews and the need to prevent their population from growing. The concern voiced by the nobleman who wrote the proposal is based on statistics that testify to the increase of the Jewish population at the time. The author also suggested an alternative method to prevent the Jewish population's natural growth—sending them for resettlement to remote areas. He predicted that the majority of the Jews would die as a result of the harsh conditions. From this document we can learn of the combination of two aims—economic efficacy as well as the extermination of the Jewish nation.

C. Ideological Motives

The same nobleman, a retired captain, recommended recruiting Jews to the army with a quota double that of Christian soldiers, with the additional conscripts being a penalty for the taxes not paid. This and other proposals for solving the "Jewish problem" include:

---

13 Gessen, *Istoriia*, 146.
14 It was written by a member of the Russian nobility, whose written language was French, not Russian.

- antisemitic motives—namely, ideological motives;
- the need to prevent natural population growth;
- financial benefit;
- conscription in exchange for non-payment of taxes.

In short, these were the main points of Nicholas I's policy toward the Jews. Already during the reign of his older brother (Alexander I), there were various draft proposals, but with only one case, as far as we know, in which the idea of forced conversion was raised.

For example, a proposal that was written and sent in the 1820s from the Third Section of the Tsar's Own Chancellery,[15] offered to clearly prove the Jews' intentions of undermining other religions in the Russian Empire. From the point of view of its author, the Jews constituted a threat to all other nations, and they also cooperated with the criminal world in Russia. The writer, who claimed to be an expert, gave a historical review of the Jews from time immemorial, in the style of the French author Voltaire and other antisemitic historians. In his conclusion, the "expert" proposed enlisting the Jews for military service, with the aim of turning them into a productive element within Russian society, after being trained in the army in beneficial crafts in the fields of the military, agriculture, and transportation. In this way, combat soldiers would be released from superfluous jobs.

At the end of the third page, he writes:

> A Jew who enters military service will feel that he can no longer observe his former religion. Furthermore, he will fear the penalties and severe actions that he will experience on becoming a soldier. Therefore, without the ability to observe the religion of his forefathers, he will abandon his religion of his own accord. This will make it easier for him to concern himself with his inner world, which yearns for calm and peace.[16] I wish to prove that neither is there anything cruel nor any injustice in this proposal. . . .

---

15 Central Archives for the History of the Jewish People, Jerusalem, HMF815. The Third Section of the Tsar's Own Chancellery was a secret police department established in Imperial Russia by Count Benkendorf, who served as the first chief of gendarmes—uniformed security police.

16 It is interesting to look into the mindset of a Russian noble of the time, and to study the tools with which he analyzes the inner world of people in general, and of Jews in particular.

According to the author, the Jews had ignored the payment of conscription tax during the Napoleonic War, so it would be only fitting that they should be conscripted according to a quota twice higher than that of the Russians, thus compensating Russia for the deficit in tax payments.

He continues:

> The recruitment will apply to young ages (from age seven or ten), not only because under these conditions they are fitter for military service, but also because *the fact that they are young will make it easier for them to leave their erroneous faith, unlike adults who are more faithful to their religion.* Minors can be drafted within the framework of military schools for cantonists. Thus, it will be possible to teach them Christianity and to baptize them before their active conscription.

In a different section, the writer refers to Jewish girls who could be put into closed educational institutions. Girls above the age of twelve would be doomed to marry Christian settlers who lived in new outposts in Siberia.

> One need not be concerned that these girls will spread the Jewish religion in the colonies. They are not proficient in the laws of their religion and will not be capable of influencing the settlers. On the contrary, the settlers in these outposts come either from a criminal background or from areas in Malorossiia [Little Russia—Ukraine] and are known to be tough people and devout Christians.

Although this ostensibly is not relevant to our discussion, one can learn from this malicious plan about the mindset and ambitions of the instigators of the conscription of Jewish boys.

Beyond the hatred of Israel that emerges from these pages, it follows that baptism into Christianity was the ultimate aim of conscripting minors. Importantly, the final draft ordinance of 1827 seems to be an exact, word-for-word repetition of these recommendations. The document implies that indirect pressure should be exerted to convert—through education or creating conditions that prevent observing *mitzvot*. Later, these ideas were received well and were accepted in practice.

This document presents one of the foundations of the conscription scheme. Other plans and proposals are also very similar to each other and testify to a clear trend within the Russian public already at the beginning of the century and before the reign of Nicholas I.

When discussing the ideological aspect, one should not limit the discussion to the antisemitic factor. The process of the acceptance of the decree recruiting mature youth and cantonists should be viewed through the wider lens of trends in Europe in general, and in Russia in particular, after the French Revolution and the Russian Empire's victory in the war against Napoleon. This topic warrants separate research, but for our purposes it is enough to say that it seems to represent the opinion of Count Uvarov, the minister of education. The quotation that follows was written much later, after the acceptance of the decree, and to explain the concept of the "rapprochement" (*sblizhenie*) between the two populations post factum, but it still seems relevant in the context of the conscription decree. Uvarov writes:[17]

> The elders of Israel say about the new schools initiated by Uvarov together with Lilienthal in 1843: "These institutions are wonderful. Their spirit is a true Jewish spirit, but the studies lead to conversion to Christianity." The meaning of these words in the language of those faithful to the erroneous and old-fashioned philosophy of Judaism is: "Studies in the institutions being established are likely, in the long run, to smother the Jews' fanatical desire to be separate from others, and to have them partake in the general principles of good citizenship." If that is the case, they do not err in their conjecture. And what better expresses good citizenship than the religion of the cross? ...

The same tone appears in the regulations for implementing the law to establish special schools for the education of Jews, passed in November 1844.

> ... the aim of educating the Jews is expressed in their continuous rapprochement with the Christian population and the abandonment of erroneous beliefs and harmful prejudices that exist in Talmudic studies.

---

17 *Sbornik postanovlenii po Ministerstvu narodnogo prosveshcheniia* [Collection of resolutions of the Ministry of Public Education] (St. Petersburg: Ministerstvo narodnogo prosveshcheniia, 1876), 233–234.

"Good citizenship" (*grazhdanstvennost'*), according to the understanding of the Russian intelligentsia of the time, involved participation in the advancement of the state from a place of personal responsibility. The state was considered a goal in its own right, and strengthening it and serving it was a critical test for every loyal citizen. The Jews were far from this worldview, something intolerable in the eyes of those who worshipped the state and order. Our claim is that there is a significant difference between the desire for conversion and the "rapprochement" plan, not only in theory, but also in practice. Indeed, the rapprochement that took place between Jews and non-Jews at the end of the nineteenth century and the beginning of the twentieth century was manifest in the assimilation of Jews into the Christian-Russian culture, but not necessarily in conversion.

The tsar's advisors saw in the "rapprochement" of the two populations, by teaching the Jews Russian culture, the best way to achieve their good citizenship. In other words: the goal was to make the Russian Empire's population uniform. The establishment of schools for the cantonists in an effort to crowd people into social and political institutions according to arbitrary planning was the first indication of Nicholas I and his ministers' policy.

D. Economic Motives

Iulii Gessen showed that the Ministry of Finance was even more interested in the conscription law than the military administration. According to the February 1820 memorandum of the ministerial committee,[18] the then minister of finance, Gur'ev, proposed conscripting an additional Jewish soldier for every 1000 rubles of deficit in the payment of community taxes. Special attention should be paid to this proposal, which was temporarily rejected at the time. Ostensibly, there is no connection between conscription of soldiers and compensation for lack of payment or paying that deficit. The persistence in this demand, which was implemented only in 1854 according to the tsar's direct orders, seemingly testifies to the officials' trend to cut corners. The arrears in payment only increased, and it was clear to the officials that there would be no improvement in the future, and that the Ministry of Finance's reports would testify to failure of tax collection. Therefore, exchanging the deficit for conscripted soldiers was intended to

---

18 Arkhiv Ministerstva vnutrennikh del, departament politsii ispolnitel'noi [Archives of the Ministry of Internal Affairs, department of police enforcement], file 349 (1827), quoted in Gessen, *Istoriia*, 32.

"beautify" the ministry reports. At the same time, this step constituted sanctions against the community with the intention of speeding up the payments and as a penalty for the arrears in payment. It seems that these considerations ultimately created the Ministry of Finance's position, but one cannot take the "whitewashing factor" lightly, either. As we will see below, even the *kahal*, which generally opposed conscription, sent a request to the authorities, asking them to offset the deficit in tax collection by additional conscription.

Four years later, the government committee met again to discuss conscription. It is interesting that the then minister of defense expressed the opinion that the time had not yet arrived for the conscription of Jews. Namely, the army did not need, and was not interested in, additional soldiers of an unknown disposition. In contrast, the new minister of finance, Count Kankrin,[19] claimed that *"the most efficient way of limiting the birthrate among the Jews* is by imposing actual mandatory conscription" (instead of taking financial compensation). According to Kankrin's proposal, boys between the ages of thirteen and fifteen were to be conscripted, with half being sent to work in factories (vocational education), and the rest trained for military service. He also suggested that, after their release from the military, Jewish soldiers would only be allowed to live within the Pale of Settlement, "excluding those who had converted during their service in the army."[20] From this comment it can be concluded that, at least at that early stage, none of the initiators of the legislation thought that there would be total conversion to Christianity among the Jews. From the cautious style, we can assume that Kankrin did not expect such a mass phenomenon, and that he preferred that soldiers who had undergone "reeducation" in the army should return to their people to exert a reformative influence on them. From a political-economic perspective, only craftsmen, farmers, and merchants who were members of guilds, were considered to be efficient professionals. Landowners, innkeepers, peddlers, and petty traders were not considered "efficient." This was despite the fact that progressive governors, such as Prince Vorontsov of Novorossiia, indicated that these vocations were essential for the village economy.

Other opinions were voiced in the ministerial committee, according to which only those not studying in public schools were to be conscripted, and farmers and craftsmen should be released from mandatory service. In either event,

---

19   See portrait below.
20   *Kniga no. 368.66 Osobogo komiteta ministrov* [Book no. 368.66 of the Special ministerial committee], November 20, 1823, as quoted in Gessen, *Istoriia*, 321.

this proposal bears a distinctly economic nature, even if it was necessary to use enforced tools to execute it.

In contrast, it was proposed in a committee meeting that there should be additional conscription in exchange for the community's non-compliance in tax payment, where the conscription of an adult soldier cancelled a debt of 1000 rubles, and that of a minor, 500 rubles. It is clear from this proposal that the preferred trend was drafting adult soldiers, in contrast to the claim that it was preferable to draft minors in order to increase the chances of conversion among Jews. The proposal was rejected because of Kankrin's opposition. He claimed that it was "not ethical to take people in exchange for money." If we assume that someone as influential as Kankrin did not need to put on a pretense in the small circle of ministers, we can learn from this statement something of the liberal state of mind among those who planned the legislation.[21] Attention should be paid to the date of the document for the purpose of a more exact documentation of the decree's preparation. In one of the meetings of the committee, the minister of defense claimed that "the Jews should not yet be drafted," that the time was not yet ripe for it.

Senator Novosel'tsev took the same stand in a document ordered by the tsar stating his opinion. He claimed that one had to achieve conscription in a slow process of Russification. That is to say, first integrate and then draft them.

From the committee's documents one can assume that the trend was:

- to limit the birth rate by removing men of a fertile age from married life;
- to give vocational education, directing Jews to industrial sectors of the economy;
- to change the social structure of the Jewish community;
- to convert Jews to Christianity.

It is interesting to note that the desire of the authorities to make the Jews more efficient stemmed from difficulties in collecting taxes. The government was doubly aware of these difficulties, as the Jews conveyed their financial distress through their emissaries. From several documents it can be seen that the tsar accepted their complaints with a certain amount of understanding. When the governor of Grodno reported terrible impoverishment in his region, particularly

---

21 From a draft of regulations concerning drafting Jews for military service, prepared by the ministerial committee. Gosudarstvennyi arkhiv Rossiiskoi Federatsii [State archive of Russian Federation], f. 1409, op. 1 (1823), as quoted in Gessen, *Istoriia*, 33.

in the towns of Endor (present-day Sviataia volia), Krynky, and Vole (present-day Indura), Alexander I ordered "the acceleration of the legislation concerning alleviating the collections of tax arrears from the Jews."[22] As a result fines of those caught avoiding tax payments were cancelled.

In 1820, the minister of finance admitted that none of the steps taken for the economic "recovery" of the Jews had borne fruit, and that "very many Jews are impoverished, are losing their permanent place of residence, are engaging in beggary, are unable to support their family, and are not complying with tax payments."[23] Many Jews were walking around without identity cards, and the exact size of the Jewish population, which in a scrupulous examination was found to be more than three times that of the communities' report, was not known. For some reason, researchers underestimate the significance of this disorder as a factor in the harshening of tsarist policy toward the Jews; however, in my opinion, Nicholas I's competent regime was not capable of coming to terms with the fact that within the empire were hundreds of thousands of citizens who had never been counted. It is no wonder that together with the conscription effort, attempts were made to obtain trustworthy information concerning the number of the Jews. Thus, the recruitment order imposed an obligation on the Jewish communities to tighten the control over the reporting of births. All this led to the desire of the government, and especially of the ministerial committee, to find ways to reduce the birthrate. "It is the committee's responsibility, in addition to everything else, to find ways of reducing the Jewish population in general, and especially in areas where there is abnormal natural reproduction."

E. The Jews' Influence on the Development of the Conscription Law

Although the number of *maskilim* in Russia at the beginning of the nineteenth century was very low, we find their representatives in St. Petersburg in positions that allowed the access to the governing leadership. Iulii Gessen writes that Frank, a Jewish *maskil* from Courland who had been educated in Germany, influenced Derzhavin's opinions. He led Derzhavin to the conclusion that the nature of the Jews to "exploit" had its source in their over-adherence to the Talmud and

---

22 Arkhiv lichnoi Ego Imperatorskogo Velichestva Kantseliarii [Archive of the Tsar's Own Chancellery], file 4296 (1823), quoted in Gessen, *Istoriia*, 65.
23 Ibid.; *Pervoe polnoe sobranie zakonov Rossiiskoi Imperii*, vol. 2, regulation 2884.

to rabbis, and that the way to improve the situation was through general education and distancing them from the rabbis' influence. This view is symptomatic.

One can divide the Jews who had sway in the government, and even in the imperial court, into several groups:

1. emissaries of the communities;
2. Jews who had converted, who functioned as censors and as "experts" on Jewish matters;
3. wealthy Jews—merchants who did business with the authorities;
4. philosophers and *maskilim*.

One cannot come to a definite division—a wealthy tradesman was often categorized as a *maskil*. However, the variety of opinions represented in the empire's capital testifies to possible clashes between different Jewish lobbyists, allowing the leadership to compare their opinions and to choose the most convenient one. From this point of view, no group could claim a monopoly in presenting the interests of the Jews, and there was no uniform Jewish representation.

Two apostates had influence on Nicholas's associates:[24] Sandberg, who served in the imperial foreign office, and another convert by the name of Podelo. They both supplied the tsar and the 1823 ministerial committee with background material concerning the Jews. In the protocol of the committee from 1826, it says that a report from an apostate was brought before the ministers concerning Hasidism, Talmud, and Kabbala. This is one of the proofs that that the ministers asked for exact information about the Jews, studied it, and to that end they looked for serious experts. These experts had influence in formulating the ministers' opinions. We mentioned above the influence attributed to Leib Nevachovich on the ministers. Especially impressive was the position of the merchant Abram Perets, an associate of the Minister of the Interior, Kochubei, one of the members of the ministerial committee for reforming the Jews. Similarly, as mentioned above, Nota Notkin (Natan Shklover) presented a plan to transfer the Jews to new settlements in the south.

A representative example of the interaction between the *maskilim* and the tsar's government, on the one hand, and the *maskilim* and the traditional Jews, on the other, is the life of Dr. Max Lilienthal who championed the introduction of general education among the Jews. Even though he was a religious Jew, in

---

24 *Evreiskaia starina* 2 (1909): 251–254.

the conduct of other *maskilim* at the time, one can see parallels to Lilienthal's worldview.

Dr. Lilienthal arrived in Russia about fifteen years after the start of conscription and was immediately employed by the government even though he was not a local resident. An imperial minister, in this case Uvarov, made contact with him very easily. If we assume that ultimately Lilienthal retired from his office out of love of his fellow Jews, Minister Uvarov was certainly aware of this love. Thus, we can say that the tsar's ministers had a certain amount of open-mindedness towards Jews who were ready to cooperate with the regime in modernizing their nation.

Despite his being religious, Lilienthal set out to convince the Jews that the government's aim was "only to make them fit for good citizenship and to be sensitive to values of the accepted civilization, without attempting to harm their religion."[25] When his task met with obstacles because of the opposition of the Jewish public, the police were enlisted to help. The following is what Lilienthal then wrote to the minister of education about his people: "dirty bearded Jews who are barely touched by the rays of enlightenment."[26] Lilienthal suggested to Uvarov imposing new taxes on the reading of the Torah and on maintaining traditional teachers for the children, and thereby to support the government schools. Among other things, he helped bring about the imposition of supervision by the tsarist ministry of education of religious boys' schools and yeshivot, so as to force general education on their students.

Similarly, many *maskilim* were motivated by their belief in the need to spread education among the Jews and exerted pressure to this end. This movement is comparable to the trend of enlisting children to military schools. In his instructions for activating comprehensive education, Uvarov wrote (November 1844): "The aim of Jewish education is to create continual contact with the Christian population, and to eliminate harmful prejudices that are learned from the Talmud."[27] This goal could certainly have been written on the front page of the ordinance for cantonist conscription, although it was defined only about fifteen years later. It is illustrative that this "educational" activity was expressed

---

25 Max Lilienthal and David Philipson, *Max Lilienthal, American Rabbi; Life and Writings* (New York: publisher, 1915), 48, 247.
26 Ibid.
27 Postanovleniia Ministerstva prosveshcheniia [Resolutions of the Ministry of education] (1844), 521; Michael Stanislawski, *Tsar Nicolas 1 and the Jews* (Philadelphia: Jewish Publication Society of America, 1983), 201.

by exerting compulsive pressure to convert to Christianity in cantonist schools at the time.

Shmuel Feiner in his book *Haskalah and History*[28] notes the *maskilim*'s blind faith in the integrity of the imperial goals. One of the first *maskilim* in Russia, S. Fuenn, wrote in a letter to his friend Stern:

> The Jewish people in this time and in this country are still on the lowest rung of the ladder of national and moral enlightenment.... Now His Majesty the Tsar has taken upon himself to be the tiller of our soil, to uproot from it all rank and bitter weeds, to cleanse the hearts of the Jewish people of all evil schemes, and to sprinkle blessed dew upon the thirsting, yearning soil...

B. Gottlieber, one of the central figures of the Haskala movement, ran a passionate campaign in favor of Nicholas I, composing a song of praise in his honor:

> ... In honor of our lord and king, the mighty emperor Nicolai I, may he rise and be greatly elevated and stand to the right of true justice; may he be of support to Zion...[29]

In light of these words of praise for the oppressor of the Jews, we should ask: Did the *maskilim*, who generally lived in outlying cities, not know about the suffering caused by conscription? How were they unaware of the decree of forced conversion? Or maybe the meaning of the cantonist decree and its implementation was not clear-cut even to that generation.

According to Tcherikover, the maskilim took a stand in opposition to the Jewish people. One of the darkest pages in the history of the *maskilim* is their role in the Russian government's persecution of Jewish books. Already in 1827, Nicholas instructed that information concerning the printing of Jewish books be brought to him. Professor Tugendhold, a *maskil* from Vilna, submitted a memorandum of books printed by Hasidim. Avraham Dov Lebensohn

---

28 Shmuel Feiner, *Haskalah and History: The Emergence of a Modern Jewish Historical Consciousness* (Oxford: Littman Library of Jewish Civilization: 2002), 158.
29 Avraham Beer Gottlieber, *Kol shirei mehalelel* [A collection of songs], vol. 1 (Warsaw: Alafin Halevi, 1890), 71.

also submitted a request to Interior Minister Bludov to inspect all Jewish books.[30]

Raphael Mahler writes in his fundamental book *Hasidism and the Jewish Enlightenment* about the significant role of the censor Tugendhold, who wrote in 1831: "Anyone who knows me knows well that apart from several principles of the Jewish religion, in practice I have no connection to the Jewish religion and its members. I am constantly in contact with honorable Christians." Similarly, he wrote (in the introduction to a prayer book translated into Polish) that Jewish youth must be grateful to the Christians despite all the difficulties and harassment that are likely to harm them.

It is clear that this identification, intended to create full rapprochement with Nicholas and his policies, removed the barriers between the *maskilim* and the imperial court.

Just as the "expert" who prepared the report for the Tsar's Chancellery (see above) needed justification for his antisemitic stance, so Nicholas himself found justification for his deeds in the camp of the *maskilim*, which was smaller but much more vocal than the remote Jewish community. It is not impossible that the *maskilim*'s support for the tsar's policies, and their submitting up-to-date information and advice, were the significant factor in accepting and implementing the conscription decree.

The influence of Jewish *maskilim* on political processes in Russia at the time has not yet been fully analyzed. The censors, usually considered an integral part of the imperial system, should be seen as having great influence on the decision makers.

Nonetheless, we do not have the ability to estimate the part played by Jews close to the court in the creation of the conscription decree.

---

30 Elias Tcherikover, "Istoriia Obshchestva dlia rasprostraneniia prosveshcheniia mezhdu evreiami v Rossii" [On the history of the Society for the spread of education among Jews in Russia], *Zion* 2 (New York, 1985): 162.

2

Who Was Tsar Nicholas I?

A. The Influence of the Tsar on the Development of the Legislation

In order to fully comprehend the development of the law for mandatory conscription of Jews, we must understand Tsar Nicholas I's personality and learn about his assistants, councilors, and the executors of the plan. Nicholas I was born on June 25, 1796, and was crowned after the death of his brother, Tsar Alexander I, in December 1825, in the atmosphere of the uprising of imperial army officers, known as the Decembrist Revolt, as they demanded reforms to the administration system.

Nicholas was raised in his early childhood by a Scottish nurse, and later by a German tutor of Baltic origin. He married a Prussian princess, daughter of King Frederick William III of Prussia and sister to the prince of Holland. This international nature of his upbringing made Nicholas Romanov a member of global European culture. Therefore, it was natural that his immediate circle, his friends and the influential individuals to whom he gave governing positions, had French, English, and German education. Examples include Count Uvarov, Count Kiselev, Speransky, Kankrin, Kleinmikhel', and others.

The extent of European nobility's influence on Nicholas can be learned from a document found in the chancellery of the officer of the military gendarmes and head of the Third Section of the Tsar's Own Chancellery, Count Benkendorf, who was extremely close to the tsar. The document concerns a report on the appearance of the minister of education, Uvarov, in the ministerial committee on Jewish affairs on February 18, 1843. On that day a proposal was being discussed to transfer all the Jews to agricultural settlements in unsettled areas. The majority of the committee members supported the proposal, but Uvarov opposed it. He claimed: "It would be a cruel and unjust deed against an entire nation." Uvarov suggested an alternative: spreading educated and enlightened values among the Jews. When he heard this, Nicholas I rose and left the meeting in fury. Shortly after, a meeting was held between Nicholas and the king of Prussia (Nicholas's father-in-law), in which the two discussed the treatment of the Jews. The king of Prussia convinced Nicholas that the minister of education was correct, whereupon Nicholas reconvened the committee to dismiss the settlement proposal.[1]

It is common to see Nicholas I as an absolute antisemite and an administrator who paranoidly believed in military order as the means to solve all problems. As much as this description can be relevant, the international context must be taken into account that Nicholas ruled in Europe after the French Revolution. It is true that in the second half of his reign relations between him and European states deteriorated, but when conscription was implemented, Nicholas was still interested in appearing before Europe as a king living in the spirit of the time, who aimed at establishing a civilized state. However, the cruel methods with which Nicholas attempted to advance the Russian Empire toward the new age did not pass unseen by the European heads of state. Thus, for example, wrote Queen Victoria, queen of England, who was related to the Romanov family and knew the tsar well:

> He is serious and tough, a man of principles, an advocate of man's personal responsibility. He received a good education, but he is only interested in military matters and politics. I assume that his intentions are good, even when he performs cruel deeds, because in his naïveté he thinks that that is the only way to control people. I am of the opinion that the horrific suffering of simple people who suffer because of him escapes him. I have much evidence that he is mostly not aware of his subjects' corruption, holding himself to be an especially honest person.[2]

Before his coronation, Nicholas was chief inspector of the Corps of Engineers and established battalion schools for soldiers in order to improve their military training. It was later thought that this initiative was a precursor of his work in expanding and improving cantonist schools. In an effort to introduce general education into military institutions, Nicholas also established eleven colleges for officers who were members of the aristocracy.

---

1 Central Archives for the History of the Jewish People, Jerusalem, HMF815.
2 See J. N. Westwood, *Endurance and Endeavour: Russian History 1812–1971* (New York: Oxford University Press, 1973), 206.

As has been shown above, Nicholas was not the first who initiated the cantonist project. Everything was ready when he was crowned in December 1825. However, the implementation of the project was delayed because the ministerial committee regarded it as an integral part of the comprehensive constitution on Jewish matters, which had not yet been finalized.

Nicholas's attitude towards the conscription of the Jews changed over the years. One can understand the changes in his policy by studying the changes that occurred in his personality. At the very beginning of his reign, he found himself in the chaos of the Decembrist Revolt and its suppression. In fact, Nicholas never enjoyed absolute quiet on the home front. The French Revolution of 1830 led to the cancellation of the results of the Russian victory in the Napoleonic War. At that time, the Polish revolution, the November Uprising, took place, which increased his suspicion that there was subversive activity within the kingdom. The year 1848 saw a wave of revolutions in Europe, which necessitated Russian military intervention in Austria, and naturally caused a radicalization of the tsar's political and social position.

One should take into account that the beginning of the restlessness in Europe was connected to tension between religions and to the status of holy sites. In 1853 the harsh Crimean War broke out, which continued until the tsar's death on February 2, 1856, and ended with the full submission of the Russian forces.[3] The Crimean War was of a religious nature, and its goal was influence on the Holy Land. This undoubtedly contributed to the religious extremism of many Russians, and of the tsar in particular. Thus, one can see the changes in Nicholas's policy toward the Jews as a direct result of political developments within the empire and without.

Nicholas certainly had a very definite attitude toward the Jews as part of the xenophobia that was common in those days, which was mixed with scorn for the Jews and Christian prejudices. However, surprisingly, we find him praising Jewish soldiers in his diary, conducting parades for his conscripted soldiers, and appointing them to elite units including the life guard of his Imperial Guard, without taking their religion into account. This treatment testifies to the tsar's ambivalence toward Jews he was not personally acquainted with. As mentioned above, there were many Jews in the imperial court and government ministries. The tsar would often hear warm recommendations of Jews from his

---

3   In this war, Jewish soldiers, especially, excelled in their heroism, among them graduates of cantonist schools.

aides (whether given in exchange for bribery or as an expression of genuine admiration).

Together with all of the above, two types of accusations raised anew against the Jews—blood libels and spreading the Jewish religion among the Christians—should be seen as significant factors in forming the tsar's attitude toward implementing the conscription law. Paradoxically, Nicholas was particularly attentive to the accusation of the Jews missionizing, and may very well have viewed converting the Jews to Christianity as a means of fighting back.

In 1811, Jews were accused of converting two gentile girls to Judaism and in 1823 came the accusation of the conversion of a Christian by the name of Yohanan of Dvinsk, who was later murdered. At the same time Jews were accused of murdering a Christian baby of the Terent'ev family in the town of Velizh. An amazing detail in this event is that Nicholas himself undertook the case, ordering the governor of the Vilna (Vilnius) district to investigate the affair and report to him: "We must discover who the miserable murdered babies are. It can easily be clarified whether or not a despicable lie is present."[4] From Nicholas's reaction, one cannot unequivocally assume that he believed the blood libel; perhaps the opposite is true. Whatever the case may be, the investigations and the publicity around this case lasted several years, and framed the creation of the law for conscription of the Jews. Several years later, the deputy minister of justice, Panin, submitted his report stating that it had been a false accusation. This verdict was supported by the head of the department for civil and religious affairs, Admiral Mordvinov, and in 1835 the Jews were exonerated. Nicholas ratified the final decision, but commented: "I cannot be convinced that the Jews did not commit the murder."[5] One can understand the feelings of the tsar when a bill was presented to him permitting Jews to employ Christians in their homes. The tsar wrote on the bill "... it should be forbidden for them to live permanently in Jewish homes ... Similarly, Jews were allowed to operate post offices but were to prevent the presence of Christians in them."[6] Out of concern

---

4 Iulii Gessen, *Velizhskaia drama: Iz istorii obvineniia evreev v ritual'nykh prestupleniiakh* [The Velizh drama. From the history of accusing Jews of ritual crimes] (St. Petersburg: Tipografiia Rozena, 1904), 79.
5 Ibid.
6 Arkhiv Gosudarstvennogo soveta, departament zakonov [Archive of the State Council, department of laws], *Vtoroe sobranie zakonov* (1827), no. 1487: "O dozvolenii evreiam imet' v usluzhenii khristianok i t.p." [On allowing Jews to have Christian women in their service etc.], quoted in Gessen, *Istoriia*, 29.

of spreading Judaism, a law was passed in 1825 limiting the religious movement of Subbotniki.[7]

Nicholas certainly feared the Jews and saw himself as being responsible for protecting the Christians from them. Paradoxically, we should ask: If Nicholas believed to such an extent in the threat to Christianity by the Jews, how did he not fear drafting them into the army? And indeed, we read in the documents of complaints that the Jews were a negative influence on the Christian soldiers.

In 1855, at the age of fifty-nine, the tsar died from pneumonia during a large military training operation, in a desperate attempt to overcome the disease in field conditions.[8]

B. Hatred of Jews

In summer 1816, when still a twenty-year-old prince, Nicholas toured Russia in order to become acquainted with the kingdom. In accordance with his mother's request, he recorded his impressions in a diary. This is an entry made during his visit to White Russia:[9]

> In practice, the Zhids control everything [instead of the nobility and landowners, Y.M.], and they literally are impoverishing this miserable nation by their business activities. They have succeeded in controlling all branches of business. They are also tradesmen, tax agents, lessees and operators of hostels and inns, owners of flourmills, craftsmen, etc., etc. In this manner they are very successful in harassing the poor and driving them crazy. They are even ready to receive yet-unplanted produce as a pledge. *True blood-sucking leeches*, completely drying out this miserable area. It is surprising that in the 1812 war against Napoleon they displayed exemplary loyalty to the Russian crown, and were even ready to endanger their lives for us.[10]

---

7 From the word *subbota*, Sabbath in Russian. Subbotniki were Russian gentiles who chose to observe the Jewish Sabbath.
8 The circumstances of his death are not so clear, and there are various hypotheses.
9 Nicholas's knowledge is, of course, based on what he heard from his travel companions, and not taken from a primary source
10 From the diary of Aleksandr Maierovitz, *Evreiskaia starina* 2 (1912–1913): 542.

Twenty-four years later, as tsar, Nicholas once again passed through the area. On his way from Kyiv to Warsaw, he decided to tour the central fortress of Brest-Litovsk (present-day Brest, in Yiddish: Brisk). The tsar was accompanied by the governor of the district of Vilna, F. Mirkovich, who described this visit as follows:

> The tsar toured the walls of the fortress. Suddenly, he glanced at a large crowd of Jews standing below. He stopped for a moment and asked: "From where do they earn their bread? We must think of some useful employment for them. These lazy souls must work. But actually, I am supposed to expel them from here."
>
> The tsar remembered how, in Odessa, he had met a tribe of roaming gypsies who were almost naked from poverty, and they were forced to work at his command, so to speak.
>
> Later on the tour, the tsar commented, "We have to find a way to draft them into labor battalions so that they will renovate the fortress."
>
> When the tsar's chariot passed through the town streets, Nicholas noticed that the houses were on the verge of collapse, and yet the committee that examined the state of the houses had determined that they were in good shape. The tsar commented, "There is deceit here. The Jews must have bribed the audit committee. There is no one whom these Jews are not capable of bribing. A new composition of the committee must be appointed immediately."[11]

On analyzing these quotations of the tsar, we see that Nicholas was very surprised at the Jews' unreserved support of his reign at the time, and was unable to explain it. One can assume that there was some ambivalence in the tsar's attitude toward the Jews. In addition, it is instructive to compare Nicholas's different opinions in the two citations above. On his first tour, his impression was that the Jews were very active, while twenty-four years later he was of the opinion that the Jews resembled the gypsies. Nicholas sounds energetic and decisive: "We must expel...", "We must make them work...", "We must draft them into labor battalions...", "They bribe everyone...." He seems eager, attentive, and curious, with his own sharp opinion on everything.

---

11 From the diary of Aleksandr Mirkovich, *Evreiskaia starina* 2 (1909): 542.

It was only in 1840 that a new plan was submitted by Minister Kiselev at the request of the tsar, with the aim of changing the Jews' way of life completely, and an executive ministerial committee was established for that purpose. We should ask: What were the tsar and his ministers doing without a plan until 1840? After all, they were harassing the Jews constantly; why did they need a new program? Furthermore, the order to expel the Jews from areas near the border, including Brest, was given only three years later, in 1843. We are faced with a gap between the tsar's intentions and their execution. The explanation to this contradiction seems to lie in the fact that the tsar's commands passed through many systems, with his counsellors waging struggles over many questions. It was because of such disagreements that both Uvarov and Kiselev were removed from their posts at the end of Nicholas's reign.

C. The Army as a Supreme Value

In order to understand the tsar's policy in changing the structure of the state and accelerating the formation of the conscription law for Jews, it should be remembered that Nicholas viewed the structure of the army in an exaggerated way as being a model for the entire state. For example, he wrote the following about the army:

> Here there is order, there is strict unconditional legality, no impertinent claims to know all the answers, no contradiction, all things flow logically one from the other; no one commands before he has learned to obey; no one steps in front of anybody else without lawful reason; everything is subordinated to one definite goal, everything has its purpose.[12]

In other words, his aim was to achieve unreserved obedience and discipline, a clear division of duties, a uniform, standardization of procedures, and, generally, an uncomplicated reality, without any fear of contradictions, conflicts, and power struggles. It is no wonder that during his reign the military regime was copied into Russian social life in general, and became rooted in the public consciousness. With this in mind, Nicholas saw the army as the most convenient means of training the younger generation of Jews to be loyal citizens of the Christian state.

---

12 N. V. Riasonovsky, *Nicholas I and Official Nationality in Russia, 1825–1855* (Berkeley: University of California Press, 1959), 1; Stanislawski, *Tsar Nicholas I and the Jews*, 15.

3

Changes in the Tsar's Policies during the Course of His Reign, 1825–1855

A. Who Influenced the Tsar's Decisions?

1. Egor (Georg) Kankrin (1774–1845) was a German of Baltic origin. His father was invited to Russia as a scientific expert. During the Napoleonic War Kankrin served as head of the General Staff's supply division. In 1824, Alexander I appointed him minister of finance. He introduced annual reports and poll tax in Russia. Kankrin researched state economy and wrote many books on the subject. In 1823, in a meeting of the ministerial committee for the "reformation of the Jews," he claimed that there was an immediate need to limit the Jews' natural birth rate, and the best way of doing so would be drafting thirteen- to fifteen-year-old boys to be sent to work in factories. On the other hand, when it was proposed to draft additional soldiers for the purpose of erasing the community's debts, Kankrin stated: "It is not ethical to take people in exchange for money."[1]

2. Count Sergei Uvarov came from a family of noblemen, studied in Paris, was fluent in several languages and authored books (in French) about philosophy and sociology. Uvarov advocated the promotion of education in general, and among Jews in particular. After serving as rector of the university in St. Petersburg, he was appointed as deputy minister of education, and in 1832 he became minister of education. It was Uvarov who coined the formula for good citizenship, which

---

1 Arkhiv Ego Imperatorskogo Velichestva kantselliarii, Vypiski iz pravil, predvaritel'no priniatykh evreiskim komitetom ob obrashchenii evreev v voennuiu sluzhbu [Archive of His Imperial Majesty's Chancellery, Extracts from the regulations provisionally adopted by the Jewish Committee on the conscription of Jews to military service].

became accepted as the symbol of loyalty to the Russian Empire: "Orthodoxy, Autocracy, and Nationality." This triad was foreign to Russian Jews. Indeed, the Russian historian Solov'ev wrote that Uvarov himself was not Orthodox and hardly believed in his religion, and that, being a liberal, he did not consider the imperial regime as just. In a recent study of Uvarov, testimonies are brought of him being a flatterer, who would humiliate himself before those stronger than him.

In the 1830s, before his promotion in the field of education, and after he finished his career as ambassador in Europe, he traveled to Count Kleinmikhel' (whom the tsar described as "unreservedly loyal") to gain his support. He even looked after Kleinmikhel''s baby, something considered as the lowest form of degradation in the imperial court. His sycophancy led to a rapid career advancement. In addition, he was also known for his lust for money and honor.

From this negative analysis it can be concluded that, despite Uvarov's relatively progressive opinions on education, he operated out of submission to Nicholas's wishes.[2] His main influence on Nicholas was not in the development of the law on Jewish conscription, but in forming the tsar's policy toward the Jews during the time of the cantonists. In addition, similar to the tsar, Uvarov opposed granting equal rights to the Jews and to severing their connection to their permitted area of residence in the Pale of Settlement.

Uvarov's worldview was full of contradictions. His opinions were a mixture of advanced thinking and medieval philosophy, and those concerning the Jews were extremely confused. It seems that, in the first place, he did not strive to convert the Jews to Christianity, but his field of vision did not grant him a sufficiently advanced perspective. In this connection, his disdain for the "elders of Zion"[3] should be noted. On the other hand, after meeting Rabbi Schneersohn and Rabbi Yitzchak of Volozhin, Uvarov wrote:

> From my contact with them, I was convinced of their loyalty to the kingdom and their total submission to the tsar, not only because of fear of royalty, but as a result of their worldview.... Loyal, honest people, with impressive personalities and without any fawning ...

---

2 Tsintiia Vitteker, *Graf Sergei Semenovich Uvarov i ego vremia* (St. Petersburg: Akademicheskii proekt, 1999), 78.
3 In Uvarov's language "the elders of Zion" are members of a hidden Jewish leadership.

3. Count Pavel Dmitrievich Kiselev (1788–1872) was a military commander who fought actively in the 1828–1829 war against Turkey. He abolished the penalty of lashes in the units under his command. He took a sharp stand regarding the need to free the state-owned serfs from slavery. In 1835 Nicholas appointed him as head of the agricultural administration of the tsar's estates, and shortly afterwards as head of the bureau of imperial property. Till 1848 he enjoyed the tsar's full trust and stood at the head of the committee for the reformation of the Jews (established in 1840). When Alexander II ascended the throne, Kiselev advised him to open a new program for the "reformation of the Jews," in connection with which he initiated the annulment of the cantonist decree.

4. Prince Mikhail Semenovich Vorontsov was the governor-general of the settled areas in southern Ukraine (then called Novorossiia). He was known as a liberal, and supported granting equal rights to the Jews. Vorontsov felt that the Jews were fulfilling an important role in the economy and that they were not "useless."

From 1843 on, we see the growing influence of Chernyshev, the minister of defense, and Protasov, the chief procurator of the Synod, the governing body of the Russian Orthodox Church, which in Protasov's days became the state ministry for Church affairs, a bureaucratic government office in every way. On these two people, the tsar laid the responsibility of accelerating the conversion of the cantonists. At the beginning of my research, I thought that the beginning of an extensive conversion campaign in the 1840s could be dated specifically to 1843, when these two active personalities entered the scene. Indeed, when the names of Protasov and Chernyshev arose during the course of the study, it seemed to me that they would be responsible for this change. However, my assumption failed on studying their life histories.[4] It became apparent that they both served in their positions before 1843. The reason why their names do not appear as part of the conversion process earlier still needs to be explained.

5. Prince Aleksandr Ivanovich Chernyshev (1785–1857) apparently was the tsar's most trusted officer. On the day of Nicholas's coronation, Chernyshev was promoted to the post of deputy chief of staff and received the title of count. Soon after, he was appointed as minister of war, a post he held till 1852. In 1848, he was appointed as chairman of the ministerial committee and granted the title of prince. During his term of service, the number of soldiers in the army

---

4   *Entsiklopedicheskii slovar' Brokgauza i Efrona* (Berlin: Brokgauz i Efron, 1898), XXVa.

increased by forty percent, and the maintenance expenses of the army increased by seventy percent compared to the beginning of that period.

6. Concerning **Count Nicholas Alexandrovich Protasov**, it was said that he would drink water out of Nicholas's hands as an expression of absolute submission to the tsar. In 1835, he served as deputy minister of education under Uvarov. His duties included the supervision of the teachers' colleges and educational institutions of Belarus, which was populated by hundreds of thousands of Jews. In 1836, he was appointed as the chief procurator of the Synod. He transformed the Church into an organized system, similar to a government ministry. For example, he introduced into colleges for priests general studies such as medicinal sciences, natural sciences, agriculture, etc.

7. Last but not least, we must focus on **Count Aleksandr fon Benkendorf** (1783–1844). Benkendorf, of German heritage, rose to greatness already in the days of Alexander I as he led some of the most significant battles in the Napoleonic War. He was very close to Nicholas I. He assisted Nicholas I in subduing the Decembrist Revolt, after which he initiated the establishment of a political police force that, in 1826, became the Third Section of the Tsar's Own Chancellery. A year later, in 1827, he established the Corps of Gendarmes, the executive arm of the Third Section. He particularly liked to follow the actions of famous intellectuals like Alexander Pushkin and Alexander Herzen and to "educate" them.

Concluding this list of the tsar's counsellors, one can say that Nicholas gathered around him intelligent people, with general and philosophical education, who were well aware of the trends in contemporary Europe, and advocated for the advancement of industry, technology, and education. They presented a range of different opinions, which made the decision-making processes in the court very complex. Decisions were made not based on absolute dogmas, but after much discussion and the voicing of various positions.

Some earlier influences that led to the passing of the military service law for Jews are revealed by the British missionary Lewis Weill, who visited Tsar Alexander I back in 1817. Weill attempted to convince the tsar that it was forbidden to forcibly convert Jews, and that peaceful ways should be used. This position of enlightened European Christianity seems to have led Prince Golitsyn, one of the most prominent members of Russian aristocracy, to oppose the policy of forced conversion. He established the "Bible Society" to explain Christianity and spread the religion among the Jews, but he did not wish violent methods to be used for this purpose. There is no testimony that such moderacy with regard to conversion to Christianity was acceptable to Nicholas, but he undoubtedly knew that sensitivity to it existed among European nobility.

B. The 1840s: A Turning Point in the Treatment of the Jews

We mentioned above that the 1840s saw a worsening of the tsar's antisemitic trends. The submission of Minister Kiselev's memorandum on "methods of organizing Jewish matters" can be seen as the turning point. Kiselev was one of the most influential officials in the tsar's court. He referred to the "Jewish Torah" (meaning the Talmud and the *Shulḥan Arukh*, that is, a collection of rabbinical guidelines opposing the Christian worldview) as being "the reason for the Jews' alienation from state life."[5] He therefore proposed weakening the influence of the "Talmud" on the Jews by opening state schools. In addition, Kiselev recommended conducting a comprehensive enlistment of the majority of the Jews (three times more than was in practice), while at the same time shortening their term of service to ten years. He proposed teaching them, during their service, "useful" vocations (such as medicine, engineering, etc.). Then, on returning from the army, the Jews would improve their life quality. Kiselev thought that this could reduce the number of "useless" (in his opinion) Jews, while increasing the number of "useful" ones. Nicholas accepted his recommendations and created the Committee for the Determination of Measures for the Radical Reorganization of the Russian Jews. Kiselev's memorandum and the activity of the ministerial committee undoubtedly left their mark on the tsar's policy toward the conscription of Jewish soldiers. They laid the framework for the drastic change that occurred in 1843 with the introduction of forced mass conversion.

A further testimony that the tsar's attitude toward the Jews became harsher is given by the 1852 blood libel trials in Saratov.[6] This town, located on the banks of the Volga River, far from the Pale of Settlement, was home to forty-four Jewish soldiers who had been released from the army after twenty-five years of service. They lived in their own homes and had a synagogue and a Torah scroll. Some of the Jews lived there without permission but with the tacit consent of

---

5   Gessen, *Istoriia*, 79.
6   See M. Trivus, "Ritual'nye protsessy" [Ritual processes], *Evreiskaia starina* 3–4 (1912): 246–262.

the authorities. Among other things, many apostate Jews lived in the town, and even they did not completely cut off their relations with their Jewish families.

When a Christian child disappeared, the blame immediately fell, as usual, on the Jews.[7] The interrogators exerted pressure on the witnesses and the accused to extract an admission of murder. Although not all the testimony was accepted, after eight hours of interrogation, severe sentences were passed and Jews were sent to forced labor. It is clear that a staged trial such as this, that stemmed from the Christian population's anger at the neglect of the authorities to deal with these Jews, could not have taken place had the officials not been aware of the mood in the tsar's palace.

C. Changes in the Russian Empire—a List of Events

To show the gradual development of the Jewish conscription and conversion initiatives, it is necessary to sketch a general outline of events in the Russian state in order to give a comprehensive analysis of this process and its background, as well as to understand the political, social, and national factors that determined it. It seems that previous researchers who dealt with this topic did not attempt to see the intensification of these initiatives as part of a complex development. Of course, this period also saw the extensive activity of the ministerial committee and officials of the tsar to reform the Jewish population, but here I make do with events connected more immediately to conscription to the army.

1. A List of Main Events Connected to the Conscription of Cantonists

1795: The last partition of Poland. Jews are exempt from conscription in exchange for a payment of 500 rubles.
1800: Derzhavin's tour and report on ways to reform the Jews, conducted at the request of the Senate.

---

7   Only during the Beilis trial at the beginning of the twentieth century, Russian scientists proved that there was no basis for blood libels. See *Russkie uchenye o evreiskom verouchenii: Zakliucheniia prof. P. K. Kokovtsova, P. V. Tikhomirova, i I. G. Troitskogo na protsesse Beilisa* [Russian scholars on Jewish creed: Conclusions of Profs. P. K. Kokovtsov, P. V. Tikhomirov, and I. G. Troitskii at the Beilis trial] (St. Petersburg: Tipografiia L. Ia. Ganzburga, 1914).

1802: Establishment of the ministerial committee for Jewish affairs (reestablished in 1823).

1803: Formation and meetings of the ministerial committee for Jewish affairs, which includes the Jews Notkin, Perets, Zandberg, Dillon, etc.

1804: The ministerial committee proposes and regulations concerning the Jews, which include their expulsion from the villages and categorization according to "usefulness" to the public.

1812–1815: The Napoleonic War.

1817: The establishment of a Christian-Jewish association under Prince Golitsyn's Bible Society.

1823: Renewal of the ministerial committee's activity after the Napoleonic War.

1823: Preparation of a draft of the law for mandatory military service of Jews.

1825: Establishment of the committee consisting of the heads of ministries to implement the "Jewish" policy; the decision to transfer Jews to the cities.

1825: Death of Alexander I; the Decembrist Revolt; coronation of Nicholas I.

1826: Mandatory service imposed on Cossacks, Moslems, and pagans.

1826: Nicholas proposes introducing a penalty clause for conversion to Judaism.

1826–1828: War against Persia and the annexation of Armenia.

1827: Establishment of the Third Section of the Tsar's Own Chancellery, which can bypass the Senate.

1827: Passing of the law on mandatory military service for Jews.

1827: Nicholas proposes drafting two children under the age of twelve in exchange for one adult.

1828: Representatives of the *kahal* request renewal of permanent representation in the imperial court.

1828: Amendments to the conscription law. The *kahal* requests permission to draft according not to birth records but to the opinion of its administration.

1830: Uprising in France. The Polish revolt for political independence. Nicholas I suppresses the revolt.

1830: Nine tradesmen from Bohuslav complain that the *kahal* administration is burdening them with the payment of the entire community's deficit, including the draft obligation.

1830: The Senate proposes to allow offsetting tax arrears in exchange for additional recruits; the minister of finance attempts to halt this initiative.

1831: Changes in the structure of the army and the draft ordinance began and continued for several years.

1832: Count Uvarov appointed as minister of education.
1834: Annual recruitment is introduced. The empire is divided into regional recruitment zones ("strips," first from north to south and later from west to east). Recruits are taken from odd or even strips in alternating years, with the exception of the Jews who were conscripted annually.[8]
1835: The government acquits the Jews accused during the blood libel trial in Velizh.
1835: Kiselev is appointed minister of state property, including military colonies and cantonist institutions.
1835: Most researchers agree that this year saw the passing of new regulations concerning the Jews: responsibility for recruitment procedures handed to the *kahal*; forced recruitment permits issued for people without passports, vagrants, and people with harmful behavior.
1836: Prince Dolgorukov (governor of Lithuania and Belarus) proposes drafting children instead of collecting debts: one child in exchange for a debt of 500 rubles. The *kahal* asks to permit drafting an adult in exchange for a debt of 1000 rubles.
1840: Nicholas demands rearranging Jewish community life in towns, and limiting the functions of Jewish courts of law.
1840: Nicholas appoints Count Kiselev to prepare a comprehensive program to arrange Jewish life. Kiselev prepares a memorandum with the help of the *maskilim* Feigin, Levinson, and Gazanovsky. They regard the Talmud and the rabbis as the main obstacles to making the Jews more efficient.
1840: **In December, Nicholas approves Kiselev's memorandum and appoints a new ministerial committee for a radical reorganization of the Jewish way of life and conscription procedures.** The reorganization includes sorting the Jews according to their "usefulness" and aiming for a threefold increase in the number of conscripts. Count Kiselev proposes shortening the term of service up to ten years. The plan is to train conscripted Jews in useful vocations and send them back to their communities.[9]

---

8   *Stoletie Voennogo ministerstva 1802–1902* [Centenary of the Military Ministry 1802–1902], vol. 4: *Glavnyi shtab* [Main Staff], part 1, bk. 1, section 2: *Istoricheskii ocherk. Komplektovaniie voisk v tsarstvovanie Imperatora Nikolaia I* [Historical overview: recruitment of troops in the reign of Emperor Nicholas I] (St. Petersburg: Vol'f, 1907), 72–74.
9   Gessen, *Istoriia*, 79.

1841: The tradesman Samsonkin submits a complaint concerning the violation of the recruitment procedures by the *kahal*.
1842: Uvarov invites Lilienthal to prepare reforms in Jewish education.
1843: A harsh year for the Jews in Russia. The events of this year are so important that they will be given in more detail in the several entries below.
April 29, 1843: The tsar instructs Chernyshev to start the mass conversion of the cantonists. Chernyshev passes the order to Protasov.
August 1843: The establishment of the committee of representatives of the Jews to promote secular education, which includes Rabbi Yitzchak son of Rabbi Chaim of Volozhin, and the Rabbi Schneersohn, head of Chabad.
November 1843: Passing of education law, imposing Ministry of Education supervision on yeshivas and religious boys' schools.
1843 (specific date not available): The army's head priest, Katovich, sends out instructions to convert the cantonists.
1843: The tsar orders the resettlement of Jews from areas within fifty kilometers of the border.
1844: The revolt in Mstislavl (Mstislaw).
1844: Kiselev proposes to prevent the promotion of Jews who did not convert, and Nicholas approves this proposal. The abolition of the institution of the *kahal*. Responsibility for conscription and tax collection is placed on the public administration.
1846: Moses Montefiore visits Russia and demands equal rights for the Jews. His visit is a failure.
1846: The ministerial committee decides to conduct, from 1850, categorization of the Jews according "efficiency." Nicholas moves the starting date to 1852 as he meets the opposition of district governors.
1847: The tsar's response to Montefiore's request for equal rights for the Jews: "This is not feasible. I will not allow it so long as I live."[10] Nicholas's and Kiselev's responses to Montefiore's proposal are publicized abroad.
1848: A series of revolutions in European countries. The establishment of new borders and new states. Russia's military involvement. Russia becomes "Europe's gendarme."

---

10 Gessen, *Istoriia*, 110.

1848: Uvarov is fired from his post as minister of education because of his liberal opinions, and seemingly as a result of developments in Europe. Kiselev's influence decreases.

1850: According to a new law, three additional Jews will be enlisted for every case of failure to meet the recruit quota. An additional soldier can be recruited in exchange for cancelling 2000 rubles from the community's debt.

1851: Radicalization of Nicholas's position. He directs to increase the recruitment quota to twenty-five men out of every thousand, but this directive is not carried out.

1851: Rabbi Yisrael Salanter travels to St. Petersburg to supervise the efforts of the lobbyists to relieve the severity of the draft decree.

1852: According to a new directive, in every draft, ten Jews are to be enlisted for every thousand taxpayers. The amount of tax debt offset is lowered from 2000 to 300 rubles for each additional recruit.

1852: A penalty for not meeting the conscription quota is imposed on household heads and community leaders.

1853: The outbreak of the Crimean War.

1853: According to a new law, any Jew without a passport, who is not a local resident, can be drafted instead of a local resident. The growth of the *khapper* phenomenon.

1854, 1855, 1856: Wealthy Jewish tradesmen submit requests for rights equal to those of Christians.

1855: Port Sevastopol surrenders in the Crimean War.

August 1855: The cantonists' revolt in Arkhangel'sk.

February 18, 1856: Tsar Nicholas I dies during military training. His death is claimed to have been the result of a common cold.

March 14, 1856: Kiselev suggests that Alexander II reexamine the means of "reforming" the Jews.

August 26, 1856: The ministerial committee abolishes the law on recruitment of minors and the seizing of those without passports, vagrants, and criminals for recruitment. The cantonist decree is finally abolished only a year and a half after Alexander II ascends the throne.

January 1, 1857: The cantonist schools are transformed into military academies. Cantonists who converted to Christianity are transferred to these institutions.

2. A Summary of Events in Chronological Order

The period of the implementation of the conscription law in general and the cantonist law in particular can be divided into three:

- from 1826 till the beginning of the thirties: routine operation of the law;
- from the beginning of the 1830s until 1846: active efforts to transform the nature of the Jewish community, with attempts to use Jews for this purpose;
- 1846–1855: constant exacerbation of the treatment of Jews, with the climax in the years 1852–1853, followed by a certain calm.

There is a connection between international events and the recruitment activity. First, 1830 marked the beginning of the period of revolutions and saw the revolt in Poland. Nicholas responded by beginning to recruit Jews in Poland. The tsar and his government attempt to follow the new trends in Europe, with an overemphasis on general education. In 1848, the tsar's position harshens in all fields following upheavals in Europe. 1851 sees a deterioration of Russia's relations with France and Britain. Nicholas again worsens his politics towards Jews, as he believes that the Jews have great influence on European countries, and probably that the world is controlled by the Jews. This was a widely accepted belief at the time: a probably unfounded rumor had it that the Austrian foreign minister, Metternich, who outlined European policy in the first half of the nineteenth century, was of Jewish origin.

The stages of the tsar's own aging should also be taken into account. In 1826 he was thirty years old; in 1856, forty; and the harshening of his position is evident as he grew older. He had to rethink his previous initiatives. Thus, the reestablishment of the ministerial committee in 1840 can be seen as an admission of failure of the previous policy toward the Jews.

Passing to more specific developments, there are grounds to assume that the recruitment quota was changed already in 1852, and therefore, till then the conscription was of five taxpayers per thousand. Also, hunting down Jews with no permanent place of residence, those who lacked passports, was practiced only from 1853, and lasted just three years. One can assume that these harsh phenomena remained in the national memory as being characteristic of the entire cantonist period.

Part II

IMPLEMENTATION OF THE CONSCRIPTION LAW

1

Community Preparations for the Implementation of the Decree

The preparations for the passing of the recruitment decree are detailed in the memoirs of an official from the Ministry of the Interior, Osip Przhetslavskii (in Polish, Józef Emanuel Przecławski), who published them under the pseudonym Tsiprinus. He testifies that the Jews knew of the preparations and attempted to prevent the passing of the legislation. They were absolutely surprised when it was actually passed.[1] According to these memoirs, Nicholas placed the responsibility for preparing the law on his brother Constantin, who was governor of the Kingdom of Poland, and he in turn transferred the task to Senator Novosel'tsev. Nicholas waited for Novosel'tsev's recommendation for three weeks, but Novosel'tsev opined that the time had not yet come for such a decree. He proposed taking some additional steps to prepare the Jews for military service. However, the tsar did not agree to wait and ordered the minister of the interior to prepare the text of the statute "making the obligation of the Jews' recruitment equal to that of all citizens."

Tsiprinus tells of his acquaintance with Rabbi Mordechai Lipschitz, who arrived in St. Petersburg on a community mission, and visited Tsiprinus for discussions of the Torah and Kabbalah. The rabbi admitted, by the way, that he had succeeded in bribing Senator Novosel'tsev with 20,000 gold rubles. When Tsiprinus informed Rabbi Lipschitz that the decision had been made, the rabbi turned pale and fainted.

---

1 Simon Dubnov, "Kak vvedena byla rekrutskaia povinnost' dlia evreev v 1827 g.," *Evreiskaia starina* 2 (1909): 257–266.

Dubnow describes the efforts to collect a large amount of money to be used by the Jewish lobbyists to abolish the decree; confirmation of this has yet to be found in the communities' documents. Stanislawski comments[2] that the rabbis imposed a special tax on all the communities for that purpose. Each Jew was obligated to reduce his expenses by three quarters, and to bring the rest to the recruitment abolishment fund.

An anonymous report concerning the collection of money[3] reads as follows:

> At the beginning of December 1827, the rabbi of Berdichev [Berdychiv] came to Kherson [a new colony in southern Ukraine, about 500 kilometers from Berdichev (!)] to hold an appeal for Jewish emissaries to Petersburg. He claimed that one hundred thousand rubles had to be collected. The name of the rabbi of Berdichev is Isaac Rappoport. Similarly, an official by the name of Nechai announced that that on the occasion of the publication of the conscription law, an order was issued for every Jew to donate fifteen gold coins. This has been the practice since September 1826 [!]. All the money collected was entrusted to the rabbi of the town of Ovruch, Avraham Buger, and also to the rabbi of the town of Chernobyl [Chornobyl].[4]

---

2   Stanislavskii, "K istorii kantonistov."
3   Central Archives for the History of the Jewish People, HMF60, Documents of the Third Section, file 196 (1828).
4   Rabbi Mordechai Twersky (known as the Maggid of Chernobyl, 1770–1837). He was the second grand rabbi of Chernobyl.

2

The Statute

The law was implemented speedily. Already in 1828, we find a memorandum concerning the admission of Jews to a course for military medics as well as requests of rabbis to supply kosher food for Passover to Jewish soldiers. This shows that within a year after the law was pased all the procedures of conscription were in full swing.

When discussing the law of mandatory conscription of Jews, one must remember that the draft was called "the law of equal mandatory conscription for Jews," but in practice it was a special ordinance that applied only to the Jews. The following are the main points of the statute:[1]

A. The Text

An Imperial Ordinance to the Ruling Senate:
Out of a just principle of equality in the obligation to join the army for all those liable for enlistment and to make it easier for our loyal citizens, I hereby command:

1) to oblige the Jews to actively comply with the recruitment requirement;
2) to cancel the financial levy previously imposed on them in exchange for mandatory recruitment;
3) to implement their recruitment into the army according to the guidelines established for this type of recruitment alone, as attached hereto.

---

[1] See Central Archives for the History of the Jewish People, HM2\8280, copy from Rossiiskii gosudarstvennyi voenno-istoricheskii arkhiv [Russian state archive of military history], f. 1, op. 1.

> We are convinced that the education and skills that the Jews will acquire during the course of their service will contribute also to their families[2] at the end of the service determined by law, so that they will ultimately benefit due to the reinforcement of their settlement and the thriving of their individual economy.
>
> Personally signed by the hand of Nicholas I: I hereby command the execution of this law.
>
> August 26, 1827

The following is an appendix to the tsar's directive:

> I hereby request His Majesty's directive to be publicized in every location.
>
> Director general of the Ministry of the Interior, V. Lansky
>
> His Majesty's chief of staff, Leontii Vasil'evich Dubel't
>
> August 26, 1827
>
> The Imperial Ministry of Defense, August 28, 1827
>
> To the deputy director general of the Ministry of the Interior, Lieutenant General Aleksandr Chernyshev
>
> Order to circulate the law.
>
> According to the report of the director general of the Ministry of the Interior and the chief of staff, the following should be printed and circulated among the civil authorities to be announced and publicized:
>
> 1) the tsar's statute of August 26;
> 2) the regulations of mandatory recruitment and mandatory service for Jews;
> 3) guidelines for the civil authorities;
> 4) guidelines for recruiting officers and those receiving the recruits: a framework for receiving and transporting the recruits.

---

2 About what sort of help to the family can one talk after twenty-five years of separation from the family?!

Statute on the Obligation of Recruitment and Military Service of Jews

Section 1. General laws applying to the Jewish people
Clause 1. All general recruitment obligations apply to Jews equally and according to their appropriate civil status. The general law and guidelines determined for other sectors of the population apply also to the Jews, except for specific cases.

Section 2. Recruitment procedures and exemption of Jews
Clause 5. If and when an exceptional right is granted for an exemption from service in exchange for a fee, the exemption shall apply under the following conditions:

a) the community has no tax payment arrears;
b) the community has no commitment to any public body or private individual.

Clause 9. Males below the age of twelve and above the age of twenty-five are not to be enlisted.

Section 3. Method of dividing the burden of recruitment among the Jews
Clause 13. The conscription ordinance for Jews applies to the entire community, separately from all other conscription groups and regardless of the conscription of Christians.

Section 4. The obligations of the public authorities[3]
Clause 24. The responsibility for handling the recruitment procedures in a proper and accurate manner rests with the community in accordance with the orders given by the district (*guberniia*) administration.

Clause 25. All the instructions of the community for this purpose shall be accepted only in the form of a decision of the management of the community and shall be based on the approved regulations.

---

3 The term *kahal*, the community institution of the time, is not mentioned here. In 1844 the *kahals* were abolished and the *obshchestvo*, an institution responsible for recruitment, was established.

Clause 26. Any ruling by the community administration regarding recruitment issues shall be reviewed in advance by the governor's office. It shall come into effect after receiving the governor's approval.

Clause 27. The community is to choose between three and six appointees to carry out the recruitment order.

Clause 29. The expenses of the community regarding recruitment shall be attached together with its approval to the general account of the expenses of the community, and shall be honored according to the accepted process.

Clause 32. In the event that candidates for recruitment or ransom in exchange for recruitment are not presented at the determined time, the district administration shall collect the requested amount from the *obshchestvo* through proactive operations.

Clause 33. Superiors who have not fulfilled their duties properly shall be held responsible for the failure. They shall be fined for the damages or recruited themselves in an impartial manner.[4]

Clause 34. According to the community's decision, any Jew can be drafted at any time for non-compliance with tax payments, vagrancy, or for any other public disturbance that the community will not be willing to tolerate. (All this if the recruit meets the requirements of the conscription regulations).

Section 5. Prioritization during recruitment; management of priority registers

Clause 37. Every Jewish community must maintain a family priority register for conscription. All family members shall be registered in the register according to the accepted method.

Clause 38. This register shall be updated every three years according to the true number of Jews belonging to the community to whom the obligation of recruitment applies.

Section 6. Obligations of the individual

Clause 44. A family whose turn has come for conscription according to the priority register, and who has a candidate for conscription to whom, based on his qualifications and age, no section exempting him from

---

4   Some studies state, seemingly in error, that the penalty was only determined later.

conscription applies, shall not be entitled to receive an exemption for any reason whatsoever.

Clause 48. A family whose turn it is to bring their family member for conscription shall not be permitted to present an alternative candidate unless the following conditions are met:

a. the substitute will declare that he came of his own free will;
b. the substitute will be a resident of that conscription district;
c. the substitute's family has already met the conscription obligations or has another son eligible for conscription.

Section 7. Granting exemptions from conscription

Clause 58. Merchants shall be exempt from military service in accordance with the general [Christian] regulations.

Clause 59. Exemption from conscription shall be given to rabbis who are legally authorized and hold a certificate of approval.

Clause 61. Youths who have studied in recognized elementary schools, middle schools, and high schools and met all the educational requirements of the institution (apart from religious studies), shall be totally exempt from the obligation of conscription, subject to the presentation of certificates of successful completion and positive behavior.

Clause 62. Young people who have studied for at least three years in institutions of general education or with a recognized craftsman shall be exempt from military service until the end of their studies, each on his own terms.

Clause 63. Craftsmen with the rank of master, who practice their craft in a recognized Jewish factory according to accepted criteria, shall be exempt from conscription into the army, each on his own terms.

Clause 64. Jews who were transferred to colonies specially allocated for agricultural settlement shall be exempted from conscription for fifty years.

Clause 65. Jews who successfully engage in agriculture on agricultural farms shall be exempt from conscription for twenty-five years.

Clause 68. Any given authorization of this type will expire once the business activity ceases.

Section 8. Conscription of minors

Clause 70. A minor under the age of eighteen shall be enlisted without being sworn in. Minors are sworn in on their transfer to active service.

Clause 74. A minor who has not reached the age of eighteen will be directed to preparatory training establishments for military training [in other words, will become a cantonist].

Clause 90. The military service of such minor for the purpose of calculating the service period shall be considered from the age of eighteen.

Section 12. Deserters

Clause 80. A Jew who escapes conscription will be considered a community deserter. If he is caught at the end of the recruitment, he will be considered a captured deserter and his recruitment will not be included in the community's recruitment quota.

Clause 84. Whoever gives shelter to a deserter is liable for immediate conscription, without being included in the conscription quota of the community.

Section 13. Religious routine of Jewish soldiers

Clause 91. A soldier is permitted to observe all the customs of his religion during free time from active military service. The commander will maintain strict supervision so that no one prevents the soldier from observing the tenets of his religion.

Clause 92. A soldier is permitted to visit a synagogue and rabbis in the vicinity of his service only with the approval of his commander.

Clause 93. The commander may permit a gathering for the observance of a religious tenet in the base in a place specially designated for this purpose. The approval applies in places where there are no synagogues outside the base, especially on religious holidays.

All religious activity will be conducted under the supervision of the commander appointed for that purpose.

B. Order of Recruitment Procedures for the Civil Administration of the Province

Clause 1. When carrying out the conscription order, one should not be too strict with the Jewish community or with any of its members.

Clause 2. Resolving problems—those dealing with recruitment should turn to the courts of the regional authorities to solve any problems. Below is a list of institutions to which one can turn:

a) the recruiting office;
b) *kazennaia palata*[5]—the regional administration;
c) the civil governor;
d) the office of the attorney general of the province.

Clause 3. The location for the recruitment procedures is the recruitment office (*rekrutskoe prisutstvie*).

Clause 9. The recruitment priority registers must be managed according to the information in the census (*revizskaia skazka*).

Clause 11. For each family, the rank of each candidate must be noted in the recruitment priority books according to the following classifications: "has fulfilled his enlistment duties," "exempt from enlistment," "released from enlistment duties for the following reason: ..."

Clause 14. The decision of the community administration, the *kahal*, regarding a change in recruitment priority will be valid if it is accepted under the following conditions:

a. in the presence of at least seven elected members of the *kahal*;
b. in the presence of some of the community dignitaries.

Section 9. Confirmation of release from service

1. Confirmation of release from service will only be given in the presence of a police clerk/attorney, two members of the local council, and at least two town dignitaries.
2. The required documents for receiving a confirmation of exemption:
   a) confirmation of the title of rabbi signed by the general manager of the institution for matters of foreign religions;
   b) an agricultural occupation permit issued by the state colonies administration;
   c) confirmation of being an apprentice signed by local council members and the management of the trade union.

---

5 The local office of the Ministry of Finance that dealt with registering citizens and tax collection.

Section 10. Below is an example of the management of priority registers

Absentees, reason for absence, deletion from the list, additions to the family list, reasons for changes in family composition after the last census, eligibility for exemption, personal details, reason for granting the exemption, list of family members by age, names of family members as listed in the census.

Order of the chief of the General Staff of His Majesty the Tsar, Count Dibich, and director general of the Ministry of Interior, V. Lansky

Clause 2.0. Jewish minors aged eight to twelve are to be transferred immediately, and adults after having been sworn in, to the command of an appointed senior officer for assignment to units according to the order. Minors must be kept separate from adult conscripts.[6]

Clause 4.0. During the recruitment, a residential apartment for recruits shall be rented from Christians only.[7] The Christian landlords shall provide the recruits with food of improved quality financed by the Ministry of Finance.[8]

Clause 6.0. Guarding the recruits. At the head of a group of recruits shall stand:

a) above fifteen men—an acting officer;
b) under fifteen men—a non-commissioned officer.

Escorting recruits. The escort unit shall consist of a senior officer, a non-commissioned officer; and for every group of fifteen, a private. The non-commissioned officer must be literate and trustworthy.

Clause 7.0. Care must be taken, especially in an area with a Jewish population, to house the recruits with Christians.

---

6   According to Merimzon, "Rasskaz starogo soldata," 290–301, this rule was violated.
7   According to Itzkovitz this rule was violated. See Itzkovitz, "Vospominaniia evreiskogo kantonista" [Memoirs of a Jewish cantonista], *Evreiskaiia starina* 5 (1912): 54–65.
8   All the recruits point out that they received good food.

> Clause 9.0. Each non-commissioned officer shall receive the group of recruits from the recruiting commander according to his instructions. An escort officer must be equipped with a copy of the regulations.
>
> Clause 10.0. In order to prevent absenteeism, a recruit must not be allowed to have personal belongings in excess of what is allowed according to the list.[9]
>
> Clause 13.0. Funding must be allocated for the rental of a wagon to transport conscripts at the rate of twelve soldiers per wagon,[10] and for the sick—one wagon for two soldiers.

These directives include exceedingly exact guidelines on appointing officers and the personal details of the escorts, renting houses from Christians, allocating transport according to criteria of quantity and quality (for the sick). The authors of the document tried to prevent any improvisation or independent initiative of the escorts.

This is important to remember when discussing the likelihood of escorts acting not according to the directives, including coercion to convert. The clause regarding religious rights seems surprising, and below we will present directives concerning observance of Sabbath and festivals, appointment of rabbis, kosher slaughter, etc. Ostensibly, those directives were supposed to apply also to minors, and there is no legal mention in all the clauses of the statute of differences between the rights of an adult and those of a minor, other than the obligation of the oath.

C. Procedure for the Civil Authority That Carries out the Recruitment

> **Appendix to the Regulations on Conscription of Jews**[11]
>
> Clause 1. The main supervisory task of those appointed to carry out the draft regulations is . . . to prevent anything excessive that would burden the Jewish community.

---

9 Religious articles were confiscated on the basis of this clause.
10 According to the memoirs of the cantonists, this order was carried out in practice.
11 Central Archives for the History of the Jewish People, HM2\8280, copy from Rossiiskii gosudarstvennyi voenno-istoricheskii arkhiv [Russian state archive of military history], f. 1, op. 1.

Clause 16. Attention should be paid that presentation of unscheduled conscripts on the pretext of some sort of defect should not be used against poor people with positive behavior, when the true reason for bringing them to be drafted lies in some superstition or conspiracy on the part of the Jews.[12]

Clause 20. The oath is to be administered inside a synagogue or study hall that is used as a place of pray, in front of a Torah scroll. To ensure the trustworthiness of the oath, the Torah scrolls shall be those used at prayer times.

At the time of the Torah reading in the synagogue, the district authorities are to seize the Torah scroll temporarily to verify its suitability for religious use.

No oaths are to be administered on Saturdays and festivals. (Attached is a calendar of festivals.)

Clause 24. The rabbi administering the oath shall be appointed specifically for this task, **and shall not be the community rabbi.**

Clause 30. The rabbi shall give the recruits religious guidance. Two lit candles will be on the table.

Clause 34. Before taking the oath, the recruit is to wash his hands in the ritual manner, wear a tallit and a *kittel*, lay tefillin, and stand in front of an open Holy Ark.

Clause 36. In certain districts, when taking the oath, Jews are accustomed to placing the Torah scroll under their right arm, or placing their right hand on a verse . . . in the book of Leviticus. **The authorities shall collect reliable information concerning the local custom.**

Clause 37. A converted Jew or a Christian familiar with Jewish customs can be appointed to supervise accuracy in the execution of the ceremony.

Clause 38. At the end of the ceremony the shofar will be blown in the order of *tekiah, teruah, shevarim.*

Clause 42. The rabbi administering the oath will present the authorities with an authorizing document approved by the managing director of the Ministry of Religious Affairs.

---

12 This is to prevent apostates from being brought to be drafted as a form of harassment.

> The text of the rabbi's sermon should be as follows:
>
> "... Any violation of this oath shall be considered a serious offense and shall not be expiated by any other permit, cancellation of the oath, transfer and announcement, nor by any *Kol Nidrei* or *Al Ḥet* prayer, nor by any other means, not on Yom Kippur or at any other time."
>
> (Note of the author of these regulations: The regulations were written according to *Midrash Tanḥuma*, the writings of Rabbeinu Baḥye, and Rabbi Yitzḥak Abuhav.)

This document is amazing in its accuracy, scope, and knowledge that its author demonstrates in the laws of Judaism. It is implied that it was extremely important to the army that a Jewish soldier fulfill his duty with complete faith and adherence to the Torah (out of fear of divine punishment). Clearly, the authorities regarded the recruit as a Jew who would remain Jewish in the future. If they had reckoned on the majority converting, they would not have seen any reason for a Jewish oath. The authorities were assisted by knowledgeable Jews who served faithfully, otherwise they would not have arrived at the details of the local customs and the intricacies of violating the vow by bringing their halakhic source.[13]

D. Who Was Fit for Conscription and Who Was Exempt

From the draft regulations brought above, we can arrive at several conclusions concerning procedures for granting exemptions. The recruiting institutions were supposed, initially, to recruit all those obligated according to the law. They had to do this in order of dates of birth as they appeared in the community registers. However, a free hand was given to determine obligation or exemption. All these specifications also applied to the general population.

According to the conscription law, it was possible to enlist tax evaders, criminals, people of negative behavior, and people whom the community wished to get rid of not according to priority of age. The authorities were concerned that the community might to rid itself of people who did not observe *mitzvot* and

---

13   On the close relationship between the *maskilim* and the tsar, see Gessen, *Istoriia*, 141.

who were planning to convert by having them drafted into the army. In order to prevent this trend, the statute specifically states in that exceptional drafting is forbidden when performed out of prejudice and superstition.[14]

Exemptions were given according to vocation to tradesmen listed in a guild; apprentices during their training period; priests (that is, rabbis with recognized certificates) and yeshiva students; students in state schools and other academic institutions and their graduates; as well as residents of new agricultural settlements (the exemption applied to all the years of conscription, but in some colonies there was no blanket exemption). Thus we see that exemptions were given to those who were already involved in "useful" activity that matched the government's plans. Social groups that operated in the spirit of the reform were naturally exempt from conscription. This fact demonstrates that the aim of the conscription policy was social integration, and not necessarily national assimilation of Jews. There was no doubt, however, that this trend would lead to assimilation.

Apparently, the creators of these extremely detailed regulations expected their executors to understand the complexity of the task and act accordingly. This is surprising considering the low caliber of people available to the tsar for enforcing the regulations. The guidelines were written by scholars in the capital city, but those who implemented them in practice were junior and non-commissioned officers. Although it is known that there was a strict requirement to enforce the regulations, it is not possible to learn whether they were implemented correctly and in full.

Another striking point is the instruction not to burden the Jews and not to be overly strict with them during the recruitment. The very need for the authorities to mention this in the documents indicates their concerns about the arbitrariness of the recruiters' behavior. Still, this sensitivity is quite surprising. In order to understand the contradiction between the cruelty of the law recruiting minors and this seemingly considerate statute, we should perhaps mention the words of Queen Victoria of Britain that the tsar was unaware of the arbitrary nature and cruelty of his commanders in the field.[15] Did the tsar really not know of this, or was it a pretense?

---

14   See the story of the Russian author Nikolai Leskov, "Monastyrskii sad" [The abbot's garden], about such an attempt.
15   See also Nicholas Riasanovsky, "Nicholas I," *Encyclopedia Britannica*, https://www.britannica.com/biography/Nicholas-I-tsar-of-Russia.

3

The Positions and Activities of the Community, Its Spiritual Leadership, and Its Members

A. The Legal Status of the Community Institutions in Implementing the Conscription Law

The law assigned to the community institutions the responsibility of bringing candidates for recruitment and meeting the quotas determined by the army. The community was required to maintain birth registers in order to determine the order of recruitment according to age, and to establish its own recruiting body, according to clause 27 of the statute. After the dismantlement of the *kahal* in 1840s, the authorities provided the framework for another recruiting body in the Jewish community. The recruitment institutions were to enlist all those legally obligated, and to do so according to priority of age according to the community registers. At the same time, a free hand was granted to determine who was obligated and who exempt (clause 74 of the statute). The local state authority was to appoint Christians to the local recruiting committee, and the military authorities established a military framework that dealt with recruitment, including a medical board. Thus, the stature gave the community authorities power, which naturally caused many possibilities of conflict and tension between the members of the community, and between the members and the community administration.

B. Changes in the Position of the Community Administration (*Kahal*) and the Relations between the *Kahal* and the Community Members

Our goal in this study is to examine the procedures of conscription, service, and the forced conversion to Christianity of Jewish boys in the Russian army.

The functioning of the Jewish community as a mechanism and its relationship with the Jewish public are important and respectable issues in themselves, which in my opinion require a separate study. However, I will here comment on the interaction and changes in the relations between the three main elements within the Jewish community: the community members, the spiritual leadership, and the community administration, with reference to the cantonists.[1]

Stanislawski[2] sees the implementation of conscription as the turning point and the beginning of the crisis in the relationship between the community and its administration, and as the cause for the public's loss of trust in the *kahal*. Without invalidating this view, in our opinion there is no room for the idealization of the institution of the community administration, even in the generations prior to the conscription decree. According to the definition of its role, the community administration was to stand between the state authority and the Jewish public. It is convenient for a regime to make use of such an establishment in order to achieve its goals which, in the natural way of things, oppose the interests of the individual and the public in general. Even if the establishment sees the interests of those it represents as its goal, it must, even if for the sake of this goal, present a good performance to the regime whose interests are in opposition to the community. The only room for maneuver left to the establishment is in manipulation of the law. The result is that the establishment is doomed from both sides, for any true reform required exerting strength not found in a single community. (A permanent organization on the national scale did not exist, anyway.)

It is no wonder that we find tension between the *kahal* and the community as a whole. This tension was one of the causes for the founding of the Hasidic movement in Ukraine about a hundred years prior to the conscription decree. See, for example, the book *Toldot Ya'akov Yosef* by one of the pioneers of the Hasidic movement, Rabbi Ya'akov Yosef of Pollonye. As Shmuel Ettinger points out,[3] the erosion of the relationship between the community administration and its members began in the middle of the eighteenth century, as a result of the changes in the political structure in Eastern and Central Europe (and it is

---

1 See also the audit committee's report: Central Archives for the History of the Jewish People, RU450, copy from Gosudarstvennyi arkhiv Rossiiskoi Federatsii [State archive of Russian Federation], f. 109, 1 eksp.
2 Stanislawski, *Tsar Nicolas I and the Jews*, 123–155.
3 Shmuel Ettinger, *Toldot am Yisrael ba-et ha-ḥadashah* [The history of the Jewish people in the modern era] (Tel Aviv: Dvir, 1972), 52–53.

possible that such has been the balance of power in the Jewish communities since time immemorial).

Moshe Rossman[4] presents a fascinating analysis of the status of the community administration in the second half of the eighteenth century. He comes to the conclusion that, already then, a limited oligarchy of wealthy individuals controlled the community administration and as a result, its decisions were arbitrary and tainted by the interests of the wealthy stratum of the community. Such was, for example, the character of one of the community leaders in Medzhybizh, Itzko Ognisty. He was notorious "for his evil activity. He deceived widows, expropriated goods from craftsmen, extorted money from the people, testified falsely in court against Jews, and harassed the city's residents in all kinds of ways."[5] It is obvious that such a character would have no problem dealing in kidnapping, falsifying documents, etc. Thus, there was no drastic change in the behavior of the community leaders before and after the passing of the conscription decree.

When the institution of the Jewish community came under the control of the Russian authorities, it was already in a state of internal disintegration. The authorities needed time to understand the "new creature" that had fallen into its hands. Their natural goal was to annul the community's autonomy, while still exploiting it for concentrated tax collection and other burdens, such as conscription.

C. The Struggle with the Authorities over the Status of the *Kahal*

Ever since the Napoleonic War (1812–1815), two Jews, emissaries of the communities, were in the imperial court and in the army headquarters: Zundel Sonnenberg and Leizer Dillon. In addition, in 1816, representatives of the communities of Lithuania and White Russia (but not of the Hasidic Ukraine) gathered in Minsk to formulate a uniform position vis-à-vis the authorities and a permanent relationship with the imperial court. The communities' relatively strong position is proved by the fact that they succeeded in annulling the obligation to wear European clothes and in obliging the landowners to repay their

---

4   Moshe Rossman, *Ha-Besht, meḥadesh ha-Ḥasidut* [The Ba'al Shem Tov, the renewer of Hasidism] (Jerusalem: Shazar Center, 1999), 118.
5   Ibid.

debts to the Jews. On their side, the authorities demanded that the communities be particular in managing registers and tax payments. In 1827, the duty of tax collection was imposed on the community. This led to a demonstrative shutdown of the *kahal* administration. The members of the *kahal* justified the shutdown by saying that, according to the new directive, no one was allowed to hold a public office without knowing Russian or another foreign language.[6] As the authorities attributed much importance to the *kahal*, contrary to the law, approval was given to appoint members who only spoke Yiddish. At the same time, the Ministry of Finance agreed to spread the payment of debts over a period of fifteen years.

The additional responsibility placed on the *kahal* did not change the authorities' general aim of annulling Jewish autonomy. The government did not even agree to continue meeting with Jewish representatives and, in 1827, it was proposed to the *kahals* to prepare letters of requests to be presented to the governor. This signifies a serious decline in their status. In the course of the years it became undoubtedly clear, also to the authorities, that the *kahal* was not an efficient tool for either tax collection or conscription. Inept procedures, corruption, and deceit in the community administration's systems, together with the elimination of the community's independence, led to the abolition of the *kahal* institution in 1844.[7] In its stead came the administrative institution called *obshchestvo*—a sort of community administration on behalf of the authorities. The change was significant as from then on, the communities were directly subordinate to the local councils. The decline in the status of the *kahal*, both socially and institutonally, affected the communities' ability to deal with the recruitment problems and their willingness to do so.

D. Activities of the *Kahal* in Relation to Jewish Conscription

At the beginning of the process, the community institutions worked vigorously to annul the conscription decree. The emissaries of the community achieved success in the imperial court of Alexander I and Nicholas I in their campaign for the cancellation of the cantonists statute, gaining constant postponements

---

[6] Arkhiv Ministerstva finansov [Ministry of Finance archive], file 22: "O pravilakh predpolagaemykh dlia vzyskaniia podatei s evreev" [On the rules proposed for collection of taxes from the Jews] (1827), 157; quoted in Gessen, *Istoriia*, 62–64.

[7] *Vtoroe sobranie zakonov*, no. 18546, quoted in Gessen, *Istoriia*, 94.

of its application. At the last stage, already in the days of Nicholas I, the communities were aware and connected enough to grasp the change of atmosphere in the imperial court. Following the early warning, nationwide fundraising was announced and up to 200,000 rubles was collected. With this money, certain Jews knew how to reach the person responsible for the legislation, Senator Novosel'tsev, and apparently also knew how to transfer the bribe to him. Secondary evidence for this is the fact that Tsar Nicholas decided in an unprecedented way to intervene personally and bypass the accepted legislative system.[8]

The method of conducting the fundraising, as seen in the documents quoted here, indicates organizational abilities at the national level. A general austerity order was announced to reduce spending on personal needs by seventy-five percent, and rabbis went to outlying towns for the purpose of fundraising.

With the implementation of obligatory conscription for Jews, and Jewish minors in particular, the communities mobilized to give aid to the conscripts, particularly to the cantonists. In the years 1828–1829, the communities of Vilna, Mogilev, and Vitebsk sent many requests to the military authorities to allow the supply of *matzot* to cantonists. Lobbyists were sent to the capital for this purpose, and their efforts were successful. The tsar gave his personal approval to transfer *matzot* to the Jewish sailors in the navy's central base in Kronshtadt.[9]

Moreover, after the imposition of the conscription decree, the community leaders took various measures to weaken or reduce the effect of the conscription. These included improper registration in birth registers, forgeries, bribery, and more. In addition, informers were mobilized from among government officials, who let the community know of upcoming conscription dates and provided other useful information. As a result of these efforts, the authorities lost their ability to conduct an annual conscription; they did not have the cooperation of the heads of the community, and there was no understanding between them. In practice, the military authorities were dependent on the community administration. There was reason for the members of the tsar's audit committee to complain that they were unable to understand the recruitment procedures as administered by the heads of the community.[10] In this way, the community

---

8 It should be noted that from a legislative point of view, the recruitment decree was classified as an imperial command with the power is stronger than that of a law.
9 Gosudarstvennyi arkhiv Rossiiskoi Federatsii [State archive of Russian Federation], f. 109, d. 330, l. 16.
10 See the report of gendarmes at work, Central Archives for the History of the Jewish People, RU450, f. 105, copy from Gosudarstvennyi arkhiv Rossiiskoi Federatsii [State archive of the Russian Federation], f. 109, op. 450.

administration gained a certain independence in determining which candidate for conscription would have priority, as reflected in the recruitment announcement of the community in Minsk (see below in this chapter).

However, the community administration was under constant threat of punishment. Obviously, in the complete chaos and lack of proper administration, it was not possible to find men eligible for recruitment in sufficient numbers, as we learn from the descriptions of the recruitment procedures in Mstislaw and Berdychiv. Did the authorities suspect that, despite the pretense of cooperation, the community administration was hiding the recruitment reserves of which it alone knew?

E. Was There Any Point in Passive Resistance

It must be admitted that these methods were applied only at the community level and were short-sighted. They did not have the potential of solving the problem in its entirety. The inability of Jewish communities to conduct conscription in an orderly manner led to radicalization of positions in the military, and led to drastic measures such as the use of military units, patrols, arrests, imposing blockades, forced recruitment of foreign residents, and abductions. In the next round of decrees, the heads of the communities themselves faced conscription and forced labor that was imposed on them.

An additional change in the *kahal's* position concerned offsetting the tax liabilities in exchange for additional recruits. If, at the beginning of the period, the community administration was opposed to this type of offset, at the end of the 1840s we find requests from the administration to the authorities to allow them to use this measure. This indicates that the difficulties in complying with the tax payments exceeded the difficulties of conducting the recruitment in all its aspects. For the treasury it was the wealthy in the community who were required to cover the deficit, while the lack of recruits was covered by the poor.

It should be noted that, in granting priorities in conscription, the community administration found itself in a severe dilemma. Lacking unmarried men fit for conscription, they had to choose between enlisting small children and adults who supported their families. It was obviously easier to enlist one child than the father of a large family, with all the cruelty that such a decision entails. From the list of conscripts available from the community of Minsk, we do not see the full picture yet, because at the beginning of the conscription period there were still unmarried young men capable of using weapons, and despite this, seventy percent of the conscripts were boys between the ages of twelve and sixteen.

In estimating the efficiency with which the *kahal* operated for the good of the community, one must take into account that its members worked under absurd conditions and knew that not fulfilling the conscription order would bring trouble for them and the entire community. If there had been a responsible national leader capable of seeing the whole picture, it would probably have been possible to ease the suffering and maintain public morale. But, as is known, such responsible and united leadership did not exist in the provinces of the Russian Empire, not even among the spiritual authorities. Nevertheless, the Jews' passive resistance to the conscription decree, as a community and as individuals, was a defined social phenomenon, to a certain extent neutralizing the efforts of the military. In parentheses it should be noted that methods of forgery, desertion, and deception were common also among the Christian population, mainly on the individual level.

This passive opposition was not calculated and planned. Therefore, it is only natural that we find a contradictory trend in the functioning of the community: the effort to reduce the community's debt by additional conscription, especially of minors by way of abductions.[11] Conscription regulation no. 34 granted the community administration the possibility of enlisting Jews who were behind in their tax payments or those who led a disorderly life. Thus, a free hand was given to the members of the *kahal* to choose the draftees arbitrarily. The existence side by side of contradictory aims in the administration's functioning, testifies to a state of dire distress of the Jewish people in the Russian diaspora. One can learn of these aims from requests submitted by communities to the governors of the provinces.[12]

The *kahals* of Mogilev in White Russia and of Shklov in Lithuania (both in present-day Belarus) requested permission to ignore the order of priorities of conscription of families, and to act only according to the community's judgement, with the aim of sending to the army all those who did not meet the tax demands or who disturbed the functioning of the community. In their letter, they claimed that conscription should not follow the official list of priorities, explaining that people who did not own property could easily escape at the time of conscription, and then the community would constantly be forced to enlist householders who owned real estate. In order to demonstrate their loyalty, the members of the *kahal* noted that they would not send for conscription those

---

11 See below, 161; see also the Central Archives for the History of the Jewish People, HMF759/a–b.
12 See, for example, below, 95n32.

not strong in their faith, as under military conditions they would not know how to observe the tenets of their religion. (This corresponds completely with the Ḥatam Sofer's ruling; see below in this chapter.) When the government refused to allow the *kahal* to determine the order of conscription arbitrarily, the *kahal* persisted and resent the request the following year, under the pretext of "proposals for the benefit of the people."[13]

In contrast, the community of Vilna did not raise the notion of conscription without a defined order in its proposal for improvements, but demanded comparing the conscription tasks of the Jews with those of the rest of the population.

As we see, it was not by chance that the community members suspected the *kahal* of collaboration with the authorities. Matters could reach violent clashes as in the revolt in Starokostiantyniv, in which town residents laid siege on the *kahal* offices. The ambivalent position of the community heads finds expression also in international activity to abolish the decree.

F. International Efforts to Abolish the Conscription Decree

According to Aryeh Morgenstern,[14] it is not the date of the Damascus blood libel that should be determined as the first attempt at international action for the sake of the Jewish people, but the time of the Jewish conscription law in Russia. Morgenstern investigated the office of *Pekidim ve-amarkalim* in Amsterdam, an organization that managed funds distributed to European Jews who lived in Jerusalem and studied Torah. The documents relating to the office's support in the absorption of the followers of the Vilna Gaon in the Land of Israel showed that, already in the fall of 1827,[15] a secret missive was sent by the heads of the Vilna community to the banker Lehren, the head of the Dutch office and an owner of the private bank Lehren and Hollander. The authors of the letter were the head of the Vilna rabbinical court, Rabbi Avraham Abeli; the head of the community, Rabbi Aryeh Leib Peseles; and the secretary, Rabbi Avraham Strashun. They asked Lehren to use his personal connections with the heads of European countries to try to abolish the conscription decree. The letter was

---

13 Arkhiv Ministerstva vnutrennikh del, departament politsii ispolnitel'noi [Archives of the Ministry of Internal Affairs, department of police enforcement], d. 461 (1828), quoted in Gessen, *Istoriia*, 61–62.
14 Aryeh Morgenstern, *Ge'ula be-derekh ha-teva* (Jerusalem: Orot, 1997), 57–59.
15 September 26, 1827, between Rosh Hashana and Yom Kippur.

probably written in cryptic language, and therefore Lehren was unable to understand whether it was only about the draft decree or also about other decrees, such as desecration of the Sabbath and more.

Apparently, Lehren turned to, among others, the chief rabbi of England, Rabbi Shlomo Herschel Berliner. Lehren asked him to activate his personal connections with the philanthropist Nathan Rothchild and others. Immediately on receiving the letter, Rabbi Berliner approached Rothchild, who volunteered for the mission, but his efforts did not go well. The lobbyists did not know which decree was being referred to. The matter did not come to the attention of the British press (!), and the Russian ministers did not take the unclear request seriously. It was agreed that Lehren would discretely clarify the matter at the Russian embassy in Holland, and similar efforts would also be made in England.

At the same time Lehren tried to approach the heir to the throne of the Netherlands, who was the Russian tsar's brother-in-law (his wife's brother). He turned to one of the Dutch government ministers requesting him to speak to the prince: that "he speak favorably to His Majesty the Tsar about the Jews, and that he examine the details of the command to take soldiers from our people.... Although [the prince] did not give him a clear answer that he would do so,"[16] Lehren recommended that the aristocrats in Vilna should attempt to meet that prince when he next visited Russia.

Thus, the heads of the Vilna community made an exceptional effort to abolish the decree, out of a sense of responsibility for the Jewish people. In addition, we understand from the document that Jews in European countries were capable of influencing Nicholas. Nicholas did not live in a vacuum. He too had rules according to which he was expected to function before European nobility.

In his reply to the heads of the Vilna community, Lehren emphasized the difficulty in dealing with the matter, explaining that the conscription laws in European countries applied also to the Jews. It is difficult to estimate, but his efforts may have been fruitful, somewhat moderating the cruel plans of Nicholas I.

---

16 Aryeh Morgenstern, "Igrot ha-pekidim ve-ha-amarkelim me-amsterdam ve-ḥeker ha-yishuv ha-yehudi be-eretz Yisrael" [Letters of the officials and merchants from Amsterdam and the study of the Jewish settlement in Eretz Israel], *Cathedra* (December 27, 1982): 108–185.

G. The Jews' Immediate Response to the Conscription Decree

E. Tcherikover[17] presents in his study of the *maskilim* many facts concerning the response of the Jews to the conscription decree. In 1827, in Starokostiantyniv, in the district of Vilna, the Jews demanded that the local rabbi issue a ruling to refuse the conscription edict, and they threw stones at the *kahal*[18] leaders.

Rabbi Barukh ha-Levi Epstein (author of the Torah Temima commentary on the Torah) wrote[19] that in 1853, in Grodno, Rabbi Eliyahu Shick (author of *Ba'al Hidushei Shik* on the Talmud) called the locals to break into the "kehila house" where the adult recruits were being held. Holding an axe, he even led the mob and released them.

Rabbi Yaakov Berlin[20] from the town of Mir (father of the Netziv of Volozhin), mentions in his memoirs that his father, head of the local rabbinical court, ordered the residents to release the children who had been forcibly taken by the *kahal*. Rabbi Berlin was taken to court for this, but acquitted (!). Rabbi Yaakov Berlin add that similar actions were carried out in other towns, and that the public opposition significantly deterred the *kahal* members.

Tcherikover also found copies of documents of the Third Section of the Tsar's Own Chancellery,[21] including a report of insurrectionary activity against the conscription, according to which, in 1843, a recruit from Vilkomir (Ukmergė), Lithuania, was released. In the same year, a Jew accused of smuggling draft evaders into Poland, and in 1852, a conscript abducted from Radin, Lithuania, was released from conscription.[22]

I. M. Dik relates that, when the conscription law was publicized in Vilna, Jews left their houses, and going from house to house, banged on the windows shouting, "What, are you sleeping? The world is going up in flames!"[23]

In 1836, two informers, Schwartzman and Ochsman from the town of Nova Ushytsia in the district of Kamianets-Podilskyi were sentenced to death in a local court on account of the crime of *rodef* (one who is "pursuing" another person

---

17 E. Tcherikover, "He-Hamon ha-yehudi, ha-maskilim, veha-memshala bi-yemei Nikolai ha-Rishon" [The Jewish mass, the *maskilim*, and the government in the days of Nicholas I], *Tziyon* 4, no. 2 (1938–1939): 159–160.
18 Dubnov, "Kak vvedena byla rekrutskaia povinnost'."
19 *Mekor Barukh*, vol. 1 (New York: New York Public Library Yizkor Books, 1954), 965.
20 According to Stanislawski, *Tsar Nicholas I and the Jews*, 36.
21 E. Tcherikover, "Fun die Russische arkhiven," *Historishe schrift* 1 (1929): 688.
22 Stanislawski, *Tsar Nicholas I and the Jews*, 136.
23 I. M. Dik, *Der erster nabor* [The first draft] (Vilnius: Romm, 1871).

so as to murder him or her). The ruling was issued by Rabbi Yisrael Friedman of Ruzhin, who later became the Rebbe of Sadigura. After the murder, eighty people were arrested, with twenty receiving harsh punishments.[24]

Benjamin Goldveiss informed the authorities that the members of the *kahal* that they were submitting falsified birth registers to the recruiting office in order to make conscription more difficult.[25] Another such informer, Herzl Prohorovkin, was murdered by three Jewish soldiers for telling the authorities of forgeries on the part of members of the *kahal* in 1837.

Thus, the *kahal* did not always help the informers and the authorities, and the possibility of opposition existed. It seems that there were influential factors within the community beside the administration.

The authorities' responded to such activities by means of new decrees in the course of the years. It is clear that these laws were passed as a reaction to events during the years of the decree. Below is a partial list of these laws.

1. A recruit who deserts when conscripted will not be added to the sum of recruits.
2. A community which has not caught the deserter is obligated to bring an additional recruit.
3. Whoever aids in deserting or gives shelter to a deserter will be enlisted without waiting his turn, or will be sent to harsh labor.
4. Whoever finds the deserter will receive a reward of 100 rubles.
5. Whoever inflicts a wound on himself in order to avoid the draft will nevertheless be recruited. In addition, another member of his family, preferably a minor, will be recruited. If such a case occurs, the community will be obliged to enlist soldiers at a number one third higher than the quota fixed.
6. A foreigner may not be conscripted in place of a native countryman.
7. Communities that smuggle minors abroad, will be obligated to supply two soldiers for every on minor.

---

24 S. Dubnov, "Popytka empansipatsii evreev v Rossii" [The attempt at emancipating the Jews in Russia], in idem, *Perezhitoe. Sbornik, posviashchennyi obshchestvennoi i kul'turnoi istorii evreev v Rossii* [Experience: Collection dedicated to the social and cultural history of Jews in Russia], vol. 1 (St. Petersburg: Brokgauz i Efron, 1908), 1–7.
25 Iakov Brafman, *Kniga kagala* [The book of the Kahal] (Vilnius: Tipografiia vilenskogo gubernskogo pravleniia, 1869), 192.

> 8. Anyone who is about to be drafted will be sent as a punishment to harsh labor for twelve years if he is found unfit for regular service [namely, even if his old or sick!].
> 9. A community which hides a draft candidate will receive a fine in the amount of 300 rubles.

H. The Position of Jewish Spiritual Leadership

Stanislawski quotes a halakhic responsum concerning *agunot*: "A soldier who converted to Christianity, but agreed to give his wife a divorce, but was not accurate, calling his wife's father a *kohen*, where in fact he was an Israelite. How can one release the woman from her *aguna* status?"[26] This is just one example—in the responsa literature, there are dozens of rulings concerning *agunot*, among them the case of a certain Polish soldier who was engaged, but because of his conscription did not get married; or the soldier who did not return to his wife, and the questioner wished to know the status of the woman with reference to remarrying. These rulings do not give us additional details concerning service in the Russian army.

Stanislawski also recounts four cases in which rabbis initiated an uprising against the recruiting office and even the release of conscripts, some of them minors. He mentions the public opposition of Rabbi Israel Lipkin (Yisrael Salanter) on that matter.[27] In light of the paucity of facts on deliberate rabbinic activity regarding conscription, Stanislawski demonstrates surprise about what he calls the silence of the rabbis. In our opinion, a lack of documents does not testify to lack of activity. We may be talking about the rabbis' wish not to openly display opposition for obvious reasons.

Rabbi Fishman-Maimon[28] presents the story of Rabbi Eliyahu Shick of Kobrin (Kobryn), author of *Ein Eliyahu*, a commentary on *Ein Yaakov*. On his visit to Grodno, he initiated the release of abducted children from the community center, and determined that the abductor should be prosecuted according to the

---

26 An *aguna* is a woman who cannot remarry as she is still halakhically bound to her first husband.
27 The head of the *mussar* movement. See Imanuel Etkes, *Reishit tenu'at ha-mussar* [The beginning of the *mussar* movement] (Jerusalem: Magnes Press, 1982), 247.
28 Y. L. Fishman-Maimon, *Sarei ha-me'ah* [Princes of the hundreds], vol. 4 (Jerusalem: Mossad Harav Kook, 1965), 247.

law mentioned in the Torah (Ex. 21:16): "One who kidnaps a man and sells him . . . shall surely be put to death." This ruling matches the decision of the Ḥatam Sofer. Rabbi Yaakov Lorberbaum of Lissa (Leszno), author of *Mishkenot Ya'akov* and *Kehilot Ya'akov*, summoned the heads of the community of Karlin in the Minsk district, and warned them not to have any dealings in child abduction. As we are talking about great rabbis, whose influence was recognized beyond their locale, it is clear that rabbis took a stance of clear opposition to the activity of the community establishment.

From the rabbis' activity in the army, we also learn of their self-sacrifice in ensuring the observance of the *mitzvot*. In the archives of the navy, we find a 1828 letter[29] from rabbis in White Russia asking to appoint a rabbi in Kronshtadt to manage prayers, and to encourage halakhic observance of the festivals from Rosh Hashana to Sukkot. The tsar gave his personal approval. This testifies to the influence that Jews had in the imperial court concerning religious matters. Probably the request to send a rabbi or a cantor for the Days of Awe was a sophisticated method of securing a rabbi's tenure at the naval base. Similar requests are found in other archival material: for example, Jewish sailors request to appoint a rabbi from among them. The personal qualities required of the rabbi are listed, as well as the demand (in Russian) that he be fluent in holy books and halakhic rulings, kind to people, and humble in his ways. The one elected was Rabbi Eliyahu Romm. We should mention that the very ability to elect a rabbi at the height of the reign of Nicholas I, and the active participation of the soldiers in appointing him, should raise questions concerning the conditions of Jewish soldiers in the Russian army. In this case the appointment was for a rabbi on a central navy base in the Baltic Sea, where the strictest discipline was imposed, with everything subject to the pursuit of excellence in the art of combat. On the other hand, the centrality of location is probably what gave the rabbi special status in comparison to other places.

Regarding the concern of the rabbis for the individual, one can come to fresh conclusions after studying archival material on the appeal of the Volhynia community to the commander of the Smolensk division for a supply of *matzot* for the minors.[30] In the ongoing correspondence between the commander of the

---

29 Central Archive for the History of the Jewish People, HMF15, copy from Gosudarstvennyi arkhiv Rossiiskoi Federatsii [State archive of the Russian Federation], f. 109, 1 eksp., d. 330, l. 131.

30 Central Archives for the History of the Jewish People, HMF759, copy from Gosudarstvennyi arkhiv Rossiiskoi Federatsii [State archive of the Russian Federation], f. 109, 1 eksp., d. 330, ll. 28–31.

district corps division and the commander of the Smolensk division, it is clear that the base commander's opposition to the proposal was based on the assumption that this could lead to the separation of Jewish minors from gentile minors, as well as to the additional demand of giving furlough for Passover and granting advantages to the Jewish minors. In the community's letter of request, they write that the said privilege had been granted on other military bases.

Thus we learn of the strenuous efforts exerted by rabbis very soon after the passing of the Jewish conscription statutes. In a document written just a few years later, the topic of giving soldiers leave for Sabbath and festivals was raised again. The main headquarters of the fleet demanded information about the festivals, and amazingly, we find organized calendars of the Jewish festivals issued for the use of unit commanders in giving leave to the soldiers. The festivals are ranked as "most important" and "secondary" festivals, testifying to the fact that the calendars were put to use. In addition, the main unit headquarters issued an unambiguous, explicit order to grant leave for Sabbath and festivals. Similarly, the headquarter documents discuss determining a place for prayer, when necessary outside the base, at a distance of several dozen kilometers.

Finding these guidelines together with His Majesty's directive that Jewish soldiers were to be given rest even on Christian holidays, even though the Jews thus received additional days of rest, testifies to the fact that the rights of Jewish soldiers were protected, on the one hand. We also see that constant efforts were being made by the rabbis over many years to increase the Russian army's consideration for the needs of the Jewish soldiers. Below, we will expand on the bewildering contrast between the reasonable level of religious freedom allowed to the Jewish soldiers, as seen here, and the descriptions of the mass forced baptism of Jewish minors.

Another aspect of the topic of the rabbis' role in conscription are the guidelines given to the conscripts. Several testimonies show that there were rabbis who tried to instill in the boys a hope of the imminent abolishment of the decree. In one informer's letter, a soldier who had converted to Christianity tells of the "rabbis' conspiracy to eliminate Emperor Nicholas" as well as their call to the soldiers not to give in to the pressure to convert in anticipation of imminent salvation. The head of the Irkutsk community, S. Beilin, gives similar testimony.[31] He tells that when he himself was conscripted many years earlier, as the conscripted children were taken away, the local rabbi stood on a table at the

---

31 Beilin, "Iz rasskazov o kantonistakh," 115–120.

side of the road and turned to the children with a moving call not to convert to Christianity.

We find rabbinical reference to a similar problem in the *Ḥatam Sofer*'s responsa concerning the draft of Jews into the Austro-Hungarian army at that time. As the rulings of the great rabbis were not limited to geographical borders,[32] it seems that the ruling of the Ḥatam Sofer constituted the guidelines also for the Jews in the Russian Empire. The Ḥatam Sofer wrote as follows:

> And concerning the topic of Jews being taken to the state armies,[33] it is better for us to be silent about this, and the great sages should turn a blind eye (!) and let those appointed **from the community** to do as they see fit at the time; and now is the time to be silent. But nevertheless, I will say, that it is the practice of the state to impose a levy on the entire nation to draft people into the army, and that is the state law and must be upheld. Therefore, it is the individual's responsibility that **anyone who is fit to go out and does not have a wife and children must go according the state law.** But this does not apply to boys who learn Torah who, even if the state has not explicitly exempted them, nevertheless from the Torah's law they are exempt, as stated in the first chapter of Bava Batra (8a). And several times when, for citizens in our country, I testified that they are learning and would be successful in leading a community, they were exempted from conscription to the army; and if that is the case anyone who touches them touches the apple of [God's] eye.
>
> Thus, it would be fitting that they all stand equally in front of the community and draw lots. The one on whom the lot falls will attempt as much as he can to obtain an exemption through payment, or to find someone in his stead, or he should go himself, but all the Jews are obligated to help him redeem himself.
>
> **But to force people without drawing lots and to say that they are reckless and emptyheaded, and even act immorally and desecrate the Shabbat, in my opinion, that is like someone who "kidnaps a person and sells him." For who gives permission to exchange one person for another. The state obligation and ordinance applies to everyone equally.** . . . The best of those who are forcibly conscripted transgress the

---

32 The Ḥatam Sofer's ruling matches the stand taken by the Grodno community in its letter of request to the district governor. See above.
33 Namely, the ruling is a general one, to be implemented in all similar cases.

> mitzvot perforce and rarely, but those would be doing so willingly, and we would be rolling [a stone] onto one who has already fallen according to what is written in the first chapter of Kiddushin regarding one who sold himself to gentiles, etc.[34]

Thus, the Torah view (*Da'at Torah*—a ruling given by a supreme Torah authority that obligates all Jews) on conscription is divided into several aspects. First, the state law must be obeyed because to the Talmudic principle: "The state law is the law." One should turn a blind eye to the activity of the community administration, although it is clear that negative deeds are performed. All are equal before the law, but yeshiva students should be released from conscription even if there is no explicit permission from the authorities. Under no circumstances may one hand over people for conscription claiming that they do not observe *mitzvot*—that they are "emptyheaded"—in exchange for "worthy" Jews. On the contrary, it is preferable to submit for conscription people who are particular about observing *mitzvot*, as it is forbidden to cause someone to completely stop observing *mitzvot*. However, it is permitted to change candidates for conscription for those ready to enlist for payment.

An identical stance was presented in the letter of the Mogilev community to the governor of Belarus, showing that the Ḥatam Sofer's ruling was accepted throughout Eastern Europe. But more often, the heads of the *kahal* in the Russian state acted in opposition to this rabbinical opinion.

---

34 *Shut Ḥatam Sofer*, vol. 3, section 29 (June 1830).

4

The Implementation of the Jewish Conscription Law

A. How Many Soldiers Was It Possible to Enlist from the Jewish Community in Russia?

In order to understand the significance of the draft quotas and the number of conscripted children, we must look at a demographic model of a Jewish community of the time. However, reliable district population censuses were conducted only from 1830, about three years after the start of the recruitment. The obligation of conscription applied to those who pay poll tax (*podushnaia podat'*), namely, every male; therefore, to calculate the number of conscripts per thousand, we must examine the number of men alone.

Below is the calculation presented by Stanislawski:[1]

District	1830	1838	1847	1851
Grodno	31,813	33,918	45,403	43,178
Kyiv	45,000	55,883	65,757	78,182
Minsk	37,000	49,000	43,500	45,800
Mogilev	36,700	46,000	44,500	49,500
Podillia	70,000	82,000	81,000	85,000
Vilna/Kovno (Kaunas)	46,600	69,000	73,000	64,000
Volhynia	94,000	101,000	83,400	86,500
TOTAL	404,309	494,412	491,579 (a little less than in the previous conscription)	535,670

---

1   Stanislawski, *Tsar Nicholas I and the Jews*, 163.

Stanislawski notes that this chart is based on several sources, because there is no statistical sequence from one source. In addition, there was no uniformity in the administrative division, which changed every so often. To make the matters more complicated, Jews who lived outside the Pale of Settlement were not included. Moreover, it is impossible to count the number of Jews who "disappeared" and were never counted in any census. The assumption is that at least a third of the whole Jewish population was not registered. To make a gross estimate, the total size of the Jewish population at the end of this period was about 1,500,000 people, of them 750,000 men.

According to the draft quota of four per thousand, we can conclude that each year an average of about 2,000 Jewish soldiers were enlisted, at least at the first stage. According to the military report[2] on the number of cantonists conscripted between 1827 and 1840, the number reached a total of 15,050—about 1,100 each year. This number constitutes about half of the Jewish conscripts annually. If we estimate one year's conscription as about 1.5% of the population as a whole, the boys enlisted between the ages of eight and twelve were about 8% of the 500,000 Jewish men seen in the chart above; namely 40,000 boys.

Thus, each six years, 7,000 Jewish boys of these ages were taken to the army; a significant percentage. One has to take into account that about half the children were exempt from service because of physical disabilities, so that just a little less than half of the healthy boys were taken. Accordingly, the conscription of boys into service reduced the birth rate among the Jewish community, to the satisfaction of the tsar's officials.

B. Changes in the Recruitment Procedures among the Jews

In order to understand the processes of the decree's implementation, let us first examine when the recruitment actually started. It can be assumed that after the tsar's decree was given, the implementation was handed over to a cumbersome bureaucracy and that the organization of institutions and positions needed to carry out the order would continue for a long time. It is therefore quite surprising to learn from a (Yiddish) notification of a list of conscripts in the town of

---

2 Y. Petrovsky-Shtern, *Jews in the Russian Army, 1827–1917: Drafted into Modernity* (Cambridge: Cambridge University Press, 2014), 125, according to the documents in Rossiiskii gosudarstvennyi voenno-istoricheskii arkhiv [Russian state archive of military history], f. 405.

Minsk, published on November 27, 1827, that the conscription started immediately, within three months of the law being passed. The very need of the community to publicize such information is interesting (see the next section).

The first draft statute[3] included a general ordinance for the conscription of two men out of every five hundred taxpayers. Only later did they change to calculating a certain quota per thousand. At any rate, the quota of four per thousand seems to have been the average quota also for non-Jews.

In 1831, when new military regulations were put into practice, conscription quotas for Jews and non-Jews were now different from one another. Whereas the draft age for the general population was between twenty and twenty-five, for the Jews it was brought down to eighteen.

An additional question is the conscription quota itself. The main source for this information is the full collection of the laws of the Russian Empire's army, and the collection of laws and government edicts concerning the Jews edited by Levanda. It is generally believed that the most extreme quota was introduced in 1854: ten per thousand tax payers. In Levanda's collection, we find a draft ordinance from July 14, 1831 of a quota of ten Jews per thousand in the areas of Mohilev, Kyiv, Podillia, Volhynia, Minsk, Grodno, Vilna, Kovno, and Vitebsk. It is not possible to explain the significance of the ordinance and whether it was ever implemented. It is interesting to note that in this draft the conscription areas are divided going from west to east. Later, in 1834, the division was changed and now went from north to south. Ostensibly, this change did not apply to the Jews.

The fact that the conscription began immediately in 1827 is also verified by Korobkov,[4] who claims that in that year the plan was to draft 1,637 Jews, a number that matches the figure of 400,000 men,[5] assuming that the quota was four per thousand. The authorities were to have drafted 56,284 men from the general population, such that the Jewish share in the conscription was 2.5.%, corresponding to the percentage of the Jewish population in the empire.

According to the collection of military laws, in the years 1834–1839 the quota was five per thousand. In 1832 there was no conscription at all. These numbers show that the quotas and times of conscription were discussed anew each year, and often changed. It is clear that the limit of the quota stems from demographic

---

3 V. S. Levanda, *Sbornik zakonov, kasaiushchikhsia evreev* [Collection of laws concerning the Jews] (St. Petersburg: N.P. 1874).
4 Kh. Korobkov, "Evreiskaia rekrutchina v tsarstvovanie Nikolaia Pervogo" [Jewish recruitment during the reign of Nicholas I], *Evreiskaia starina* 6 (1913): 233–244.
5 The number of conscripts demonstrates that Stanislawski's data are correct. See the chart above, at the beginning of this chapter.

and social considerations, the number of men fit to carry weapons being quite limited. Despite all the increases in the required quota, the number of actual conscripts was not enough to supply the required number.

It is interesting that in Itzkovitz's conscription certificate it states that he was drafted at his young age because of the draft evasion of older Jews. This phrasing was standard, and it was customary to write it on conscription documents of minors. Apparently, adults and not minors were supposed to be drafted in the first place, but, lacking a sufficient number of adults, the people who managed the conscrption inevitably turned to minors.

We do not have an orderly record of numbers of conscripts till 1840. Only in 1841, after new regulations were passed, reports of the numbers of those serving in specific units began to arrive at the army offices.

C. The Activity of the Draft Committees (Analysis of the Gendarmes' Report on the Regularity of the Conscription)

This report of the gendarmes brings additional information about conscription processes:[6]

> April 22, 1840
>
> To: Count Benkendorf, commander of the gendarmes
>
> Reporter: Major-General Shnell, commander of the fifth district of the gendarme brigade
>
> Inspection report on the recruitment procedures in Western recruitment area—partial recruitment and non-scheduled recruitment of the Cossacks—concerning the draft of November-December 1839
>
> Clause 1. The community reports are so confused that they are absolutely incomprehensible.
>
> Clause 2. The community administration exploits the approval in order to combine families, and it combines rich families with poor families.

---

6   Central Archives for the History of the Jewish People, RU450, copy from Gosudarstvennyi arkhiv Rossiiskoi Federatsii [State archive of the Russian Federation], f. 109, 1 eksp., d. 330, ll. 28–35.

As a result, members of poor families are drafted, and the entire conscription burden falls on the poor.

Clause 3. The chairman of the local conscription committee prevents the conscription committee from conducting a comprehensive audit and getting involved in draft procedures.

In the area of Volhynia the audit committee cooperates with the local draft committee and the draft procedures are implemented properly.

Inspection report for 1839, partial third conscription, district of Kiev

Reporter: Lieutenant Colonel Bekker

General draft quotas: Six recruits per thousand men; owners of small farms:[7] five per thousand.

Clause 4. In the city of Zvenigorod the local conscription committee took several recruits who do not suit the age of conscription, and some of them are real children. This negative phenomenon is a routine characteristic of the draft [Lieutenant Colonel Bekker's opinion].

Clause 5. The commander of the gendarmes in the town of Skvira [Skvyra][8] complains that the Jews of the community who were responsible for the draft procedures set up a warning system ahead of audits, and accordingly, when the auditor comes they freeze the entire process in such a way that an audit cannot be conducted.

Clause 9. Those appointed by the *kahal* and the Jewish delegates disregard the recruitment procedures in the severest manner. They turned the conscription into a profitable trade for themselves and the *kahal* under the pretense of dark and unjustified reasons. On the basis of illegal rulings they send whomever they want to military service.

Clause 11. The Jew Avrum Goihman from the community of Uman coaxed a townsman by the name of Bershanovsky to enlist to the army under a false name in exchange for the sum of twenty-five rubles, and for the promise that he (Goihman) will ensure his release from service within two months.

---

7   *Odnodvortsy*—a category of state peasants in Russia until 1866. Evidently, the quotas changed according to social status.
8   A city with its own Hasidic movement, not far from Kyiv.

Clause 17. The person in charge of absorbing recruits, the commander of the unit of army veterans in the city of Zvenigorod, Captain Rimkovitch, is regularly found drunk. Being in such a situation he housed the Jewish conscripts in Jewish homes in gross violation of the regulations.

Clause 18. The head of the gendarmes in the Kiev region reports that the adults entice Jewish minors to enlist in the army by bribing them with gifts, temptations, and intimidations. The minors agree to enlist without understanding the significance, and when they grasp the matter, they complain that they were deceived and refuse to enlist. On the basis of this, Lieutenant Colonel Bekker proposes to the head of the Third Section of the Tsar's Chancellery, commander of the gendarmes, General Count Benkendorf, **to completely abolish the conscription of minors**. In his opinion, the minors are a burden on the army.

Clause 19. The total arrears in the recruitment quota in the Volhynia district: 209 people, of whom 24 are Jews.

As this report shows, the authorities took trouble to conduct an audit, which testifies to an attempt to properly manage the conscription. However, the gendarmes, the Tsar's secret police, failed in enforcing the law on the leaders of the *kahal*. The Jews drove them crazy with stories and strange ("dark," "murky") claims. The population registration books could not be used. The gendarmes were of the opinion that people were being conscripted according to the decision of some Jewish court of law.

In fact, the members of the *kahal* turned the draft into a profitable trade. Giving the officers vodka and money, they blocked the auditing and prevented the conscription committees from being involved in the conscription processes. During recruitment, wealthy tradesmen fraudulently recruited people by giving them a small amount of money and guaranteeing immediate release (as if it were child's play, and as if the authorities were in their hands). They probably had evidence of being able to release people after conscription, and that is why they were believed. Other sources, such as an apostate's informing on Rabbi Aimes,[9] also mention promises given to conscripts that they would be released.

The situation with the minors was similar. The *kahal* drafted children without any effort, through lies, bribery, and gifts. The army was not interested in

---

9   Central Archives for the History of the Jewish People, RU347, copy from Gosudarstvennyi arkhiv Rossiiskoi Federatsii [State archive of the Russian Federation], f. 109, 1 eksp., d. 186.

enlisting minors and did not see in it a religious or educational challenge. From the point of view of the army, the children were a burden.

The average quota was five to six per thousand. We do not have other evidence that there was a difference in the conscription quota according to the size of the household, so that small householders (*odnodvortsy*) were drafted according to a lower quota. But that fact probably refers only to Christians.

To sum up: The tsar received information from the gendarmes about the improper behavior of Jews in the conscription processes, including the conscription of the weak, the poor, and children. Perhaps, the abolishment of the *kahal* (the community administration) can be seen as a reaction to this activity. Whatever the case may be, these acts were undoubtedly likely to increase the scorn for the Jews among the antisemites, and to legitimize the idea of "reforming" the Jews. Nevertheless, the *maskilim* were incorrect in casting the blame for the distortions on the Jews, who were in fact the scapegoats of the tsar's policy. It was as a result of being placed under inhumane conditions that they did not function properly. The true solution would have certainly been to grant equal rights. But with the tsar unwilling to do so—"This is not feasible" as was his response to Sir Moses Montefiore's letter—he and his ministers bore responsibility for the distortions of the *kahal*'s leaders.

The report of the gendarmes can be compared with the report of the governor's office, also in the district of Volhynia, from 1850, which was addressed to the Ministry of the Interior.[10] The report states, among other things:

> The Jews succeed in receiving advance information of the conscription, and immediately escape from their homes. The community appoints agents to search for the evaders, but these connive with the evaders and declare that the evaders cannot be found. As a result, the priority in conscription moves to the minors, and people not determined by the *kazennaia palata*[11] come to *the conscription office.*

This report gives the numbers of draft evaders in the province. The number increased five-fold within thirteen years: from 355 people in 1833 to 1,875 in 1846. Evidently, the Jews learned the art of dodging military service, and the authorities could not find a way of dealing with the problem. The governor of

---

10 Central Archives for the History of the Jewish People, HMF665, copy from Gosudarstvennyi arkhiv Rossiiskoi Federatsii [State archive of the Russian Federation], f. 109, 1 eksp., d. 330.
11 The Ministry of Finance's office of the city administration.

Volhynia complained that only the lame, the handicapped, and the minors came to the conscription center, out of whom no one could be found fit for service. He claimed that those appointed to manage the conscription on behalf of the community turned the whole matter into a source of earning money, and that much money was invested in draft dodging. The Jews knew how to bribe even the members of the jury in district courts.

It is important to note that the governor's report makes mention of the *kazennaia palata* as the state institution that dealt with conscription, particularly with composing lists of candidates for conscription and of deserters. Originally, this body was responsible for drawing up population censuses for tax collection purposes. It is very interesting that matters of conscription were classified as relating to the tax collection department.

As we have seen, the governor also repeats the claims of Lieutenant Colonel Bekker in his 1839 report, according to which minors were drafted because of the widespread draft evasion by adults and the high percentage of those unfit for service. This is also stated explicitly in the memoirs of Israel Leib Itzkovitz.[12]

The governor of Volhynia was writing to his superiors. Had there been an explicit order to catch children, the governor would have had no reason to note the justifications for the increasing conscription of children in an internal document.

D. The Method of "Comprehensive" Conscription

The stories of conscription in Mstislaw and Berdychiv supply a lot of material to analyze the draft process in practice.

1. The Revolt[13] in Mstislaw

An example characterizing the government's activity concerning conscription appears in the documents about the revolt in Mstislaw, a Jewish town on the border between Ukraine and Poland. Based on a file of the police department in the

---

12 See above, Itzkovitz, "Vospominaniia evreiskogo kantonista."
13 The label "revolt" was given by the authorities with the malicious intent of incriminating members of the community.

Ministry of the Interior,[14] the rebellion started at the end of 1843, when a military unit confiscated goods smuggled from Poland. The Jews, who were owners of the merchandise, expressed a certain amount of opposition. On the basis of a biased report of a "rebellion" submitted by the local authorities, Nicholas initiated a draft with the abnormal quota of one recruit for every ten Jews. Following the order, the local governor imposed a blockade on the Jews of the city and ordered to seize every Jew aged from twelve to thirty-five[15] who was registered as a local resident in nearby areas and transfer them to Mstislaw. Following the rabbis' call, Jews flocked to the cemeteries to pray and beseech day and night, but to no avail. The recruitment unit broke into houses at night, and its members captured every male from the age of seven, but at the same time they were ready to release any of those abducted in exchange for a bribe. A few days later, they managed to recruit thirty-two people. According to the registers, they needed to recruit 161 more, but these could not be found. The Jewish population began to starve because of the blockade. In light of the local authorities' inability to carry out the tsar's order, the governor of the province and the Minister of the Interior intervened. It soon became clear that there had been no trace of a revolt, and the decree was cancelled.

What is amazing here is the ease with which the tsar imposed the decree, staging the recruitment of the Jews as a military operation in every way—bringing in army units, imposing a blockade, and using excessive brutality. The use of conscription as a punitive tool is an important characterization of the tsar's arbitrary practices.[16]

On the other hand, we learn that the tsar had no tools to enforce his orders, and that in the face of total resistance from the community, the authorities failed miserably, and the recruitment level did not even reach fifteen percent. This showed the recruiting authorities that they needed cooperation and dialogue with the community for the success of their mission. To achieve this goal, the recruitment authorities in general and the local government in particular had to take a tolerant position towards the community, to protect its needs vis-à-vis the central government, and to seek a common language with the community's activists.

---

14 Arkhiv Ministerstva vnutrennikh del [Archives of the Ministry of Internal Affairs, department of police enforcement], d. 479 (1844), quoted in Gessen, *Istoriia*, 113; Central Archives of the History of the Jewish People, RU678, copy from Gosudarstvennyi arkhiv Rossiiskoi Federatsii [State archive of the Russian Federation], f. 109, d. 101.
15 The age of recruitment was up to twenty-five according to the law.
16 Central Archives of the History of the Jewish People, RU678.

2. Conscription in Berdychiv. Conscription as a Punitive Tool

The events in Berdychiv in 1850, seven years after those in Mstislaw, show that using conscription as a punitive tool was routine. On December 27, 1850, it was decided to enlist three additional recruits for every recruit missing in the general conscription, as a warning and in order to speed up the cooperation of the community in the future.[17]

In Berdychiv, forty-five men were missing from the conscription. Since, according to the tsar's order, only adults from the age of twenty could be drafted, the community had to supply 135 adults (3x45). Conscription of adults was a severe punishment for the community, as it immediately affected the recruit's family. It became clear that there were no additional men of conscription age (between twenty and twenty-five) in the community, or that the adults were the sole breadwinners of their families, and therefore could not be drafted. The governor of the province decided to deviate from the tsar's order and to enlist minors as well.[18]

In order to verify the lack, a committee was established with a senior officer at its head. The committee found that the *kahal*'s register listed 840 Jews aged from twenty to twenty-five. Taking into account that many had left the area and did not actually live in Berdychiv, and that the breadwinners could not be drafted, 192 men were left for conscription.[19] At the time of the draft, none of them could be found, but even had they appeared, it is doubtful whether it would have been possible to enlist 135 of them. This can be concluded from the fact that in the previous conscription, out of the 207 enlisted, only ten men were found to be fit for service—about five percent. A manhunt was conducted, and 720 men were caught, of whom 339 were registered as residents of the town. Again, only ten were found to be fit.

The results of this extensive military operation made it legitimate to decide on the indiscriminate conscription of minors. The number of children from the age of twelve (and in fact, much younger, seven to nine years old) that were caught and imprisoned was 496. Of these eighty-one (sixteen percent) were fit

---

17 Gessen, *Istoriia*, 114. Central Archives of the History of the Jewish People, HM2\9423/12, copy from Gosudarstvennyi arkhiv Rossiiskoi Federatsii [State archive of the Russian Federation], f. 109, 2 eksp.
18 From here we see that the policy of drafting minors was not uniform.
19 Less than twenty-five percent of those registered for conscription, before the health screening. From here we see that the actual conscription reserve was four times lower than the register's data, and the authorities therefore turned to the more available minors.

for service. It seems that this unusual method also did not help reach the quota of 135 young men, and the conscription potential in Berdychiv was exhausted for many years with this last effort.

Evidently, the authorities had great difficulty carrying out the conscription orders for the following reasons:

a. unreliable registration of conscripts in the community registers;
b. absence of conscripts at the time of conscription;
c. population mobility;
d. unsuitability of candidates for recruitment;
e. the conscription quotas were made up not according to who was available, but according to the authorities' wishes.

The imposition of the penalty of tripling the recruitment quota indicates that this step was taken out of desperation. The authorities were not capable of constantly dealing with the Jews' draft evasion.

The fact that ninety percent of the candidates were not fit raises questions. There is no other source that presents a similar percentage among conscription candidates. If this really had been the routine in conscription, the authorities would have taken it into consideration from the start, one way or another. So, there is no explanation for this. Another assumption is that the majority evaded conscription through bribery. This is difficult to accept, considering the severity of the order that came from the tsar himself. The high percentage of those exempt for health reasons during a punitive operation raises a question concerning the common claim that the health boards were negligent in fulfilling their duties and listed even very sick people as healthy.

As we see, the draft committee consciously set itself the goal of recruiting minors against the wishes of the tsar. This demonstrates that the officials and the community wanted to ensure an "easy life" for themselves by taking children, who were more available than adults. If this assumption is correct, the aim of conscription changed from converting the Jewish boys to Christianity to a necessity stemming from the need to fill the quotas. It was also easier to give up one child than many breadwinners. Was there, then, a cruel but logical calculation?

Here we should ask: Why did the tsar not want to enlist the minors according to this order from the beginning? Does this not demonstrate a change in the tsar's approach to the conscription of boys as a means of limiting natural reproduction? Is this not an admission of failure? Indeed, the cantonist decree was abolished soon after Nicholas's death without, as far as we know, any effort on the part of the Jewish leaders. Could it be that already in Nicholas's lifetime a plan was prepared for the annulment of the cantonist decree, as it was an inefficient means that did not serve its purpose and cost the state treasury a lot of money?

E. Jewish Conscription in the Mid-1850s, and the "Tithe" Decree of 1852

The answer can perhaps be found in the last conscription decrees issued in the days of Nicholas I.[20] On the same day (December 27, 1850) as the order was given to enlist three men for every absentee,[21] another order was issued: A conscription order in exchange for arrears in the payment of community tax debts, according to which an additional Jewish soldier was to be conscripted for each debt of 2,000 rubles.[22] The minister of defense stated that, if the decree brought a significant increase in the number of soldiers, he would not know what to do with them. In addition, there was concern that the *kahal* would prefer to bring recruits in exchange for tax payment, and this would harm the state income. Thus, there was an internal contradiction in the policy which can only be explained by the fact the one who promoted the idea was involved in tax collection and not in building the budget. It seems that only in that way can the high exchange rate of 2,000 rubles be explained. Someone was interested in "zeroing" the arrears as proof of the successful functioning of the collection authorities.

This is where the damage that the decree brought to the state coffers became clear. The Ministry of Finance decided that conscription would not cancel the payment of the debt, but only postpone it for one year. But that was not enough. Those who opposed the "whitewashing" seem to have succeeded in lobbying the tsar, and in July 1852 the rate was reduced from the sum of 2,000 rubles per conscript to just 300 rubles. The ministerial committee explained the decision by saying that in that way it would be possible to cover the arrears (!). The authorities decided to deceive themselves by painting a rosy picture.

On August 4, 1852 it was decided to increase the conscription quota, and to draft each year ten Jews per thousand, in contrast to the previous quota of five per thousand. Seemingly, this increased quota was introduced in light of the war.

---

20 Levanda, *Sbornik zakonov*, 790–791 (nos. 675 and 676).
21 Gessen, *Istoriia*, 114.
22 Levanda, *Sbornik zakonov*, 237.

Among the Christian population, too, nine people per thousand were enlisted (one fewer than the new quota for the Jews). At the same time, that month, the horrific decree was enacted allowing abductions of those without identifying documents and deserters—anyone who was not a local resident. Beforehand the communities were only allowed to draft those Jews listed in the community's register lists (*revizskie skazki*, population census to the level of detailing the family composition), now permission was given to abduct almost anyone. Stanislawski[23] notes that the permission to abduct vagrants and those without permits had been made legal long before, and therefore when it was renewed it bore the character of a local act of the community administration. Thus, the balance in the mutual relationship between the Jewish establishment and the community members was broken once and for all, and their relations took on a hostile nature.[24]

In this way, the 1850s marked several important developments in the history of Russian Jewry. It should be examined to what extent each such event contributed to the cancellation of the cantonist decree and to the introduction of uniform regulations for Jews and gentiles during the times of Alexander II.

One of Nicholas's final efforts was to introduce the procedure of *razbor* (sorting and deportation of "inefficient" Jews). Later, in 1851, came the attempt to increase conscription, which succeeded in 1853. At the same time, conscription in exchange for cancelling the community's debts was introduced. All these steps testify to increased attempts to control the processes within the Jewish communities. It is impossible to claim that the quota of ten conscripts per thousand tax payers was introduced as a result of a need created by the Crimean War, as the campaign started earlier.

The worsening of recruitment measures should be seen from the same point of view. The ministerial committee raised the concern that the demanded number of Jews could not be found, and that the tsar's order could not be carried out. The tsar decided to proceed with his decision at all costs, and therefore permission was given to abduct whomever possible. Historians usually describe the various steps taken at that time simply as an expression of antisemitic cruelty. We suggest seeing the increasingly severe conscription methods as an integral part of the tsar's renewed efforts towards the proper implementation of the law, in a final attempt to impose his social administrative doctrine on the Jews.

---

23 Stanislawski, *Tsar Nicholas I and the Jews*, 184.
24 About the abductors, see above, chapter 2.

In the national memory, in Jewish folklore and songs, this last period sums up Nicholas's rule, even though, as we have shown, changes regarding Jewish conscription took place during the whole course of his reign. There was no uniform policy; there were ups and downs, including postponements and cancellations of annual conscription. Against the background of the increased effort to fulfill the conscription order, the tsar's officials caused impoverishment and collapse of the Jewish economy in particular, and of the state's economy in general. It is unclear why they did not calculate correctly the human reservoir of Jews fit for service. It is clear from all the reports that more than half of all Jewish conscripts was pronounced unfit for service. The failure of the conscription policy undoubtedly stemmed from the lack of tools with which to assess the situation and arrive at relevant decisions. The tsar's decision to enlist 6,000 men annually was unrealistic. We are witness here to the fact that with all the tsar's wishes to be rational, it was his desires that dictated his deeds and not the reality.[25]

F. The Struggle of Groups within the Community to Receive Exemptions

As mentioned, tradesmen with the recognized status as members of a guild (whoever dealt in business but did not meet the criteria set by the authorities did not benefit from the status of tradesman) would pay tax directly to the state treasury, not via the community. This favored status motivated the members of the community to strive to achieve the status of tradesmen, especially of the first guild. However, moving to a higher was difficult because, among other considerations, it required great expense on the part of the candidate. Nevertheless, people were prepared to get into heavy debt in order to be released from dependency on the community and the draft obligation.

Another condition, which also was almost impossible to achieve, was receiving exemption from the community. Naturally, the community was not interested in its wealthier members leaving the fold. Such a situation would mean imposing an increased burden of tax payment and conscription on the rest of the community members. Therefore, the *kahals* usually stipulated that an exemption from community membership could only be granted if the applicant was not in arrears with his tax payments to the community and on condition that

---

25 Concerning conscription of Jews in 1853 and 1854, see below, "Abolishment of the Conscription Decree," 259.

he was not required to enlist in the army. Thus, for example, the Vitebsk community determined that all its members would be in the category of "required to enlist," and therefore would not be able to change their civil status. Wealthier people were ready to pay a ransom fee in exchange for this exemption.[26]

From their point of view, the community was not interested in breaking away from merchants with a recognized status. In the police archives[27] there is a complaint from nine tradesmen in Bohuslav concerning activity of the community administration, which, "lacking means to fund the conscription operation, and because of arrears in tax payments to the treasury, imposes those debts on families of the tradesmen. Property has been taken by force from some of the families."

It is interesting to note that the authorities sometimes supported the communities' demand to require the tradesmen to participate in the expenses. This was because the tradesmen were a more stable source of funding than the poor members of the community.

Craftsmen, too, struggled to change their status to a higher one. An example is the activity of craftsmen in Dubrovka in the Mogilev district. In 1827, a group of craftsmen established an independent administration, but the *kahal* dissolved the organization.[28] In 1838, a group of sixty-eight people approached the governor complaining of embezzlement on the part of the community administration. Yitzchak Samsonkin headed the protest. In 1841, continuing his struggle against the community, Samsonkin submitted a complaint to Tsar Nicholas stating that the community administration violated the recruitment procedures when drafting people into the army. Ten years later, in 1851, his complaint was transferred to the court. From this procrastination it seems that the community had the upper hand in the struggle with the craftsmen.

However, the craftsmen were not always in conflict with the *kahal*. In the archives of the Senate there is a complaint from the community of Shargorod against the heads of the *kahal*. It appears that in 1834 representatives of regular members of the community accused the heads of the *kahal* of forging the public's decision concerning the draft procedures and that, according to the forged

---

26 This decision appears in *Vtoroe sobranie zakonov*, no. 3161 (1829). Gessen, *Istoriia*, 68.
27 Arkhiv Ministerstva vnutrennikh del, departament politsii ispolnitel'noi [Archives of the Ministry of Internal Affairs, department of police enforcement], d. 858 (1830), quoted in Gessen, *Istoriia*, 69.
28 Arkhiv Ministerstva vnutrennikh del, Khoziaistvennyi departament [Archives of the Ministry of Internal Affairs, economic department], d. 205 (1843): "Po zhalobe Samsonkina na pritesneniia" [On Samsonkin's complaint about harassment], quoted in Gessen, *Istoriia*, 73.

lists, recruitment priority was violated. In this quarrel the craftsmen stood on the side of the *kahal*. Several significant conclusions can be drawn from this event.

First of all, the polarization in the community reached such a point that the community itself set up an agreed representation from within that acted against the heads of the *kahal*. Furthermore, the craftsmen acted within the community as a cohesive body of influential people until even the heads of the *kahal* needed their support. In general, we see that there existed in the communities united forces that opposed the activities of the *kahal* heads.

After the *kahal* institution was dismantled on December 19, 1844,[29] the craftsmen continued to strive to achieve a status similar to that of the tradesmen, hoping to receive total exemption from conscription. They claimed that their knowledge was crucial for the public. In 1854, craftsmen from the town of Bila Tserkva submitted a request to the Senate to establish a separate administration for Jewish craftsmen, dividing them into guilds according to their vocation, to introduce order into their matters, and to make them exempt from the burden of belonging to a Jewish community.

> This community treats us according to an old Jewish custom, belittling craftsmen and burdening us in a discriminatory manner by imposing financial and personal charges.

They claimed that if a separate union were established for craftsmen, it would pay all the debts, and the burden imposed on the general public would automatically be reduced. One of the aims of this request was to receive exemption from conscription similar to the tradesmen.

In 1853, craftsmen in Vladimir (Volodymyr), in the Volhynia district, also turned to the Ministry of the Interior with a complaint about discrimination during conscription.[30] In 1855, the craftsmen of Dubno submitted a request to the Ministry of the Interior to appoint one of their representatives to the town council, and at the same time to establish a separate union for Jewish craftsmen, so that their conscription would be conducted separately through the union. They explained their request by saying that "the community looks down on craftsmen and does not grant them the favored status they deserve according to law." These craftsmen complained that the community maliciously sent the craftsmen to three different draft offices in the town, thereby sending

---

29 Levanda, *Sbornik zakonov*, 509–510.
30 Arkhiv Ministerstva vnutrennikh del, Khoziaistvennyi departament [Archives of the Ministry of Internal Affairs, economic department], d. 205 (1843), quoted in Gessen, *Istoriia*, 74.

more craftsmen to the army than required by law. Although only four craftsmen needed to be drafted, the community enlisted eight or even more. This claim needs explanation: why was a quota of four of a certain social class determined, when the quotas were fixed per thousand tax payers? If there had been an agreed internal division within the community, this agreement had been violated.[31]

This section of our study expands the list of factors within the community that were involved in sharing out the burden of conscription, and possibly even in determining the policy and priorities that were in practice. Till now the role of the community administration alone has been emphasized, whereas we have arrived at a list of actors that determined the draft priorities: the kahal administration, and after its abolishment the *obshchestvo*; representatives of the community who were selected independently; its wealthy members; the craftsmen; the spiritual leadership; and last of all, the ordinary members of the community.

G. The Army's Attitude towards Jewish Conscripts—an Analysis of the Sources

Two interesting documents shed more light on the service of Jewish soldiers.[32]

Document A

Ministry of Defense

General Staff department, St. Petersburg, September 18, 1828

The Acting Inspector of the Engineering Division hereby reports that work at the port of the Kronshtadt naval base is being delayed because the labor battalions are not adequately staffed, or the soldiers are unfit for the required work due to old age or lack of understanding.

Decision of the General Staff supervisor: "To approve the appointment of required workers from among recruited Jewish groups."[33]

---

31 Arkhiv Ministerstva vnutrennikh del, Khoziaistvennyi departament [Archives of the Ministry of Internal Affairs, economic department], d. 183 (1852), quoted in Gessen, *Istoriia*, 74.
32 Central Archives of the History of the Jewish people, HM2\8451/2, copy from Rossiiskii gosudarstvennyi arkhiv voenno-morskogo flota [Russian state archive of the military sea navy], f. 283, op. 1.
33 Later in the correspondence, the supervisory department asks from which areas the conscripted Jews come. There seems to have been a discrepancy in the quality of the conscripts according to areas.

Although in the discussions concerning conscription, scorn for the fitness of the Jews was expressed, the army personnel in the field saw the conscripted Jews as an asset, and tried to obtain approval from the General Staff for their employment. Of course, the army was interested in adult soldiers and not in minors. The demand for Jewish soldiers was likely to neutralize pressure to convert. Importantly, this need was felt already in the early years of implementing the conscription decree. The interest in the draft location can indicate a distinction in different qualities of the recruits according to their place of residence.

Document B[34]

> His Majesty the Tsar, according to the report of the Minister of Defense, has done the favor of issuing the order:
>
> **On formation of training divisions of infantry from *karabiner* units**[35]
>
> In order to promote methods of forming infantry training divisions and manning them with those qualified, I hereby command:
>
> [Clauses 1–6 do not deal with the Jews, Y.M.]
>
> 7. Without any differentiation in the method of forming the divisions, Jewish cantonists should be appointed at the time of their annual assignment to units.
> 8. Jews with a combat profile who have adopted the Orthodox religion should be assigned to combat units of the aforesaid divisions. They should be given the rank of junior officer. Jews who have not adopted the Orthodox religion and who do not have a combat profile should be assigned to the auxiliary battalions of brigades 1 and 2. Those cantonists will be trained as musicians, drummers, trumpeters, and violinists.
>
> Hence, I hereby command to immediately provide the military colonies division with lists of cantonists from among the soldiers' sons and Jewish boys over the age of 16 who are eligible for regular service.

---

34 Levanda, *Sbornik zakonov*, 540–541 (no. 469).
35 From the French *carabinier*—one who carries a carbine gun.

> Officers of the *karabiner* brigades will be directed to the cantonist units in order to select children who have reached the age of conscription according to a special order of the military colonies division.
>
> Submitted by the department of military colonies, May 12, 1842.

From this document we learn that, despite the severe lack of manpower in the *karabiner* divisions, cadets from military schools were not sent there in an organized manner. The document does not state unequivocally that Jewish children are not to be taken for regular service. Perhaps we should be precise and conclude that the Jews who did not convert to Christianity were discriminated against only in their military rank, but not in their assignment to combat units. Notably, the document also includes elements of planning for the future.

Below we will present more documents that describe the terms of the Jews' military service.[36]

Document C. Assignment of Jews to auxiliary units and the labor battalion of the imperial palace

> July 12, 1848
>
> His Majesty the Tsar has done the favor of issuing the following order:
>
> > Nineteen Jewish soldiers are now serving in mobile auxiliary battalions nos. 2 and 3 and in the labor battalion. The Jews should immediately be removed from these units and exchanged for soldiers of the Orthodox religion. In the future Jews should not be assigned to these battalions.
> >
> > Commander of the special corps of the Zimnii Imperial Palace guard corps,
> >
> > Major-General of the General Staff[37]

It can be understood from the document that, in 1843, discrimination was introduced in appointing Jews for the Imperial Guard. Before this time, Torah-observant Jews were able to serve in the Imperial Guard, but in 1843 there was a change in the tsar's attitude toward Jews who did not convert.

---

36   Ibid., 549 (no. 482).
37   Ibid., 549 (no. 482).

Document D. Assignment of Jews to naval units

> Circular of the Inspection Department of the Ministry of the Navy. June 16, 1845[38]
>
> His Majesty the Tsar has done the favor of issuing the order:
>
> To establish a procedure for the placement of the Jewish soldiers arriving for service in the navy, in addition to their placement in work crews and port ship crews:
>
> 1. To enroll minors aged twelve to eighteen in the naval cadet teams.
> 2. Adults:
>   a. Craftsmen must be sent to naval units and artillery units
>   b. Gunners must be placed in the ammunition depots of the units as craftsmen.
>
> Those not fit for combat service must be sent to in the printing houses of the navy office.
>
> 3. The procedure applies equally to the Jews who have not converted to the Orthodox religion by the age of eighteen.
> 4. Jews should not be assigned to the auxiliary teams of the Guard, the naval offices, maintenance units of buildings belonging to the navy's general administration, or cadet teams.

It appears that only in certain vocations there was no discrimination in the appointment of Jews, between those who had not converted and those who had. Jews who converted were still defined as Jews. There was clear discrimination in assigning Jews to certain select units. Notably, the tsar went into the minutest details in matters concerning the Jews' military service.

A framework that does not adopt equality is not able to promote a merging of populations. Therefore, in this example we see the internal contradiction between the assimilation trend and Nicholas's antisemitism, which prevented it.

---

38   Ibid., 609 (no. 521).

H. Discrimination against Jewish Soldiers Who Did Not Convert

1. Promotion of Jews[39]

A Jew with the rank of private, who has not converted to the Orthodox religion may be promoted to the rank of junior officer (*unter-ofitser*) only on condition of military excellence.[40]

Procedure for recognizing the rank of junior officer for the purpose of determining the clerical rank of *kolezhskii asessor*.[41]

1. In order to grant the title of *kolezhskii asessor*, proof of seniority required by law, proof of excellent behavior, as well as proof of the knowledge required of a clerk of this rank must be submitted. . . .
2. It has already been determined in the book of military laws that Jewish soldiers may not be appointed to the rank of junior officer unless they have excelled on the battlefield. Similarly, it has been determined that cantonists may not be appointed to secretarial positions. This is also the case regarding the appointment of Jews to the rank of junior officer in auxiliary troops.

With the tsar's approval, February 17, 1846

---

39 Ibid., 740 (no. 630).
40 Later, the directive was changed to: "Jews who have not accepted the Christian religion may be promoted to junior officer on condition that they demonstrated bravery on the battlefield, and with the tsar's approval in each and every case."
41 Levanda, *Sbornik zakonov*, 650 (no. 538). *Kolezhskii asessor* was a junior clerk in government offices.

2. Granting Rights to Jewish Paramedics[42]

> Office of the Imperial Navy, December 29, 1853
>
> ... There are among the observant Jews those who have been sent to study the vocation of general paramedics in medical schools:
>
> Three were sent to the military cantonist school of Kiev in 1828.
> Seven were sent to the cantonist school in Novgorod.
> (In addition, there are paramedics of the infantry.)
> Now, according to a new order, it is forbidden to send Jews who have remained faithful to their religion to medical schools.
> The medical division of the ministry requests, despite the above directive, to allow these ten paramedics to take the exam to be awarded rank 14 (of the clerkships) since they became paramedics before the enactment of the aforementioned ordinance of 1846.

There is an additional note on the document: **"According to the directive, they are not allowed to take the officer's exam. Supervisory department, July 6, 1854."**

As we see from this document, very soon after the passing of the cantonist decree, in 1828, cantonists were already sent to study medicine in prestigious military institutions. The document mentions that a group of cantonists was sent from the military school in Kyiv, testifying to the positive attitude towards Jews there. All ten medics mentioned in this document remained faithful to the Jewish religion and, nevertheless, were sent to study medicine. Evidently, the military commanders did not see their faith as a reason to reject them. Not one of them converted to Christianity despite great pressure to do so. In other words, it was possible not to give up Judaism and to be promoted in the army.

As is known, in 1846 a change occurred regarding the persecution of cantonists who did not convert. This document as well as the one cited below help us understand the extent of the persecution. As we see, even in 1854, the medical schools dared to request a violation of the tsar's ordinance, for the benefit of the cantonists. Seeing that such a minor matter was handled personally by the tsar,

---

42   Central Archives of the History of the Jewish people, HM2\8282, copy from Rossiiskii gosudarstvennyi arkhiv voenno-morskogo flota [Russian state archive of the military sea navy], f. 223, op. 3.

we can assume that, that late into his rule, Nicholas still demanded that every issue be brought to him.

Probably, this trend was long associated with medical schools, as can be seen from the following document:

> **Imperial approval of the order of the Supreme Military Council**[43]
>
> October 12, 1854
>
> The Medical Division submitted to the Supreme Military Council a request to pass a number of amendments to army regulations:
>
> 1. In the collection of military regulations, clause 34 in the appendixes...: to add that, when there is a lack of paramedic students, junior officers serving on the battlefield may be appointed in their stead, this on condition that they are found unfit for combat units, and if they have the knowledge necessary for this medical vocation.
> 2. Junior officers from among Jews who have remained in their faith will be appointed as paramedics only in times of war, and from among them only those who will be recognized by their commanders for special self-sacrifice on the battlefield while providing first aid to the wounded.
>
> Therefore, due to his outstanding actions, private Nosson [Nathan] Zuckerman should be appointed to the post of divisional paramedic of the Irkutsk division.

Tsar Nicholas added to this in his handwriting: "I approve, October 12, 1854."

This poignant document testifies to the exceptional heroism of the paramedic Nosson Zuckerman on the battlefield. At the same time, Zuckerman, described as a Jew who did not give up his Judaism, showed self-sacrifice in observing Torah and *mitzvot*.

We see that, even for the promotion of one individual, a cumbersome procedure of changing the military regulations was necessary, requiring the tsar's special approval. On the other hand, it is noteworthy that the members of the medical division were able to bring about a change in the regulations, when the whole purpose of the change was the appointment of one person as a divisional

---

43   Ibid., 833 (no. 728).

paramedic! Perhaps this case demonstrates the variety of factors that operated in the Russian army: discrimination against observant Jews, the presence of pragmatic commanders who tried to right the wrong, and a cumbersome decision-making mechanism in which one hand approved while the second nullified.

3. Jewish soldiers in St. Petersburg, March 1847[44]

> **Report of the Ministry of Defense on the number of Jews in St. Petersburg**
>
> To the Third Department of the Tsar's Own Chancellery
>
> Below is the breakdown of the Jewish soldiers:
>
> > in Guard corps—42;
> > in naval units—27;
> > mechanics—74;
> > in labor units—254;
> > naval cadets—7;
> > **total—404**

As we see from this document, most of the Jewish soldiers (sixty percent) were sent to labor units, while forty percent were directed to select and vocational units. It is interesting to note that Jews (probably converts) studied in prestigious training institutions (cadets).

4. Nicholas I's Interest in the Jewish Soldiers

From the tsar's diary, 1844:

> ... Among the Jewish soldiers brought from Poland there are no sick and no deserters. They are upbeat and ready for combat. In short—good boys to carry weapons ...[45]

---

44 *Russkii arkhiv* 4 (1910): 499–500.
45 Ibid.

Report of the Third Section of His Imperial Majesty's Own Chancellery[46]

A parade of soldiers from the thirteenth conscription of Polish Jews was held in the imperial palace in Gatchina in the presence of His Majesty the Tsar, and he found them healthy and fit.

Appointed to the Guards—9

To the teams of navy cadets—34

Reported in 1847

Report from January 1852

(Third Section of His Imperial Majesty's Own Chancellery)

His Majesty the Tsar did the favor of holding a parade of Jewish soldiers at the Zimnii Palace, from which he derived great pleasure.

Israel Leib Itzkovitz also mentions in his memoirs that the tsar held a parade for the graduates of the Arkhangel'sk half-battalion at his palace in Gatchina. From these documents we learn of an additional aspect of the tsar's attitude toward Jewish soldiers. We see that Nicholas would hold parades of Jewish soldiers and was very satisfied with them. The fact that such parades were held in the imperial palaces shows that the tsar derived true enjoyment from them. We also see that Nicholas liked to sort the Jews personally and to send them even to prestigious military units. Notably, conversion to Christianity is not mentioned in this report.

---

46 Ibid.

5. Concerning Desertion of Jewish Conscripts[47]

> **Third Section of** His Imperial Majesty's Own Chancellery
>
> January 24, 1853
>
> **Report of events in the Volhynia district**
>
> ... From among the Jewish recruits in the battalion stationed in Zhitomir, seventeen soldiers deserted within one month.
>
> [Added in pencil, probably in Nicholas's handwriting: "To draft four adults above the age of twenty from each of the deserters' communities."]
>
> Reference to the director general of the Ministry of Defense regarding recruits in private recruitment no. 10.
>
> Signed: Adjutant Major-General, Count Orlov

We should note the fact that Jewish soldiers served close to the Pale of Settlement, making desertion easy for those who wished to do so. At the same time we should note that this document refers to new recruits. Collective punishment for the communities was proposed as a deterrent. It is possible that we have here the beginning of the imperial directive for collective punishment, which later was approved as law. Importantly, the tsar seems not to have been interested in drafting minors, although in some cases this was an accepted way of punishment.

Of course, desertion was common also among the Christians, who also used self-mutilation, false registration, bribery, etc., in order to dodge the draft. For Jews, desertion was part of passive resistance strategies. The authorities did not know how to control the phenomenon, and collective punishment was also not effective.

---

[47] Central Archives for the History of the Jewish people, HMF665, copy from Gosudarstvennyi arkhiv Rossiiskoi Federatsii [State archive of Russian Federation], f. 109, 4 eksp., op. 193.

We should also note the speed with which this document moved through the army channels. Just three days passed after the tsar's order and it was already transferred as a command to the recruiting officers, without going through any process of approval.

I. Religious Life of Jewish Soldiers

1. Religious Services for Jews in the Army. Documents, Analysis, Conclusions

a. *Religious Routine of Jewish Soldiers*[48]

> **From the imperial conscript ordinance of 1827, chapter 14:**
>
> Clause 91. A soldier is permitted to observe all the customs of his religion during free time from active military service. The commander will maintain strict supervision so that no one prevents the soldier from observing the tenets of his religion.
>
> Clause 92. A soldier is permitted to visit a synagogue and rabbis in the vicinity of his service only with the approval of his commander.
>
> Clause 93. The commander may permit a gathering for the observance of a religious tenet in the base in a place specially designated for this purpose. The approval applies in places where there are no synagogues outside the base, especially on religious holidays.
>
> All religious activity will be conducted under the supervision of the commander appointed for that purpose...

---

48 Central Archives for the History of the Jewish People, HM2\82809, copy from Rossiiskii gosudarstvennyi voenno-istoricheskii arkhiv [Russian state archive of military history], f. 1, op. 1.

b. Kosher Slaughter

> Imperial Ministry of Defense, April 30, 1842[49]
>
> Supervisory Department
>
> I request to investigate and report to me: Do the Jewish soldiers pay taxes for religious services[50] for the meat they purchase?

After investigation, the following reply was received:

> They do not pay anyone. We have been informed that in certain units the sailors buy live animals. In one of the naval bases a sailor called Berko Smerkin slaughters the animals and receives ten kopeks from each one for his work.
>
> In several of the units no meat is purchased at all, and they make do with the general supply brought for the Christian soldiers.
>
> Signed: Inspector of the unit of auxiliary boats of the Baltic navy, February 1843

> **Office of Labor Battalions and Prisoner Battalions, 1843**
>
> In Revel' [Tallinn, present-day Estonia], Jews in battalions 3 and 4 make do with meat from the general kitchen. In Arkhangel'sk, in battalions 8 and 9 they receive kosher meat from the slaughterer. In Astrakhan' and Kazan' there is no sale of kosher meat.
>
> Signed: Commander of the supply section of work units and prisoner battalions. Headquarters of the main commander of the Kronshtadt base port.

---

49 Central Archives for the History of the Jewish People, HM2\8282/15, copy from Rossiiskii gosudarstvennyi voenno-istoricheskii arkhiv [Russian state archive of military history], f. 233, op. 1.

50 *Korobochnyi sbor* (literally, "box tax"), a package of taxes imposed on Jewish religious needs.

At the top of the document we read:

> An imperial directive was given to exempt Jewish soldiers from paying tax on religious needs and kosher slaughter.
>
> December 16, 1843

c. *The Decision of the Ruling Senate on the Exemption from Tax Payment on Slaughter of Cattle, etc., Granted to Jewish Soldiers, according to the Tsar's Ordinance*[51]

> His Majesty the Tsar has done the favor of issuing the order that permission should be given to Jewish soldiers to receive the following without taxation:
>
> 1. Those with families—no more than two pounds of meat and one chicken.
> 2. Single men—no more than one pound of meat and one chicken per day.
> 3. All the above, with the approval of the commander.
>
> January 21, 1847

Similarly, there is a file in the archive with the heading:

> **File 889.**
>
> Ministry of the Navy. September 3, 1854[52]
>
> On the appointment of a kosher slaughterer in army units.

Namely, even at the end of the reign of Nicholas I, the attitude toward kosher slaughter in the army did not change.

After analysis of these documents, it can be concluded that kosher slaughter was possible for Jews in the army. But, as seen in the example of kosher slaughter,

---

51 Ibid.
52 Ibid.

conditions of religious life were different in various locations. Even though it was possible to slaughter and eat kosher, in practice it seemingly depended on the conditions of service, and the extent of the will and initiative of the soldiers.

Amazingly, the tsar took a personal interest in the Jewish soldiers' conditions of service, was aware that kosher slaughter was taking place in the imperial navy, and ensured that tax imposed on civilians should not be imposed on religious sailors while serving the state. On the other hand, the tsar's personal involvement in this relatively marginal issue is evidence of his excessive concern with the Jews.

It is not clear who brought this issue before the tsar, but it is probably connected to the activity of the rabbinical committee for the promotion of education in that year, at whose head were Rabbi Yitzchak of Volozhin and the *Tzemach Tzedek*, the Lubavitcher Rebbe.

It is interesting that the soldiers organized kosher slaughter even in Arkhangel'sk, hundreds of miles from any Jewish settlement. Similarly, it should be taken into account that in Arkhangel'sk there was a cantonist school, notorious as a base where mass conversions took place, for the brutality of the staff, and for the fact that soldiers and cadets were not allowed to leave the base or have contact with one another. Evidently, the phenomenon of mass conversion should be reappraised for this military district, which stands out for its reasonable level of religious life for the soldiers. But it is specifically against the background of the relative tolerance toward adult soldiers, that the religious hardships in the military schools is so impressive.

2. Rabbis in the Army

Document A.

> **Ministry of the Navy**
>
> **August 25, 1828**[53]
>
> **From: The minister of naval matters**
>
> **To: The commander in chief**

---

53 Central Archives for the History of the Jewish People, HMF760, copy from Gosudarstvennyi arkhiv Rossiiskoi Federatsii [State archive of Russian Federation], f. 109, d. 330, l. 31.

Jews approached me with the request to release them from regular service on the occasion of their festivals, and to allow the resident of Shklov, Eliyahu Romm, to come to Kronshtadt to conduct the festival rites.

Ordinance: A personal order of Tsar Nicholas I was given to issue Eliyahu Romm with a transit passport to Kronshtadt.[54]

Document B.
The appointment of Rabbi Markus Wolfovich

File 4812

Archives of the Ministry of the Navy[55]

On the raise in salary of the rabbi of the Sveaborg naval base, soldier Markus Wolfovich, who was chosen by the community of Israel to serve in a rabbinical role

June 20, 1839

On the appointment of the civilian Moshko Razumnyi as rabbi of the Sevastopol' naval base

To release from his position Rabbi Michael Elfenbein who has served in this role since 1837. The rabbi is retiring due to health reasons.
A total of 1,117 Jews serve in naval units in the Black Sea.
85 rubles and 75 kopeks in silver coins or 300 in banknotes should be allocated to Razumnyi.
Decision: The Inspection Department does not see any obstacle to the appointment of the citizen M. Razumnyi to the position of rabbi.[56]

The documents show that there were many requests from commanders concerning the appointment of rabbis, and there were many soldiers who demanded this. However, after several years a drastic change in the tsar's attitude to military rabbis.

---

54 The archive has a copy of the passport given to Rabbi Eliyahu Romm.
55 Ibid.
56 Ibid.

> Ministry of the Interior, Department of Religious Affairs
>
> January 28, 1851
>
> ... I hereby inform you that in the army regulations there is no mention of the appointment of rabbis.
>
> His Majesty the Tsar wishes that there should not be any rabbis at all in military units.

In other words, at the beginning of the 1850s, the tsar's position on rabbinical activity in the units changed drastically, even violating army regulations that allowed the appointment of rabbis. The tsar requested to find a round-about way of abolishing the position of rabbis, without needing an explicit change in the regulations. It was probably on the basis of this opinion that this order was issued later:

> **Imperial ordinance for the department of military colonies by the minister of defense:**[57]
>
> **Absence of regular rabbis**
>
> His Majesty the Tsar studied the military regulations, volume 1, part 3, clause 388. According to this clause, Jewish soldiers serving in locations where there is no synagogue or civilian rabbi are permitted to gather for prayers in a special place allocated for this purpose, under the responsibility of one of the soldiers appointed by the agreement of his peers. Therefore, it seems that there is no need to maintain rabbis appointed by the army.
>
> His Imperial Majesty orders: to abolish clause 389 of the regulations which allows the commanders to apply for permission to appoint rabbis for the Jewish soldiers.
>
> October 20, 1853

The logic of the order in this wording is rather vague. It seems that, according to the tsar's understanding, the rabbis existed to lead the prayers, and if it was possible to appoint one of the soldiers to supervise the prayers, there was no need

---

57 Levanda, *Sbornik zakonov*, 818 (no. 705).

for rabbis. However, it is clear that the role of a rabbi is parallel to that of any other religious official. Just as, in Nicholas's opinion, Russian soldiers needed a Russian Orthodox priest, so the Jewish soldiers ostensibly needed a rabbi. Therefore, the abolishment of this role testifies to discrimination and violation of the Jews' rights.

Thus, we see that towards the end of Nicholas's reign, he became less tolerant of Jewish life in the army. A similar development can be seen in the gradual decrease of the rights concerning observance of the Sabbath and festivals, as shall be described below.

3. Sabbath and Festivals in the Army

We present here several significant documents:[58]

> **File 2160**
>
> **The General Staff of His Majesty the Tsar**
>
> Announcement of the Chief in Command of the military port in Arkhangel'sk concerning the observation of festivals:
> "Indeed, the Jews have the right to rest on the Sabbath and festivals, and this right should be respected."

This file was opened on September 13, 1831 and closed in January 1833.

> A query to the Inspection Department at the General Staff
>
> In a reply from your office on September 6, 1831, an order was given that Jews in regular service be allowed to rest on the Sabbath. In addition, the calendar of Jewish holidays for the years 1830–1845 [attached] should be adhered to. The calendar is intended to release Jews from service on their most important festivals. I request a clarification: Should Jews also be given leave on Sundays and other Christian holidays?

---

58   Central Archives for the History of the Jewish People, HMF626, copy from Gosudarstvennyi arkhiv Rossiiskoi Federatsii [State archive of Russian Federation], f. 405, op. 30, d. 340.

Reply of the General Staff, no. 930, of March 31, 1832:

> ... Jews should not be forced to work on Christian holidays, and work should be avoided in all public places on Christian holidays.
>
> The director of the Inspection Department of the Engineering Division, Engineer Major-General Nikolinko

Order of the commander of the General Staff, Prince Men'shikov, no. 165, issued on December 24, 1832:[59]

> His Majesty has given the order that Jews who benefit from leave on their festivals should be used for work on Christian holidays, especially in navy ships that require maintenance.

> **General Naval Staff, Inspection Division**
>
> **September 4, 1834**
>
> Enclosed is a letter of request from July 4, 1834 to allow Jews to eat food that is kosher for Passover.
>
> Order from headquarters: "Please ensure that the rabbi's request is fulfilled."
>
> St. Petersburg, September 4, 1834

It should be noted that the name of the rabbi and his role do not appear in the document. But, taking into account that the reply was given several days after the request was submitted, we can assume that the rabbi was in St. Petersburg and probably came to the capital with the purpose of lobbying for his request.

---

59   Ibid.

Below is an ordinance from the Ministry of Defense:[60]

Sabbath and festivals for Jewish soldiers

His Majesty the Tsar has determined a procedure for celebrating the holidays. Below are the details:

1. The Jewish Sabbath falls on the same day as our Saturday.

In addition they have holidays as follows:

- Day of purity: Yom Kippur, occurs once a year in the month of September.
- The New Year: lasts for two days and falls in the months of August–September.
- Passover: lasts eight days in March or April...
2. On all those days the duration of prayers is on average two hours. The New Year requires full attendance at prayers for two days. . . .
6. Jews should be exempt on the three holidays on which they are required to pray in a quorum.
7. This permission does not apply to times of war or during the unit's active service, such as guard duties, training, or military exercises.
13. Any violation of the army's regulations, even if it occurs for the observance of religious laws, will be punished according to the severity of the deed.

Issued April 1, 1847

After the analysis of the above documents, we reach the conclusion that, in principle, it was possible to observe some of the *mitzvot* during military service. The law unambiguously gave freedom of worship to soldiers. The instructions regarding the implementation of this freedom were also unequivocal, including the possibility of releasing the Jews from work even on Christian holidays, except in urgent cases. There is correspondence on this matter between the communities and the army officials. The appeals of the communities were not

---

60 Central Archives of the History of the Jewish people, HM2\84521/2, copy from Rossiiskii gosudarstvennyi arkhiv voenno-morskogo flota [Russian state archive of the military sea navy], f. 170, op. 1.

rejected outright, and were legitimate as far as the military authorities were concerned, but none of them were completely successful. From reports of kosher slaughter, we hear that this was a matter of course as far as the tsar was concerned. Furthermore, soldiers were given credit for paying box tax (*korobochnyi sbor*) on kosher meat. But kosher slaughter was not practiced everywhere, and it cannot be said that this depended on distance from the center. We find kosher slaughter both in remote Arkhangel'sk and in Kronshtadt, which was close to the capital, but we do not find it in Reveal' despite its proximity to both St. Petersburg and European countries. Both kosher slaughter and the observance of other religious commandments seem to have been a result of the requests made by Jews and the will of the local military authorities, although we do find kosher slaughter in Arkhangel'sk, close to the infamous cantonist base.

From the conditions of the religious life of the soldiers one can draw conclusions about the general situation of the cantonists. It appears from the documents that there was interaction between Jewish soldiers and the cantonists. We hear about this especially from the complaints of the priests regarding the difficulties in converting the minors. Thus, the military rabbi of Astrakhan', Rabbi Michael Akhundov, not only established a prayer house for the soldiers in his area, but also engaged in religious propaganda among the cantonists, and for a long time even covered up for the local military authorities. Although we did not find a parallel to this behavior in other documents, it is likely that many cantonists knew that military rabbis were appointed and financed. The appointment of the rabbis, including the "importation" of civilian rabbis from distant places to the army units, with a high salary from the tsarist Ministry of Defense, sounds surprising. Only at the end of Nicholas's days do we hear an explicit expression of dissatisfaction with the institution of the military rabbinate in the Russian army.

This conclusion assumes a different background than the usual one for understanding the fate of the cantonists. We do not hear about coercion to convert regarding soldiers in the regular army. Conversion did indeed occur, and certainly there was departure from the Torah and *mitzvot* as a result of the difficulties of the service, but, even if the extent of the phenomenon were significant, it was not a specially initiated operation. It is also reasonable to assume that Russian soldiers abused Jews who lacked the language and the required habits and who belonged to a religion hated by the Christians. Nevertheless, the situation of the soldiers was different from that of the cantonists, and therefore the question needs to be asked: Was there a sharp difference in the religious status of these two groups or a gradual transition between them? We want to argue that it is not probable that in the same environment, in the same army, and in the same nation there were two completely different systems. Therefore we must see what was happening in the cantonist institutions in the context of the Jewish religious conditions in the army in general.[61] It should also not be forgotten that, aside from the possibility of observing certain elements of religion, there was discrimination against the Jewish soldiers who did not convert; for example in preventing promotion from the junior officer level, or in directing Jewish soldiers to remote areas with a difficult climate. This discrimination, besides manifesting a hint of antisemitism, which characterized the Russian army, also had another, and perhaps principal, goal—pressing for religious conversion. This is also how grants were determined for Jewish soldiers who decided to convert, under the hypocritical claim that "the money was needed to equip oneself for Christian life."

---

61 See below, "The Relationship between the Boys and Their Gentile Environment," 170.

Part III

THE CANTONISTS

1

Review of the Establishment of the Institution for Minors in the Russian Army. Description of Service Frameworks

There was nothing new in the existence of a framework for small children in the Russian army. Moreover, many Russian families regarded it as a privilege to have one of their children admitted into a military institution with the likelihood of promotion later on.[1] Therefore, the decision to forcibly draft Jewish children was an anomalous act for these frameworks, and even without the aim of religious conversion could be considered tyranny for its own sake.

In the year 2000, the bulletin of the Moscow University published an article about the history of military institutions for children in the Russian Empire.[2] From there and other sources we learn that in 1721 Peter the Great established within the military a section for the orphans of his soldiers. A children's unit for fifty cadets was supposed to have been established in each division. Over the years, illegitimate sons of nobility, children of Polish and Ukrainian rebels, children of prisoners, vagrants, homeless people, etc., were included in this framework. The name "cantonists" was only given to them in 1805. A significant change in the development of the cantonist institutions occurred in 1817, when military colonies were established. All the children of the military settlers were defined as cantonists. It was then that the cantonist institutions became part of the department of military colonies in the Defense Ministry.

---

1   For the history of the cantonist institution, see Lialev, *Obzor uchebnykh uchrezhdenii*.
2   V. Iagmanikhin, "Voennye kantonisty Russkoi Armii 1797–1836" [Military cantonists of the Russian army 1797–1836], *Vestnik Moskovskogo gosudarstvennogo universiteta, istoricheskii fakul'tet* [Bulletin of Moscow state university, faculty of history] 1 (2000): 47.

These institutions underwent many changes over the years both in terms of quantity and content. In 1826, a change was made also in the structure of the "units for orphans of soldiers" (*voenno-sirotskie otdeleniia*), and they were divided into units according to regular military division:

Battalion	1000 men	total of 14 units	14,000 boys
Half-battalion	500 men	total of 16 units	8,000 boys
Company	250 men	total of 3 units	750 boys

A total of 22,750 boys studied in cantonist schools, but this number corresponded to only sixty-five percent of cantonist children. In practice, a large part was sent to units outside the framework of military colonies.

Nicholas I made an attempt to limit the expenses of maintaining the children. According to a 1828 order of the General Staff, non-Jewish children below the age of ten were sent home, and later, also those below the age of fifteen. At the same time, there was a significant cut in the expenditure on the education of children in military colonies. If in 1828 sixty-five percent of cantonist children studied in these educational institutions, only eight percent remained in 1831, when such schools were abolished. The removal of the non-Jewish children up to the age of ten from the units resulted in saving 808,790 gold rubles to the treasury. The treasury calculated the saving exactly, up to the last ruble. The calculations of savings show that the cantonist institutions were a burden on the army.

In practice, the study frameworks continued to operate only in orphanages where Jewish children were sent, but even there, there were reductions. In 1835, the tsar ordered that only sons of soldiers who served in regular and permanent service should be directed to these units.

There was indeed certain progress in the education in cantonist schools. Iagmanikhin notes that already in 1808 Alexander I turned the orphan institutions into schools to train non-commissioned officers. In 1817, a special committee was established to prepare textbooks, and, in 1819, a letter was issued with instructions to establish military cantonist schools. This means that someone in the army was investing thought in the development of these institutions. Among other things the letter mentioned that the schools should adopt the educational and teaching method of the Lancasterian system. It was determined that the cadets study:

1. God's law;
2. the Russian language;

3. arithmetic;
4. an introduction to geometry;
5. drawing and sketching;
6. singing.

The children were divided into three age groups:

1. beneath the age of ten;
2. between ten and fifteen;
3. between fifteen and eighteen.

In addition, professional training units were established:

1. a carabinier training regiment;[3]
2. an artillery training brigade;
3. a military engineers battalion;
4. a military school of topography.

Nicholas I improved the cantonist institution by opening training schools for military vocations, increasing their number to ten. In the 1830s, the following were added:

- three *karabiner* divisions;
- artillery training regiments that included a thousand men;
- a secretarial school;
- a clerical school;
- an ammunition school;
- a veterinary school.

Moreover, in St. Petersburg, a training institute for teachers in cantonist schools was established.

A difference must be made between the cantonist schools and the regular cantonist units, where they also studied arithmetic, writing, and even geometry, with the most talented being sent to vocational schools. At the beginning of the nineteenth century, all the cantonist boys were assigned to one of four infantry

---

3   From the French *carabinier*—one who carries a carbine gun.

training divisions, which were divided into battalions, half-battalions, separate regiments, and schools.

According to the data from the military archives in Moscow, published by Iagmanikhin (above), there was a total of about 378,000 boys in the cantonist units at the time of their dissolution. In order to explain the contradiction between the number of students in military schools (about 36,000) and the enormous sum of those released, one should assume that some of the boys lived in the villages and colonies and were not in active service, as the Jews were, but they still had had some sort of connection to the cantonist institution.

From the reforms introduced, we understand that the Jews came to these institutions at a time of economic cutbacks, when there was no desire to expand the frameworks. On the other hand, the didactic level improved, and these schools gradually started becoming training schools for military vocations. The army needed professionals in the light of the general modernization of European military.

As mentioned, the basic cantonist unit was a battalion, comprising between 800 and 1,000 troops, divided into four companies, each with 250 soldiers. A half-battalion comprised two companies with 500 soldiers, in our case, minors. It seems, however, that not all the companies were equal in size. According to the memoir of Berko Klinger,[4] a half-battalion was divided into four companies of 120 soldiers.[5] The soldiers of each company studied in the same class, with the fourth made up of children of ages just before formal enlistment. This company adopted a position of superiority and dictated the "rules of the game" within the half-battalion. At its head was a *leitenant-podpolkovnik*, who was subordinate to the commander of the town garrison. In addition there were the officers: battalion and company commanders. The *feldfebel'*—first sergeant—was chosen from among army veterans or cantonists who remained in their units even after reaching the enlistment age, were knowledgeable, and served as a good example.[6] There were also *efreitors*—lance corporals, appointed from among the veteran cantonists, and mentors who dealt with two or three new recruits. In addition, there were school teachers with officer ranks.

There was apparently no army base dedicated just for the Jews, and one of the principles in dealing with the Jews was integrating them with the gentiles. Still, it is assumed that the integration was very sparse. If the aim of recruiting Jewish

---

4   Sergei Grigor'ev, *Berko kantonist* [Berko the Cantonist] (Moscow: Detgiz, 1934), 28.
5   This division remains to the present day.
6   Itzkovitz, "Vospominaniia evreiskogo kantonista," says that these were converted Jews.

youngsters into cantonist units was assimilation, it is unclear why one of two regiments of cantonists in Arkhangel'sk—the battalion's yearly intake—comprised only Jews.[7]

Two hypotheses can be put forward to explain this amazing phenomenon of establishing units with a Jewish majority. First, the logical desire of the military authorities to integrate the Jewish minors within a gentile majority contradicted the interest of those authorities not to cause close contact between the elite and the "problematic" cadets. There is evidence that there is truth in this assumption. It is known that army commanders were not happy that the military was being used to train soldiers toward ideological and other goals.[8] Echoes of gentile opposition to cooperating with Jews can be seen from reports of villagers' refusal to adopt Jewish children between the ages of six and twelve.[9] Secondly, the military authorities did not see any special problem in baptizing masses of Jews, even over a hundred men. The moment they succeeded in creating a dynamic of conversion, they concentrated many Jews in one place for the sake of their final goal: assimilation. Seeing that there were veteran converts on the army base, there was also no need to create a renewed dynamic. A well-oiled mechanism of conversion operated on the cantonist bases. This can be seen from the testimony of the sailors in Arkhangel'sk, who were witnesses in the military prosecutor's investigation. The sailors revealed that they knew about what was happening there even before they heard about it from the battalion graduates. The apostate Sindikov testified in Terent'ev's trial on his renunciation of Christianity[10] that the cadets who had already converted persecuted those who still resisted, abusing them, flogging them, and so on.

Together with this routine, means of passive resistance were developed, as will be shown below. However, the resistance of the Jews to conversion was not active enough to deter the military authorities from their efforts.

---

7   See the documents concerning the rebellion of the half-battalion in Arkhangel'sk, Central Archives for the History of the Jewish people, HMF626, copy from Gosudarstvennyi arkhiv Rossiiskoi Federatsii [State archive of Russian Federation], f. 109, 1 eksp., d. 340.
8   See, for example, the gendarmes' 1839 report to the Third Section, above, 101.
9   M. A. Kretschmer, *Vospominania* [Memories] (St. Petersburg: n.p., 1888), 365.
10 *Voskhod* 4 (1881): 117–118.

2

Military Training Units and Military Schools for Minors

A. Recruitment and Absorption Procedures

The following is the wording of the recruitment guidelines:

> Regulations of the Ministry of Defense and the Naval Office for the Cantonists[1]
>
> Order to transfer the cantonists to battalions and half-battalions
>
> Issued on December 18, 1828
>
> Order of the director general of the Ministry of Defense in accordance with His Majesty's order to the Ruling Senate.
>
> Department of military colonies.
>
> In accordance with the military regulation of 1798 for orphans, cantonists between the ages of seven and eighteen are permitted to remain in villages with family members. Children who have not yet turned fourteen should be returned to their parents.
> This clause does not apply to Jews, who are to remain in their regiments regardless of their age.

---

[1] Central Archives for the History of the Jewish People, HM2\8451/1, copy from Rossiiskii gosudarstvennyi voenno-istoricheskii arkhiv [Russian state archive of military history], f. 1, op. 1.

One should pay attention to the fact that Meir (Chaim) Merimzon[2] relates that at the beginning he served with the rest of the children in the village. They were billeted in the houses. This was not done as adoption, just for the purpose of accommodation, while during the day, for three years, the children received military guidance and education from the army. T. Zeidel also notes[3] that Jewish children who were brought to the Ural mountains at the beginning of the 1830s were divided between the villagers. Thus, there was transfer of Jewish children to villages, contrary to the above order. In the Central Archives for the History of the Jewish People, a document of the Ministry of Defense is preserved "concerning the unwillingness of the villagers to adopt Jewish children (cantonists)." This is undoubtedly evidence of the existence of a phenomenon that has not been considered until now. This directive was issued after the conscription decree of the Jews, with the opposite goal—to grant dispensations to Christian minors. It should be noted that the age of seven was deemed suitable for conscription also for gentiles, and if the child had no relatives that wanted to take him, he would remain in a military framework. Thus, having small children in military units was not limited to Jews.

The conscription procedure, including abductions and the *kahal*'s fraud, are described extensively in many studies. We will therefore make do with a few comments. The gendarmes' report brought above exposes the involvement of the *kahal* in the conscription of minors, including fraud and deceit in registering age, health status, etc. In the case of Chaim Merimzon, quoted above, the head of the committee gave the secretary fake names of children, which he changed as he saw fit in order to exempt from service those who had bribed him. In the 1839 report of the gendarmes' commander it explicitly says that the committee changed the ages of the conscripts. Moisy Spiegel relates in his memoirs that he was seven when conscripted, and yet was registered as twelve.[4] In our opinion, there is place to doubt the specific testimonies about boys abducted and conscripted when they were between the ages of six and eight. The difference between a six-year-old and a twelve-year-old is so significant that it could not be ignored even in the tsar's conscription office. Even if it is clear that fraud was very common, it is improbable that counterfeiters did not take basic precautions. Moreover, the army opposed conscripting children because of the bother involved. This would have been the case even more so regarding pre-school

---

2   Merimzon, "Rasskaz starogo soldata," 290.
3   T. Zeidel, "Evrei na Urale" [Jews in the Urals], *Evreiskaia starina* 3 (1912): 310.
4   In Spiegel's memoirs there are details that make this questionable, see above.

children. Even if we suppose that children who lived in poverty looked younger than their age, such a difference in age would still be noticeable.

It seems that in most of the cases those who initiated the fraud were themselves Jews. This was known to the authorities. They also benefited from bribes received from despairing parents. This was apparently the reality of conscription in all strata of the Russian population, not just with the Jews.

In addition to this fraud, there was method of deceiving the children in which adults persuaded them to enlist while cynically exploiting their innocence. After passing a medical committee, they would be locked up in the "community's" prison, from where they were transferred to the district barracks, which served as a dispersal station (also for adult units). The boys had to wait a long time, until the required quota was filled. According to the regulations, adult conscripts were supposed to have been separate from the minors, but in practice, the regulations were not obeyed and the children suffered humiliation from the adult soldiers.[5]

The children's first trial was the journey to the cantonist units. There are many descriptions of the difficulties they encountered on the way. The mortality rate was especially high, estimated at reaching a third of those recruited.[6] The journey sometimes lasted more than six months, especially when the minors were sent to Siberia or the Ural Mountains—Perm', the area near Ural'sk, etc. With all the difficulties of the journey we have to distinguish, for the purpose of the study, between regular difficulties suffered by all the conscripts and the specific difficulties of the Jewish children as described in the memoirs of Spiegel, Itzkovitz, Merimzon, Beilin, Klinger, and others. The circumstances of the journey as a whole were the result of the poor standard of living and the way of life of the Russians at that time. The circumstances changed from place to place due to a combination of factors, including, for example, the personality of the escorting commander.

The documents of the Third Section, discovered only recently, include a description of the deaths of two cantonists on their way from the absorption unit in Smolensk. They had to travel in harsh weather conditions. It was only a journey of twenty-three kilometers, but even that distance, though not usually demanding outstanding fitness, was enough to cause death. One of the children was left after his death on the side of the road. The escorting commander did not even bother to report the event to the authorities on reaching their destination.

---

5   Merimzon, "Rasskaz starogo soldata," 290.
6   The efficiency of the conscription was measured according to the number of conscripts and not according to the rate of mortality. See Itzkovitz, "Vospominaniia evreiskogo kantonista," 55–65.

When the body was discovered, a representative of the court came and conducted an investigation. One would think that the escorting commander should have known that it would be impossible to hide a case of death, and therefore it is unclear why he did not report it to the military authorities. We assume that it was because the escorting soldiers were drunk, similar to what Moisy Spiegel describes in his narrative.[7] As mentioned above, he wrote that the escort was so drunk that the cantonists had to turn to the governor of Moscow to request shelter.

Of the characteristic hardships for the Jews was not knowing the Russian language, not understanding the Russian reality, not being able to observe *mitzvot* (a shocking trauma for a child brought up to observe), antisemitism, and more. In his famous narrative of the boys' journey to Viatka,[8] the writer, Alexander Herzen, describes the escort soldiers—a description to which researchers have not paid much attention. The soldiers appear in that excerpt as having pity on the children and not treating them cruelly, taking the circumstances into consideration. We find a similar description in the stories of Klinger, Spiegel, Merimzon, etc. Accordingly, we have to admit that the scale of humaneness of the soldiers and officers ranged from "reasonable" to "cruel." There was not necessarily antisemitism, as we might assume, but all depended on specific circumstances. As we will see below, in certain instances the escorting commanders exploited the hardships of the journey to convince and force the boys to convert to Christianity.[9]

On arriving at the camp or army base, the minor was attached to a mentor who acquainted him with the institution's atmosphere, its rules and procedures. At the same time the child would receive a permanent place of accommodation, a box in which to store his belongings, and several sets of uniform. In their memoirs, Moshe Klinger, Meir Merimzon, and others mention the army underwear the cantonists received immediately after their conscription. The rough material and its low quality made a harsh impression on the children. It symbolized for them their move to a completely different life. It is interesting that just this small detail remained in the child's memory until his old age, and is emphasized in all the memoirs. Another difficulty was receiving second hand uniforms. On the one hand, there was a strict demand to be careful about the intactness of the uniforms, but on the other hand, thread, needles, buttons, and other accessories

---

7   See Moisy Spiegel's testimony above.
8   Herzen, *My Past and Thoughts*, 293.
9   See below, the chapter "Conversion on the Way."

were not provided to repair them. The commanders often used the bad repair of the uniforms as an excuse to impose harsh punishments on those who refused to be baptized. Another form of abuse and punishment was initiated theft of uniform by cadets or mentors.

To sum up the conditions of the absorption of the minors into the army: there were fixed and detailed procedures, which reflect Nicholas's worship of military order, even though the conscription itself was conducted in an irregular manner. This difference probably indicates the difference between the way civilian institutions handled matters and how the military handled them.

B. The Activity of the Abductors

The activity of the abductors, known as *khappers*, testifies to the gross impropriety of the procedures of bringing boys to conscription. Almost right at the start of the conscription a unit operated[10] in the community to forcibly bring those obliged to enlist.[11] As soon as a rumor was heard of an upcoming conscription, draft candidates would escape from the village. The community sent people to look for them. As is natural, this activity involved using violence, detective work, and other irregularities. The phenomenon became especially severe in 1851 when permission was given to members of the *kahal*[12] to catch and bring to the draft office any Jew who did not reside in the area and who was within the boundaries of the community without the required documents. In line with this permission, the *kahal* hired the services of special agents who hunted people down indiscriminately. That is how the institution of the *khappers* was created.

Abductions occurred earlier, too, writes Rotstein,[13] but from 1848 the phenomenon deteriorated to the extent that mothers would stay at home to protect their children from abductors. Mahler[14] writes that there were gangs who went from town to town, abducted children, and handed them over for conscription in other towns. Levine[15] relates that the town residents complained to the

---

10   Probably at the initiative of the authorities.
11   See S. Beilin's memories of Bentzi the *khapper*, Beilin, "Rasskaz byvshego kantonista," 116. As proven here, the "legality" of abductions was given already in the 1827 regulations.
12   After the abolishment of the kahal it continued to function by another name—*obshchestvo*.
13   S. Rothstein, *Kantonistim—me-ḥayeh ha-ḥatufim be-Rusia ha-tzarit* [Cantonists: The life of the abducted in tsarist Russia] (Tel Aviv: Sifriyat yeladim ve-no'ar, 1962), 83.
14   R. Mahler, *Divrei Yemei Yisrael* [The history of Israel], vol. 8 (Merhavia: Poalim, 1970), 239.
15   Yehuda Leib Levine, *Zikhronot ve-ra'ayonot* [Memories and ideas] (Warsaw: Schuldberg, 1904), 353.

authorities of the abduction of children by Jews from a different town. Levine writes how paradoxical it was that Jews needed the gentile court of law against the Jewish community administration. According to Gessen,[16] the important point when handing over the abducted child was to receive a certificate of approval from the draft office enabling the exchange of the abducted person for another Jew whose turn it was to be conscripted. It was therefore possible to trade in these certificates. On the other hand, the possibility of redeeming the abducted person for ransom promised income for the abductors, as Spiegel testifies. As mentioned, he was first abducted in 1851 at the age of seven, but his mother redeemed him. A year later he was abducted again.

The fear of their children being abducted made the lives of many families unbearable. They invested a lot of effort in hiding their children from the *khappers*. Mordechai Rabinowitz relates that parents would dress their children in clothes of infants in order to confuse the abductors. In Minsk, Yehuda Leib Levine[17] once saw how six men entered a house and dragged out a small boy who was screaming and trying to escape. They gagged his mouth to keep him quiet. His mother tried to resist, but the *khappers* pushed her aside, got into the wagon, and were off with their "loot."

We will now analyze several testimonies of abductions, which have not yet been published in research literature.

1. Chaim Merimzon's Testimony

As mentioned, the testimony was published in 1912 in the annual *Evreiskaia starina*, under the title "The Tale of a Veteran Soldier," edited by Simon Dubnow.

Merimzon was born in Vilkovishki, a town in the province of Suvalki, Lithuania. He was abducted to serve as a cantonist in 1854, two years before the abolishment of compulsory conscription of minors, and served for twenty-five years. His full testimony appears above, 1.

As his testimony shows, the abductors acted without the mediation of the community, but contacted the recruitment authorities directly on behalf of the governor. Besides the abductors, there were no other Jews present when the boys were handed over. No wonder that the abducted boys did not try to protest or even resist.

---

16 *Vtoroe sobranie zakonov*, nos. 24768 and 24769, quoted in Gessen, *Istoriia*, 114.
17 Levine, *Zikhronot ve-ra'ayonot*.

We get the impression that the abductors operated on behalf of the authorities. Interestingly, there was full coordination between the recruiting officer and the abductors. The clerk knew in advance which names he had to list. Especially in the case of Merimzon one sees correlation between his family name and that of the one wanted for conscription. Merimzon raises the suspicion that he was taken instead of one of the wealthy candidates, and the question is: If that is the case, how did the abductors meet him by chance?

No age check or any type of medical examination was conducted. Merimzon's story is very detailed, and it is therefore difficult to assume that he forgot this significant detail.

Notably, Merimzon calls the abductors "Hasidim." The abductors did not stand in one place during the prayers, but walked around, similar to how Hasidim pray. Could this hint to the fact that the abductors in the region of Lithuania came from elsewhere, perhaps Ukraine, where Hasidism was widespread? I asked the well-known researcher of the Hasidic movement, the late Professor Gedaliah Nigal from Hebrew University if he was aware of any reference by the Hasidic writers to the issue of the cantonists, and he replied that he had not come across any. Furthermore, he said, the popular folklore and the stories of the Hasidim from that time also do not deal with this. It seems to me that this problem should be investigated.

2. Nikolai Leskov, "Monastyrskii sad"

A different story concerning the abduction of a minor is brought in story of the well-known Russian author, Nikolai Leskov, in his story "Monastyrskii sad" (The abbot's garden). The events of the story take place in 1852, when the narrator is working in the office of the governor of the region of Kyiv. He comes across a note written in garbled Ukrainian. On deciphering the note, he is convinced that it refers to the abduction of a ten-year-old boy to a cantonist camp. The boy's father, a bookbinder, was considered a man of doubtful views in the community, and therefore it was decided to draft the bookbinder's son in exchange for a well-liked man. However, it was still possible to exchange the son for a volunteer. The father found a volunteer, a Jew of about twenty-three years old, who agreed to enlist for the sum of 700 rubles. For this purpose, the father sold his ramshackle house for 330 rubles and borrowed the remainder. However, after receiving the payment, the volunteer fled to the monastery in Kyiv and claimed that he wanted to be baptized. This would have exempted him from the draft obligation, but the obligation to enlist rebounded on the boy. The narrator decides to help the Jew and his son. He relates in a tone of scorn mixed with pity how the miserable bookbinder finally comes to his office in Kyiv. His whole body is bleeding from all sorts of injuries, and his clothes are ragged. He falls to the floor and begins to kiss the clerk's feet, begging him to redeem his son. The Jew takes out a bundle of documents, including the volunteer's declaration of his free will to enlist and a receipt for the money he received. The narrator turns to the abbot of the monastery saying that the volunteer's wish to convert was not sincere.

We do not have to accept the "happy end" of the story, according to which the abbot is persuaded, and orders that the young man be thrown out of the monastery and directed to the military authorities. However, many details concerning the circumstances of the abduction seem relevant. The story reinforces the claim that the community's policy was to get rid of unwanted Jews. It also mentions purchasing an exemption from conscription for payment, a detail that we find in other sources as well. It is fascinating that the father managed to bring all the required certificates. The existence of the documents, and the fact that the father took care to have them ready, testfy to the semi-official character of the process.

3. Korobkov's Article[18]

In his 1913 article in *Evreiskaia starina*, Kh. Korobkov reproduces a 1903 story the journal *Istoricheskii vestnik* (Historical newsletter):

> I was once witness to the following event. In the center of Vilna, a young Jew was arguing excitedly with some soldiers. It turned out that the boy was one of those abducted, and he had just escaped from the barracks. The sentinel saw him escape, caught up with him, and begged [!] him to return. The Jewish boy looked at the soldier furiously and began to push his way through. Another soldier arrived and blocked the Jew's way, but the boy was a strong guy, and the soldiers did not manage to overcome him. He held onto the door of the nearest store. People started gathering around. Suddenly two tall *khappers* appeared. Apparently they were not comfortable using violence in public, and so one of them stood in the way of the boy, while the other ran to bring reinforcement. In that way they managed to pull the boy away from the door and to drag him back to the barracks.

---

18   Korobkov, "Evreiskaia rekrutchina v tsarstvovanie Nikolaia Pervogo," 233–244.

This excerpt presents the *khappers* in a different role: preventing desertion. Together with Merimzon's story, this article testifies that the *khappers* worked as government agents of conscription. If we ignore, as much as is possible, the ethical aspect of one Jew handing another over to the military authorities (in the Diaspora), we must admit that there is justification in "hunting down" army deserters, especially in a situation of mass evasion of prospective conscripts.

4. Beilin's Memoirs[19]

> In my time, I knew a *khapper* from the town of Novogrudok [Navahrudak]. He was known as "Bentzi the *khapper*" or "Bentzi the servant" (of the *kahal*). He was a stocky fellow with the neck of an ox and a decent paunch. When hunting down recruits he was continuously cursed by mothers for handing over their sons to gentiles. **His salary came from the community administration.** They usually abducted the children of the poor. The police also participated in the "hunt." They would begin to hunt down the boys immediately after Sukkot, before the beginning of conscription. After abduction they kept them in the community house or in the prison. The conditions of imprisonment were good. They gave them tasty food, they drank vodka, and went to brothels [!]. During the revelry the members of the *kahal* would persuade the boys to declare their wish to volunteer. Volunteering would make it possible to redeem from conscription those ready to pay for an exemption certificate. And why could they volunteer? Because most of them were "the unknown," namely, people who had never registered in any census. These boys had no influential relatives in the community capable of shaking up the community—by breaking the windows of the servants, by preventing the Torah reading in the synagogue, and by shouting out during the Sabbath prayers.[20] Therefore, they had no choice but to volunteer, for which the *kahal* would pay them a decent sum. This gave the *kahal* a good feeling, as though they had been kind to them. While waiting to be drafted they lived a life of debauchery. They went wild, hit each other, played cards. All this gave the *kahal*'s assistants the opening to claim that these were

---

19 Beilin, "Iz rasskazov o kantonistakh," 115–120. Beilin wrote his memories following the publication of a similar story by Ben Ami, "Ben-Yukhid: Byl' iz vremen 'lovchikov'" [An only son: A story of the times of the snatchers], *Voskhod* 1 (1884): 151–161, 2 (1884): 131–156.
20 Methods of exerting pressure on the community.

corrupt people—incorrigible. On the other hand, the boys did not really have any choice. They had not learned any vocation. They could not find employment. But there were also those who absolutely resisted being conscripted. They used every opportunity to escape from prison. Family members would lie in wait as those who had been abducted were taken out for "some fresh air." The family would pounce on the escort soldiers, beat them, and the boys would meanwhile try to escape. How sad was the appearance of those who were caught again! They marched, pale, with their heads down, barely dragging their feet and shedding bitter tears...

As I lived next to the police prison, I saw these sad sights quite often. At night we would wake up from the screams and shouts of the abducted. And in the morning, I would already see who had been taken. There was "Leibel from the bathhouse," a good-for-nothing and an alcoholic, who lived in the municipal bathhouse. There was "Lippel *der shaygetz*," a local hooligan; and also "Leibele *der kishnik*," the pickpocket. When uniform recruitment was introduced in 1874, the need for *khappers* was eliminated. Bentzi became a miserable fellow, who didn't find any work, and then it became clear that, in fact, he had just been a community worker who had done what he had been told to do. In the end, Bentzi became the scapegoat, never complaining to a soul. He sat in his fixed place and prayed to God with great fervor.

These memoirs are worthy of analysis. First of all, we should focus on the personality of the narrator: His story is full of internal contradictions. Once he says that the abductors were men who had deteriorated morally, and after a few lines he writes that they were the victims of the *kahal*. He also finds it appropriate to give Bentzi the *khapper* the benefit of doubt. Therefore, his testimony should not be accepted unequivocally. The reality, too, was very complex. Nevertheless, some more solid points may be concluded from the story.

According to these memoirs, the *khappers* were not a special patrol unit, but ordinary workers of the *kahal*. Most of the abductions that Beilin describes are abductions of adults. These include people who were not connected to the local Jewish community, even though their existence might seem unusual in the 1850s. In addition, a significant number of the abducted were people of abnormal behavior (pickpockets, vagrants, alcoholics, frequenters of brothels, etc.).

As Beilin relates, preparation for conscription was done several months in advance. The conscription was conducted in the months of January and February (when desertion is difficult due to the winter weather), and the preparations began in October. By this sophisticated means, the *kahal* wanted to overcome the difficulties of conscription.

The members of the community were not comfortable using brute force for conscription. They did abduct people, but they then tried to bribe them or morally corrupt them. This is a very important comment, as it gives us a glimpse of the community administration's workings.

Methods of exerting pressure on the community to release someone who had been abducted were simple and did not demand much money. It was enough to protest in public, especially in the synagogue at the initiative of relatives. Thus, people who belonged to large extended families had a better chance of being released than those without family.

Interestingly, we learn of the existence of a large social group comprising people who had never taken part in censuses conducted by the authorities, and who had not been registered in the government books. On the one hand, such a status had certain advantages. However, now these people were more persecuted than anyone else. The reason for their occlusion from the registries was not always a sophisticated calculation, but rather the fact that their social status left them cut off from state life. According to various estimates, the number of those who did not appear on the register reached thirty percent or even half of the total Jewish population, depending on the locality and the year. In the eyes of the authorities, such a large human resource certainly justified the need to establish special units to abduct the "non-transparent" individuals.

C. Life in the Cantonist Units

The book *Berko the Cantonist* (the life story of Berel Klinger)[21] presents life in military school. On **Mondays and Tuesdays** the children learned the order of army roll calls, standing in rows and saluting. As is known, roll calls and military marching took central place in Tsar Nicholas's view of the army. He made entire divisions march for the sake of ceremony. Entire days were spent on practicing the military gait. The ceremonial Russian military march was strange in that first of all the soldier had to stretch out his foot in a straight line, place the edge of his boot on the ground, and only then to lower his heel. This unnatural method of marching was very painful and harmful to the spine and legs. It is no wonder

---

21 Grigor'ev, *Berko kantonist*, 62.

that most of the floggings meted out to cadets were a result of their failure in these exercises.

Wednesdays were devoted to lessons in crafts. The cadets were divided into work groups according to vocations: cobblers, tailors, locksmiths, blacksmiths, and especially those who embroidered with gold thread to create the different rank symbols for the uniforms. Learning a vocation was one of the principles of the conscription of Jewish minors, at least according to its formal definition as training for a useful vocation. It should be noted that described here is a regular cantonist institution. The gifted cadets were directed to more advanced studies, such as topography, engineering, gunnery, medicine, etc.

Wednesday was not an easy day at all. The teachers were older soldiers who viewed the minors as personal slaves, over whom they ruled with an iron hand, punishing and beating them at every opportunity. Nevertheless, there was the possibility of earning a small amount of money. The veteran soldiers were alcoholics, and they sent the children to buy vodka or to do other shopping in town. According to Klinger, the children considered Wednesdays more of a festival than Sundays.[22]

One should make note of the slovenly atmosphere that enveloped school life, according to Klinger. We find a hint of this in the guidelines for conversion given to the priests (see below), as they are warned not to criticize the lifestyle of the staff. There were obviously many reasons to warn the representatives of the Christian "spiritual morality" to ignore the way of life of the officers and mentors. Looking at this lifestyle, parallels to which we often find in other Russian-language sources, especially in the nineteenth century, raises the question: Was there ever a chance of success for the policy of forced religious conversion, which required consistent and continuous activity of the army faculty and the priests? Since they did not know how to persist in the continuous use of moderate force, they resorted to the use of physical force and threats.

Thursdays: "Health and cleanliness roll call." Beneath this respectable heading, lay a day characterized by staff abuse. On Thursdays, the child soldiers had to strictly comply with every excessive requirement regarding the intactness of their uniforms. These consisted of many cumbersome items (including the metal helmet, which had to be polished to a shine, and the worn-out items that had already undergone many repairs), and so it was almost impossible to guarantee the required appearance. One of the "bonuses" that a Jew who converted would receive were new uniforms that did not need constant repairs. In addition, bed

---

22   Ibid., 54.

linen had to be folded in a very specific way, and there were additional details likely to turn a cadet's life into hell. Failure to pay attention to these small and irritating details served as a pretext for imposing harsh punishments on the children, calculated to bring them to a mental crisis and to break their resistance to conversion. In contrast, the demands made of the converts were conspicuously more lenient.

With regard to health, Berel Klinger testifies that the regulars at the battalion clinic were the victims of beatings. Klinger himself was punished by having to stand for hours while wearing ceremonial uniform, including a long coat, a helmet, and an especially heavy gun. Klinger fainted at the end and was brought unconscious to the clinic. He did not regain consciousness for hours. One of the medics told him that had he died as a result of the punishment, they would have given the reason for death as "acute," namely: The patient died because of sudden deterioration of an illness—pneumonia, meningitis, etc. This was the source of a new concept: *akuta*—the death of a minor as a result of abuse. The higher authorities knew what was happening, but they demanded their subordinates to write favorable reports, "without problems." The lie of tacit agreement, ordered from "above," is characteristic of Russia's political culture since time immemorial.[23]

The most common disease among the children was skin fungus, which was treated with pungent ointment. The cantonists Meir Merimzon and Moisy Spiegel note in their memoirs[24] that, during the very long treks to their army base, the children were not allowed to wash themselves and they suffered terribly from bugs. Many got sick and died on the way. Merimzon mentions, however, that immediately on arrival at the base, the children were given the opportunity of washing in hot water. This means that the commanders were aware of the problem, but hot water and soap were most probably considered luxuries in those days in the Russian army.

A comparison should be made between the mortality rate during army service among minors and that of civilians. It must be noted, however, that the average life-span of non-Jews was only forty years, whereas for Jews it was on average

---

23 It is interesting to note that disguising the name of disease or the real cause for death in more innocent terms was a tradition of Russian medicine till recently. Thus, for example, in Stalin's days, jaundice in prisons was called Botkin's disease.
24 Merimzon, "Rasskaz starogo soldata," 290–301; Spiegel, "Zapiski kantonista," 249–259.

fifty-six.²⁵ In light of this fact, the rate of mortality from other sicknesses reflects the low level of medicine in Russia in general.

Fridays: On Fridays the cantonists were busy learning the correct way of marching and also the clauses of the military regulations, the *punkten*,²⁶ which every soldier was supposed to know by heart. The youngsters were divided into groups of ten, and each group was taught by a different sergeant—*punktik*. One of the *punkten* proclaimed the right of the soldier to appeal the commander's decision (!), but the cadets learned on their flesh that this clause was meaningless, and if the cadet managed to prove the commander's guilt, the commander would indeed receive a light punishment, but the one who complained would also be punished by the criminal himself.

The fact that there were those who complained and proved themselves right can help us understand what was happening in the Russian army of the time. As the author of *Berko the Cantonist* relates, the cantonists organized a protest action against the commander of the half-battalion, who robbed the children, stole their supplies, etc. The cantonists agreed among themselves that the protest would be expressed in a conspiracy of silence. When the supervising major-general arrived, the cantonists answered his question of whether there were complaints with thunderous silence. Thus, without hearing any specific complaint, the major-general understood the dissatisfaction of the minors. An investigation was launched. In this way the cantonists succeeded in hinting at irregularities without submitting a formal complaint, which the commanders did not like. In fact, Berko's commander pleads, in front of all his 500 cadets, that they not accuse him in front of the supervisor: "I am sorry, children, I am truly guilty. I am very guilty before you. I beg for the sake of my family, for the sake of my children, forgive me." We understand that he was afraid of his supervisors, who acted without favoritism.

During the revolt in Arkhangel'sk the sailors also dared to complain at the roll call at the military port about the force exerted to convert. Their commander, Podpolkovnik D'iakonov died before leaving for an enquiry in Petersburg.²⁷

On **Saturdays**, military training was conducted in the framework of a half-battalion, and later in the day the cantonists would be required to wash the floors of the rooms. Polishing the floors with special brushes was an ordeal. The boy who was polishing had to work on his knees and to ensure that the floor was perfectly

---

25 "Naselenie Rossii," in *Entsiklopedicheskii slovar' Brokgauza i Efrona* (Berlin: Brokgauz i Efron, 1913),
26 From the German word *punkt*, meaning "point."
27 See Itzkovitz, "Vospominaniia evreiskogo kantonista," 54–65.

shiny. One can understand how detrimental, for the children who were brought up to observe Jewish commandments, was the work on Shabbat, which desecrated the holiness of this day. The boys were all forced to work together, and so they unable to refuse to carry out this order. The dilemma that the cantonists faced was probably something to the effect of: "If I'm incapable of observing the commandments, it means that God is opening up the road to Christianity for me." They did not know that not observing the *mitzvot* did not mean that they had to convert to Christianity, and that there was a solution: not to observe *mitzvot*, but to remain Jewish.[28]

Sunday was a holiday for the Christians. The Christian cantonists and those who had converted were sent to the local church. This was a pleasant pastime for them, whereas the Jews stayed in the barracks to study or to do urgent jobs. Those left behind studied "articles" from the regulations, with special emphasis on the penalties for transgressions in the army. They did all this while the prayers in church were continuing, so they would not be idle during that time. Toward the end of the day, they too would go to town, to the market, and especially, according to Klinger's memoirs, to family members. This is how contact with Jewish local residents and also with family members was made, if these came to visit or if they lived in the area. This description matches the report of the chief procurator of the Holy Synod,[29] who identified the permission to leave the base as the main reason for the failure of the attempts to convert the cantonists. Another option for free time on Sundays was staying in the school and playing with other minors.

Itzkovitz, who was a cantonist in the Arkhangel'sk half-battalion in 1853–1857, tells of a slightly different schedule in his school:[30]

> Wake-up time: 6:00 am. The mentors, twelve-year-olds, wake up the cadets by flogging them mercilessly. All of them are taken to Christian prayers, without being asked or without distinguishing between Jew and Christian.

In Itzkovitz's opinion, there was no possibility of objecting, unlike Klinger, Merimzon, and others, who managed to resist.

---

28 See Rabbi Joseph Karo, *Shulḥan Arukh, Yoreh De'ah* 157: "One should be killed and not transgress."
29 Ginzburg, "Mucheniki-deti" [Martyr children], *Evreiskaia starina* 13 (1930): 67, from the Synod archive, letter from Metropolitan Anatolii of October 17, 1844.
30 Itzkovitz, "Vospominaniia evreiskogo kantonista," 54–65.

> After prayers they received 100 grams of bread.
> They then spent about half an hour on their clothes: cleaning, sewing patches, polishing their boots.
> Between 7:00 and 11:00: marching drills.
> 11:00: lunch.
> After the meal, they marched to the classrooms, where they learned reading, writing, and arithmetic, and had craft classes.

It is interesting that on Saturdays they did exactly what Berko relates: washing the floors (scrubbing with all their might). The mentors who continuously walked around rained blows on those who were not making sufficient effort.

The two stories are not completely parallel. In Itzkovitz's memoirs many details are missing, including a list of weekly activities, except for Saturdays, which match Klinger's narrative. It should be noted that, from the commanders' point of view, polishing the floors was in preparation for Sunday, which was a holy day for Christians. For the Jews, it was forbidden work, of which they were undoubtedly aware. Considering the fact that this was the routine for everyone, and not just for the Jews, halakhically speaking, they could obey, as this was not a case of *shemad* (an action intended specifically against the Jewish religion), and not complying may have been a matter of endangering their lives, *pikuaḥ nefesh*, for which one is allowed to desecrate the Sabbath. It is unclear if anyone taught the boys what was permitted or forbidden, as Rabbi Yisrael Meir Kagan, the Ḥafetz Ḥayim, did fifty years later for soldiers in the Russian army.[31] I find it surprising that a simple thing like that, which could have saved hundreds of boys, was not done.

D. Studies of the Cantonists

As mentioned in the general description of the curricula, the didactic methods in the cantonist schools were designed according to advanced methods imported from England (the so-called Lancaster system). However, it is doubtful whether it was possible to apply the methods properly, considering the extremely poor level of the teachers, a large part of whom had never received any professional training (only later was an institute for teacher training of the required type established).

---

31   Rabbi Yisrael Meir Kagan of Radin (Radzyń Podlaski), *Mahaneh Yisrael* (1881).

The Jewish boys generally knew how to read and write, which meant that at that time the educational level of the Jews was higher than that of the Christians. There was one drawback: all the studies in the Jewish boys' schools and yeshivot were conducted in Hebrew. In addition, the Jews spoke Yiddish, Polish, Ukrainian, and Lithuanian, but generally did not know Russian. This caused a lot of trouble for the boys in the army, and it can be assumed that every Jewish child strove to learn Russian as quickly as possible. Merimzon relates that for some coins and a bread roll he hired a teacher from the village to teach him Russian.[32]

Berel Klinger tells of the learning atmosphere.[33] The classrooms were on the third floor, above the bedrooms. There was a wide corridor, on both sides of which were high glass doors leading into the classrooms. There were about one hundred cadets in a class.

> The teacher sat and one student stood up and answered a question. The teacher said: "You don't know the lesson. You're making fun of me. Go to the door." The student went to the door and knelt down in front of a multiplication table that was hanging on the wall. At the end of the lesson, seven cantonists were already on their knees. The punishment sergeant, called "the drummer," was there and he raised a whip and hit the children on their palms. After each blow, the whip left two red-yellow stripes. One of the children received seventy-two beatings, could not last out, and fell flat on his face.[34]

The teacher did not check who had converted and who had not. Both Christians and converts received the punishments, and Berel Klinger himself, who did not convert, was appointed as a mentor of the students because he did well at arithmetic and received the nickname of honor: *rifmetist*. In practice, the drunkard of a teacher handed over all the students to Berko the Jew. Klinger was the one to determine the punishment given to lazy students.[35]

---

32 Merimzon, "Rasskaz starogo soldata," 290–301.
33 Grigor'ev, *Berko kantonist*, 54.
34 According to Grigor'ev, *Berko kantonist*.
35 One must, of course, take these old memoirs cautiously. Thus, for example, Spiegel cites the exact price of a half-kilo of meat, a price paid when he was eight years old. How did he know and remember?

Moisy Spiegel,[36] who served at the Tobol'sk fortress, relates that the classroom was built as a semi-circle. Five groups learned together in one room, with ten students in each group. The teacher was one of the cantonists, not an adult teacher or a commander as in Klinger's story. The children sat round a table, and they were moved from table to table according to how they succeeded in their studies, regardless of their religion. They started to learn the Russian alphabet by writing on wooden boards with a thick pencil, which they would then scratch out for the next writing assignment. They would continue on to learn neat handwriting, as some of the cadets were designated to be army scribes. At the next table they learned arithmetic. In grades 2 and 3 they learned geometry (!), geography, sketching, book-keeping, and the army regulations.

All the students were supposed to take part in classes of religion. The teachers taught the Christian prayers, and took all the children, both Jews and Christians to church. Thus, for example, Moisy Spiegel was asked to sing Christian hymns because he had a good voice.

When comparing the stories of Spiegel and Klinger, one can come to the clear conclusion that school was meant to train professional soldiers. In comparison to the peasants who enlisted at the age of twenty, and most of whom were illiterate, the graduates of the cantonist schools constituted the vocational elite of the lowest rank in the army, but had the possibility of promotion. The graduates of these schools were acquainted with the army from their childhood, and this early experience enabled them to manage better than a fresh conscript, even a Christian one.

In these schools, students advanced from one class to the next regardless of which religion they belonged to. The Jews had a better chance of progressing in studies because of their cleverness. After the initial acclimatization, when the Jews suffered more than the Christians, after having learned the "secrets" of a soldier's life, the Jews began to progress and seize positions. It was not for nothing that, already at the beginning of their conscription, Jewish cantonists were directed to medical studies that were considered prestigious (see above).

E. Living Conditions, Food Supply, Conditions of Service

According to Klinger, the dining room was huge, the size of an enclosed marching field (apparently, they had a special building for marching in the winter).

---

36   Spiegel, "Zapiski kantonista," 249–259.

A non-commissioned officer, called *tsudiner* (from German *Zudiener*, meaning "responsible for the service"), presided over meal arrangements. He distributed aprons and freshly baked bread to the group of cantonists responsible for the kitchen. They received the bread in the institution's bakery and weighed it before distributing. They then gave knives to the cantonists to slice the bread. Each child was meant to receive a large slice (Itzkovitz notes that the morning bread ration was 100 grams). The cantonists on duty put cups and jugs of *kvas*[37] on the table, as well as salt cellars. The chef distributed plates to the battalions who would enter the dining room to the accompaniment of drums. Each one would take a place by the table. At a sign given by the drum, they started a Christian prayer. At the next sign, the cantonists jumped over the benches next to which they were standing, and sat down. They were served cabbage soup, *shchi*, cooked from pork and rotten cabbage. In order not to draw attention of the mentors, the children made movements with the soup spoon, but they did not touch the soup and just ate the bread. At the end of the meal, they would be given the crumbs that had formed when the bread had been sliced.[38]

Cantonists who were sent to villages had completely different living conditions and schooling. We learn of this special framework from Merimzon's narrative. Although from other documents we hear of children being adopted (fostering), this refers only to individual cases. Merimzon speaks of a whole regiment, about 200 youngsters, living in the village, with each cantonist being sent to a private house. We know that the army paid those who gave accommodation to the soldiers well. Although the householders profited from the arrangement, the treatment of the boys changed from one place to the other. As told above, the first family to house Merimzon had him sleep in a narrow stuffy place, and fed him left-over non-kosher food. The children of the house abused him and tried to smear his lips with pig fat. In contrast, after he was transferred to another home, Merimzon enjoyed conditions "similar to Mama's house," and the lady of the house treated him humanely. He had his own money, which allowed him to buy food and even hire the services of a teacher who taught him Russian. Berko Klinger, stationed at the Arkhangel'sk port, also had money, as apparently did soldiers everywhere.

---

37 A traditional Russian beverage typically produced from rye or dried rye bread by natural fermentation.
38 The author confirms that the ceremony of breakfast had not changed in prison institutions in Russia even a hundred years later.

3

Social Aspects of the Cantonists' Lives

A. Contact with Family

It might seem sometimes that, as soon as he was conscripted, a Jewish boy was completely cut off from his family. However, some memoirs[1] mention mothers accompanying their children, even if they had been recruited long before, and that their separation was heartbreaking. It seems, moreover, that this was not always their final separation.

Meir Merimzon, for example, was abducted from a town in Lithuania and taken to serve in the district of Kyiv, a distance of almost one thousand kilometers, and yet he relates that his parents used to send him a letter with a sum of money every month.[2] Merimzon does not mention how contact was made after the cruel separation, and does not give details as to how the letters were transferred. Even after his family decided to cut off all contact with him when they suspected him of converting, he managed to correspond with his past teacher.

We must remember that, despite the distance he had traveled since his abduction, he still remained within the Pale of Settlement, where the main part of the Jewish population lived. If there had been something unusual about this contact, Merimzon would certainly have specified how the correspondence took place. Seeing that he did not do so, we can conclude that it was quite common. The simplest assumption as to how contact between a cantonist and his family occurred is that local Jews or wandering merchants helped deliver their letters.

If this is the case, then we can assume that there was often contact between the cantonists and the local Jewish community. We find confirmation of this in the report of the chief procurator of the Synod to the tsar (see above), in which

---

1 See, for example, Merimzon, "Rasskaz starogo soldata," 290–301.
2 Ibid.

he complained that the local Jewish community enabled contact between the cantonists and their families. It is correct that when there was a long distance, it was more difficult to send letters, but even then, it was possible to do so from time to time—perhaps twice a year.

The priests perceived contact with family as an obstacle to their missionary activity. The head priest of the army, Katovits, claimed that a boy's contact with his family, and his commitment to his parents, constituted a more significant motive in his resistance to conversion than his loyalty to his religion. Nil, the archbishop of Irkutsk, complained in a report of September 21, 1844 to the Holy Synod that, although only four cantonists who had not converted remained in the unit, it was difficult to convince them.[3] The priest's mission would have been much easier, if it had been possible to prevent the parents' influence. It should be noted that at the time there were only about ten cantonists in his unit, so he was not speaking about any outstanding success. The four remaining boys were probably children of Jewish settlers who lived in the surrounding area.

Several months later, Nil again wrote to the Synod,[4] suggesting to only allow cantonists to meet family members in the presence of a cantonist convert. It can be assumed that he was referring to local Jews, otherwise it would be difficult to explain how Jews in the Pale of Settlement, who were prevented from leaving the Pale, could travel such great distances. The November 1845 report of Father Grigorii to Abramov, the commander of the Tobol'sk half-battalion, reinforces this theory. As an excuse for the failure to convert the cantonists, he points to secret meetings held between cantonists and their parents, who lived locally.

We also learn of letters exchanged between the children and their parents from the report of the archbishop of Arkhangel'sk to the Synod on October 24, 1844.[5] He writes that the parents' letters strengthened the children in their resolve not to convert. From this complaint we learn that parents were able to locate their children, and certainly made every effort to do so.

If one or two letters were capable of boosting the cantonists' resilience against the pressure and coercion of an entire ecclesiastical military apparatus, we can testify to their very strong spirit. Or perhaps the Christian spiritual influence did not suffice to change the boys' basic position. Moisy Spiegel, who served in Tobol'sk, relates that the priest would often invite him to his home, entertained him and spoke to him sincerely, trying to convince him: "... because they had to

---

3   Ginzburg, "Mucheniki-deti," 68.
4   Ibid. The letter is from January 10, 1845.
5   Ibid., 60.

report on conversion from love, not force." This statement[6] seems most strange. Did the priests really obey the guidelines they received?

We learn about the significance that the authorities attributed to written correspondence between a minor and his family from the prohibition to write in Yiddish. The archbishop of Saratov and Tsaritsyn (Volgograd)[7] complained in a letter[8] to the chief procurator of the Synod[9] that the cantonists of the battalions in Saratov write to, and receive letters from, their parents in "the spoken Jewish language," and he proposed demanding that the parents write in Russian. Still, his efforts were in vain. We can assume that most of the parents wrote anyway to a local Jew and not directly to the military unit. In any case, it is clear that correspondence between parents and children took place, and it was difficult for the censorship and the authorities to control or stop it.

Matters were different for those who converted. As the letters arrived to the cantonist with his name prior to his conversion, the priests of the Saratov unit would return the letters to the sender, with the excuse: "There is no cantonist here by that name."[10]

B. Contact with the Local Jews

The archbishop of Tobol'sk, Father Vladimir, reported to the Synod in his letter of November 21, 1844,[11] that he had been very successful in converting. The priest knew that the chances of his "success" were limited in time, and depended on them ending with the minors' acclimatization in the unit. Considering the fact that conscription was in the winter, and the journey to Tobol'sk lasted at least four months, the approximate time of the cantonists' arrival at their destination was at the beginning of the summer. Thus, the ability for the priest to exert influence lasted, in the best-case scenario, only two months—till August.

What happened in August? The boys discovered the Jews living in the town. The Jewish community in Tobol'sk existed already from the beginning of the nineteenth century, but considering that this town is located in western Siberia,

---

6   Spiegel, "Zapiski kantonista," 249–259.
7   Towns on the Volga River, relatively far from the center. See Ginzburg, "Mucheniki-deti," 70.
8   Trivus, "Ritual'nye protsessy," 249–259.
9   Ibid. From the Synod archive, December 19, 1844.
10 From S. Ginzburg's archives. The child was given a Christian name on conversion. However, see Levanda's *Sbornik zakonov*, 161, for the authorities' instructions not to change the family name, ostensibly to allow identification of the cantonist, showing that he was not Russian.
11 Ginzburg, "Mucheniki-deti," 66.

thousands of kilometers from the Pale of Settlement, it can be assumed that only a few dozen Jews lived there at the time, in addition to the Jewish soldiers. Most of the residents were convicts or people who had escaped punishment, but even such a population was a threat to Father Vladimir's achievements.

As can be understood from Father Vladimir's report to the Synod, a Jew by the name of Mendel was a real obstacle for him. This Mendel had acquired a position in the town council and, as such, had contacts with officials at different levels. This smart Jew, with the help of his contacts, knew how to reduce the pressure on the cantonists. It can be concluded from Father Vladimir's report that he did not have at his disposal efficient (cruel) tools to conduct immediate conversions. His influence on the boys was limited with respect to the children's acclimatization and adaptation to the local conditions.

It is interesting that this assumption is verified by other sources, among them the memoirs of Klinger and Merimzon. So the church only had a very limited amount of time, just a few months, in which to operate. Therefore, the efforts of the clergy were concentrated within the first month of the cantonists' arrival. As we will see below, the pressure to convert started already on the cantonists' journey to the base.

Similar to Father Vladimir's complaint, the archbishop of Pskov, Father Rafael', also complained to the chief procurator of the Synod:

> The cantonists in Pskov are making contact with local Jews under various and strange pretexts. These contacts must be prevented and military supervision imposed on them.

At the same time, the metropolitan of Novgorod, Antonii, wrote to the chief procurator explaining his failure to convert the cantonists in the Novgorod battalion:

> In the village of Medved, where the cantonists are stationed, live Jews.[12] They are also in the surrounding villages. The cantonists have regular contact with these families, and this is a true obstacle when trying to direct

---

12 This document reveals that cantonist units were stationed in villages. Merimzon also mentions this practice and describes the living conditions in the village, in the homes of the peasants, something not previously mentioned in research studies.

them towards the truth. This contact undoubtedly strengthens the cantonists' spirit of resistance in an unwanted manner, as it greatly weakens the influence of the Christian instructors.[13]

In this report, too, the helplessness of the Church in coping with the local Jews is apparent. Even the priest does not point to any intentional incitement on the part of the Jews, or to the activity of any rabbi. It was only the kind encouragement that the children received from other Jews, but it was enough to thwart the influence of the Christian instructors, who were attempting to direct the boys on the "true path."

The archbishop of Tobol'sk and of all Siberia, Father Georgii, turned to the governor of eastern Siberia, Prince Gorchakov, with a request:

> **Perhaps** it is possible to remove from Tobol'sk the Jews who came to settle the area at the order of the tsar, so that they will not be an obstacle in our attempts to convert the cantonists to Christianity. (The bold is mine, Y.M.)

When Georgii received a negative reply from Gorchakov, explaining the refusal with the fact that there was nothing in the law that permitted expelling people for such a reason,[14] the priest persisted and complained to the chief procurator:

> It would be most befitting to prevent the Zhids from settling in Tobol'sk, not just to remove an obstacle in the conversion of the cantonists, but because of the nuisance [they are] to the Orthodox residents themselves.

We must still explain how contact was made in places where there was no Jewish population. At investigations of soldiers of the half-battalion in Arkhangel'sk, we hear them testify that, when a search was conducted, letters from family members were found among their possessions. When they left the base in Arkhangel'sk on a trek to St. Petersburg, they met their siblings and parents.

---

13   Ginzburg, "Mucheniki-deti," 67. Ginzburg refers to the Synod archive, November 17, 1844.
14   Ginzburg, "Mucheniki-deti," 67. From this correspondence we can understand that not every proposal of the priests was accepted. On the contrary, the military authorities did not support missionary activity. See also below, the request to dismiss Rabbi Aldukhov.

There was no organized Jewish community in Arkhangel'sk, and so a different explanation to that of Merimzon must be found.

The answer seems to be in the fact that in Arkhangel'sk there were adult soldiers who were freer, to such an extent that they could even have kosher slaughter. Soldiers of such a status undoubtedly kept in touch with their families. Each soldier was allowed to have a "home vacation," and the Jewish soldiers were not deprived of this right. In addition, after the first ten years of service, every soldier was permitted to rent an apartment in the town and live a family life.[15] From the story of Berko the Cantonist we learn that in the area of the Volga River cantonists were permitted to go to town during their days off, and they would naturally meet Jewish soldiers there, even if there was no local community. Among the opportunities for meeting with Jewish tradition was also the contact with communities of the Subbotniki, who did not have a Pale of Settlement, and lived in important centers in Russia. These communities enjoyed full freedom of movement, while completely identifying with the Jews. Therefore, we can assume that in principle it was possible for a cantonist to make contact with his family from almost any location.

On the other hand, from Merimzon's narrative we learn that his parents sent him a harsh letter in which they wrote that they suspected him of converting to Christianity, and so decided to cut off all ties with him. He did not succeed in changing their attitude. Thus, although the possibility of keeping in contact through letters existed, it was not always a mutual intention, and did not last for many years.

To understand the contradiction between the possibility of writing letters home and the lack of contact over a continuous period, it can be supposed that the idea that all cantonists converted to Christianity caused a stigma, according to which every conscript was an apostate. We don't hear any opposition to this rejection of all cantonists on the part of the rabbis, and public pressure was probably also involved. It was customary to mourn a recruited family member as dead, on account of converting.[16] The rationale for such a harsh position most probably stemmed from the wish to create strong barriers to preserve the religious framework. The concept was that parents who were tempted to continue to have contact with the child, whatever his condition may have been, were in this way creating a conciliatory and forgiving attitude towards the apostate.

---

15 This detail has gone almost unnoticed by researchers, who describe a soldier's life in very gloomy colors, while the status of permanent soldiers was not the worst in Russia.
16 Merimzon, "Rasskaz starogo soldata," 221–232.

If this hypothesis is even partially correct, it must be admitted that the same tool of self-defense also operated in the opposite direction. Excommunicating a blameless child was likely to severely harm his ability to resist the temptations of conversion. It can be assumed that the reason for severing contact with the conscript was connected to the way of life of the Jewish family in the nineteenth-century *shtetl*. The effort to continue the contact in a situation of uncertainty concerning the child's religious status was too great for most families. Similarly, it was difficult over a long period of time to worry about finding ways to transfer letters over distances of thousands of kilometers (from Lithuania to Siberia, for example).

We learn a significant detail about the minors' social situation from the memoirs of the governor of the province of Simbirsk (Ul'ianovsk), Ivan Markovits-Zirkevich. He relates that in 1836,[17] the tsar himself came to the cantonist training base in Simbirsk.[18] One thousand two hundred cantonists were supposed to be there, but in fact only three hundred (!) were present at the roll call. The commander of the base explained that the cantonists stayed in the private homes of those who adopted them, except for the Jews who were on the base to prevent them from having contact with the local Jews.[19] The tsar was annoyed and asked, "Do you also have Jews outside the base?" The commander admitted that, indeed, there were some Jews who stayed in town with special approval from "above." Meanwhile, the tsar remembered that one of the cantonists had appealed to him with a complaint, and he commanded that the child be brought to him. The tsar asked the commander about the cantonist's achievements in his studies and about his behavior, and was satisfied with the reply. Notably, he did not ask whether the child had converted to Christianity. Then the tsar turned to the boy and asked:

- And so you complain that you are your mother's only child?
- That is correct, Your Majesty!
- Benkendorf,[20] check this, and if that is the case, release him immediately. And if not... (The tsar made a gesture signifying that there would be a harsh punishment.)

---

17 See the review of new publications, *Evreiskaia starina* 6 (1913): 70.
18 A town on the banks of the Volga River.
19 The town was far from the Pale of Settlement, and yet Jews lived there!
20 Head of the security services, commander of the Gendarmes.

One can arrive at several conclusions from reading about this episode. The tsar arrived, and the commander of the base did not even bother to bring all the cantonists to the base. The fact that the majority stayed outside the base is fascinating. Till now, researchers thought that the cantonists lived in private homes only when staying in the village. The atmosphere of free coming and going testifies to sloppy and careless management. Even if most of the Jews stayed on the base, the moment the majority of cantonists were permitted to come and go as they pleased, a disorder was created that, to a certain extent, also reflected on those discriminated against.

The fact that there were Jews in the town was an additional complication, as verified also in Berko Klinger's memoirs cited above. Furthermore, the access to the tsar, when a Jewish child can turn to him with a complaint and not be beaten for his audacity, is also most unusual. Could this have been a liberal game in front of a small child?

In his 1828 report on the cantonist institution in Vitebsk, Lieutenant Colonel Merder[21] recommended transferring the boys to a base outside the Pale of Settlement, to separate them from the local community. He complained that the members of the community had sent letters to the children in an organized effort to prevent the boys' conversion. Under the influence of the letters, which included promises of redemption and threats of curses,[22] the Jews succeeded in convincing a large part of the candidates not to convert. This document strengthens our theory that the contact between the Jews in the area and the cantonists was a significant factor in their resistance to conversion. Merder wrote in his report that there was no family connection between the community in Vitebsk and the children, who had been taken from the community in Minsk. If we add to this comment the documents testifying to the fact that the Jews of Vilna cared for the cantonists who came from Riga and Mogilev and were training in the military school in Smolensk, we can probably speak of widespread coordination among the communities in adopting cantonist institutions. It should be remembered, however, that these documents are from the beginning of the conscription period.

---

21 The name testifies to his German origin. (*Mörder* means "murderer.")
22 This refers to a custom to curse Jews who left their religion, asking to bring a divine punishment down on them.

C. Relationships among the Boys

We could have expected that the reality of many Jewish boys being together would cause the group to unite and to react uniformly to life in the cantonist school. From studying the composition of cantonists in military bases, it is apparent that the authorities were not concerned about such an organized response. Evidently, the children experienced a high level of demoralization and despair on coming to the base. The missionary activity was so violent and fast that no time was left for the minors to organize in any way. In addition, the new cantonists came to bases where there were children and teenagers who had already been through the "treatment." It was they who received the novices and familiarized them with the atmosphere of what was going on in the institution. Testimony to this appears in the words of the witness Sindikov in the trial of the cantonist Terent'ev. Sindikov testified that the children who had been baptized annoyed their still-Jewish friends because it disturbed them that the latter had not given in.[23] We find a similar description from the town of Smolensk. In his report on the conversion of cantonists, Brigadier General Rebinder wrote that the children explained their wish to convert as an expression of identification with peers who had already done so. It is an evidence of their immaturity, which we must take into account in order to understand why there was no organized response.

At the same time, on the personal level, there was mutual help and cooperation, as seen in the testimonies of Merimzon and Klinger. Klinger tells of encouragement and support among the children, but he also shows cruel behavior that, we believe, characterizes of the boys in general. From the moment he was appointed as a mentor in arithmetic lessons, that same Klinger, persecuted for his Judaism, no longer showed any sensitivity, and dealt out punishments to the students for their lack of diligence.

We receive a different picture from the documents of an investigation conducted in the Arkhangel'sk half-battalion. Even if at the time of their conversion there was no agreement among their boys concerning their wish to return to Judaism at a later stage, after they converted, natural leaders appeared who initiated and organized the resistance. We understand that for this purpose they used both persuasion and social and physical pressure. The difference between accepted passive behavior, and the behavior of the Arkhangel'sk cantonists, can be explained by the fact that the Arkhangel'sk soldiers were older

---

23 See *Voskhod* 4 (1881), for more on Terent'ev's trial.

(between the ages of seventeen and twenty-one). The atmosphere of the time was probably also different.

D. The Relationship between the Boys and Their Gentile Environment

The attitude of the local population to the Jewish soldiers was, as a rule, hostile. Nevertheless, during the course of our research we came across several unexpected instances of gentiles helping the children. Chaim Merimzon's story particularly stands out for this. After suffering with his first landlady, he was sent to live in the home of Christian Baptists where he was treated very warmly. Also, later, Merimzon tells of reasonable treatment that he received from Russians.[24] Similarly, Spiegel tells of the reception and of the moving farewell of the residents of a certain town where the cantonists had been stationed. The daughter of a commander in one of the towns fed Itzkovitz with white bread, and even held him in her arms. Although it would not be correct to see these examples as being common, they seem to speak of a certain nuance that should be added to the picture of cantonist life. Not all non-Jews were hostile to the Jews. Their attitudes changed from location to location, depending on the geographical area[25] and the religious variety of the locals. To a certain extent this is also true regarding the army professionals, such as the escort officer in Alexander Herzen's story analyzed above.

---

24   Spiegel and Itzkovitz report of similar treatment.
25   Grigor'ev in *Berko kantonist* tells that the attitude of the population in faraway towns improved in comparison to Moscow.

4

The Cantonists' Religious Life—Documents and Certificates

A. Festivals

April 5, 1828[1]

To the commander of the Smolensk Fortress, Major-General Keren

We received the following letter from the Jews of Mogilev:

A request of the Jewish community of Mogilev, Belarus
We hereby request and plead that you approve the transfer of special products for the cantonist boys serving in the town of Smolensk. We would like to stress the importance of special products for the festival of Passover. One can understand this also from the permission and order given last year in the engineering division.

Signed: S. Shpungin, head cantor of the community; head of the community, Yetzke Staroslasky; the merchants Hirsch Lipschitz and Etya Frumkin.

Submitted in March 1828[2]

---

1 Central Archives for the History of the Jewish People, HMF760, copy from Gosudarstvennyi arkhiv Rossiiskoi Federatsii [State archive of the Russian Federation], f. 109, 1 eksp., d. 330. The date refers to the day the letter was filed.
2 Similar requests were submitted on behalf of the communities of Vitebsk, Smolensk, etc. Gosudarstvennyi arkhiv Rossiiskoi Federatsii [State archive of the Russian Federation], f. 109, d. 196, ll. 25–44.

Copy of a report by Major Vinokurov, commander of the military cantonist battalion in Smolensk:

> **To Major-General Keren, military commander of Smolensk**
>
> Report no. 407[3]
>
> In reply to your order of April 3, 1828, together with the letter of the Jewish community of Mogilev, I hereby inform you that the request to supply *matzot* for Passover does not seem to me to be reasonable. One cannot set aside a special table for them in the dining room without an explicit order from you.
>
> In addition, in the regulations of October 31, 1827, clause 111, it states that Jewish minors enjoy the same conditions as Christian minors and receive military and vocational education equal to that of the Christians. This being the case, if we release them from studies on their festivals, when the Christian students will be studying, the Jews will miss the possibility of studying the topics covered on those days. Then again, they will not learn on Christian holidays, thus missing studies twice. In general, such a practice will not contribute anything positive to their vocational or military studies. The General Staff will blame us for their failure in their studies, and this will have negative implications.
>
> Therefore, I recommend that you receive explicit permission from the superior command concerning exempting Jewish minors on festivals and transferring *matzot* to them.
>
> Signed: Major Vinokurov

B. Cantonists in Synagogues

One of the significant difficulties confronted by the Church in its efforts to convert the minors was the law[4] allowing Jewish soldiers to pray in the town

---

3 Central Archives for the History of the Jewish People, HMF759/a–b, copy from Gosudarstvennyi arkhiv Rossiiskoi Federatsii [State archive of the Russian Federation], f. 109, 1 eksp.

4 Central Archives for the History of the Jewish People, HM2\8451/2, copy from Rossisskii gosudarstvennyi arkhiv Voenno-morskogo flota [Russian state archive of the military sea navy], f. 170, op. 1, d. 558.

synagogues, or to establish places of worship on the base.⁵ Ostensibly, this law applied also to the cantonists. In most places the minors did not know that they could demand this right, but in others a routine of going out for prayers was created. It is surprising that for years the military authorities did not object to this. One of the reasons for this was that the non-Jewish cantonists would go to the local churches on Sunday, and a significant number of them even lived in the city. We can understand from this, that the Jews, too, could enjoy this privilege.

It is very interesting that, to a certain extent, the adult soldiers enjoyed freedom of religion, as seen from the above documents. This was especially the case in central areas such as St. Petersburg and Kronshtadt. The personal example of the adult soldiers certainly created a precedent also for the minors. Some of the adults came from the ranks of the cantonists, and even if this were not the case, they were not completely separated from the minors. As proved above, there was a strong connection between the minors and the adults.⁶

The metropolitan⁷ of Novgorod and Petersburg, relying on the reports of the military priest of the half-battalion in Revel', wrote to the Synod on October 5, 1844, that

> the reason for the obstinacy of thirty-two Jewish cantonists not to convert is based on their hatred for anything Christian. However, an additional reason is the fact that, according to the instructions of their commanders, they are released on their holidays to pray with the local congregation, where they meet other Jews. These Jews come from a variety of military units and promise the boys all sorts of fake promises and frighten them with strange scenarios. All this encourages the children to be loyal to their mistaken faith.

---

5   In 1828, a complaint was submitted that in Riga and Vitebsk Jews were not allowed to go out to pray in synagogues. Gosudarstvennyi arkhiv Rossiiskoi Federatsii [State archive of the Russian Federation], f. 109, d. 330, ll. 19–21.
6   Ginzburg, "Mucheniki-deti," 50–79.
7   Ibid.

Father Vladimir of Tobol'sk[8] wrote to Count Protasov on November 21, 1844:

> The local cantonists must be forbidden from going to the Zhids'[9] house of worship which in Tobol'sk is more like a *korchma*[10] than a place of worship

In 1844 the metropolitan of Astrakhan', Father Smargard,[11] reported to Count Protasov concerning a battalion of cantonists in the town (on the Volga River):

> The main obstacle to the success in converting the Jews of the battalion is the Jew Mikhail Aldukhov, a soldier in the *leist*[12] unit no. 8, who was appointed as rabbi by the local military authorities in the absence of a true rabbi. He was permitted to rent a special house in which the cantonists gather on their festivals ... and not only does he try all means possible to make them remain Jewish, but he also conducts visits on the base before the festivals. I appealed to the substitute of the military governor of Astrakhan', Brigadier General Rebinder, asking him to fire the sailor Aldukhov from Astrakhan' with a reasonable excuse. If, for some reason, the request cannot be fulfilled, I asked that at least he be distanced from the Jewish cantonists in the area of the battalion, under any pretext at all. Brigadier General Rebinder informed me in his reply of October 3 that he cannot fulfill my demand because of the regulations of obligatory service of Jewish soldiers [!], clauses 91 and 93...
>
> Signed: Metropolitan of Astrakhan', Smargard
>
> November 29, 1844[13]

This astounding document presents significant new information concerning both the behavior of the Jews and of the military authorities. Nevertheless, it is hardly mentioned in the research literature, except as an example of the complaints of the Christians persecuting the Jews. This document reveals tension between the representatives of the Church and the military commanders.

---

8   Ibid.
9   A derogatory expression, not usually acceptable in written correspondence.
10 A tavern operated by Jews.
11 Ginzburg, "Mucheniki-deti," 50–79.
12 Auxiliary boats in the port.
13 Ibid.

As we learn, Rabbi Mikhail Aldukhov (the source of this name is not clear) served in Astrakhan' as the Jewish chaplain. He was apparently not qualified to be a rabbi, as he did not hold appropriate certification. The local military authorities did not consider this as a factor that could preclude them from appointing him as a rabbi, and so he was appointed with the agreement of the commanders. Aldukhov was given the authority to set up a synagogue and conduct Sabbath and festival services. This place became a center of Jewish life. Adult soldiers and boys visited the synagogue and heard the rabbi's sermons and words of encouragement. Evidently, Aldukhov was an active rabbi, motivated by holy zealousness. He organized extensive educational activities and talked to the boys, encouraging them not to betray the religion of their forefathers. He even visited the boys in the lion's den, the place where the boys were baptized—a Jewish rabbi in military uniform who entered without being disturbed. The boys ran up to him, he spoke to them, and invited them to pray. There was nothing the priest of the battalion could do after such a visit. The permission given by Brigadier General Rebinder for the presence of a military rabbi legitimized the boys' refusal to convert. If a rabbi could be a soldier and loyal to the tsar, and enjoy the authorities' protection, then there was nothing wrong if the cantonists remained Jews and continued to serve the tsar.

No less surprising is the opposition of Rebinder, the military governor, to the plans of Father Smargard. Ostensibly, Rebinder was a German who adopted the Russian culture.[14] In his opposition to the priest, he refers to the proper enforcement of the regulations concerning the military service of Jewish soldiers.

The priest understood that his request to get rid of Aldukhov was problematic, and therefore he wrote of the need for a "reasonable excuse." The priest knew that it was probably impossible to drive the rabbi out of the town, so an excuse had to be invented at least to prevent him coming to the battalion. We would have expected that in Russia at that time the need to convert the cantonists to Christianity would have been enough to ease the process, but Father Smargard himself was aware that it was not legal and not acceptable!

Clearly, the priest's concerns were justified. Brigadier General Rebinder did not see any reason to disturb Rabbi Mikhail Aldukhov in his work. Smargard's appeal undoubtedly became known to the local officers, and the rejection of his demand certainly made a great impression on the cantonist battalion's commanders.

---

14   Mentioned in the documents of the Third Section, in correspondence dealing with the situation of cantonists in Vitebsk. Gosudarstvennyi arkhiv Rossiiskoi Federatsii [State archive of the Russian Federation], f. 109, 1 eksp., d. 330, ll. 22–27.

Although the metropolitan had a senior Church status, he had no authority to contend with the military leaders. He therefore complained directly to the chief procurator of the Synod, Protasov, several days after his request had been rejected by Rebinder. Protasov turned to Nicholas and presented the matter in such a way that the tsar agreed with him and gave the respective order to the Minister of Defense.

We are talking here of a conflict between the army and the Church. It cannot be said that the Church always had the upper hand, especially not in practice. The question is: Can the tension between the army and the Church be seen as a permanent and dynamic component of the conversion story? At least one other source, the guidelines given by Kutnevich, the head chaplain of the army, obliges the priests to treat the military authorities with respect, which shows that in fact the situation was different. We see similar tension in the occurrence related above, when Prince Gorchakov rejected the archbishop of Tobol'sk's request to expel the Jewish settlers from the area, so that they would not be an obstacle to the conversion of the cantonists.

Even after the prohibition forbidding the boys to go to synagogues, it can be assumed that the Church was unable to prevent contact between the cantonists and Jewish soldiers and rabbis in the area. There were probably occasions on which adult soldiers demonstrated great self-confidence, as Rabbi Aldukhov, a regular soldier in uniform, did when he confronted the army priest, a person of high status. Aldukhov's daring is quite amazing.

In response to the multiple complaints, Protasov apparently succeeded in convincing the tsar to cancel the aforementioned clauses regarding the cantonists, thanks to his personal strength of character and his activist endeavors to convert Jewish children. This is implied from the following order of the navy commanders:

Management of the navy's training units[15]

On the prohibition for the cantonists to visit synagogues, March 2, 1845

The chief-procurator of the Holy Synod submitted a report to His Majesty the Tsar concerning the reason for the failure of the means taken by the religious institutions to convert the Jewish cantonists to the Orthodox religion.

---

15   Ginzburg, "Mucheniki-deti," 73.

> The reason for the failure lies in the fact that the cantonists are released to pray in the institutions of the Jewish community, where they meet with their coreligionists. His Majesty has ordered to prevent all secret gatherings and not to release the cantonists for that purpose.
> They should be permitted to observe their religion within the institutions in which they live, under the supervision of a Jew elected for that purpose from the naval units of the town and in the presence of an officer or teacher.
>
> Commander of the management of the navy's training units, March 2, 1845

This is a document of revolutionary significance concerning the cantonists. It shows that the chief procurator of the Synod was required to explain to the tsar the reason for the failure in converting the Jews, a mission in which the tsar was still personally involved, even in 1845. Protasov was on friendly relations with Nicholas, so this was evidently a serious failure. He understood that and did not try to justify the Church or to claim otherwise.

For the first time, we see a document directly defining the activities intended for conversion as "the means taken by the religious institutions to convert...." These "means taken" are attributed only to the Church, not to the army. At the same time, most of the documents concerning exertion of force in relation to the cantonists refer to military officials. Perhaps one should separate the missionary activity of the Church and a similar activity, probably not authorized, of the military officials in the area.

This document should be compared to the guidelines given to the priests of the unit, where it was recommended to cooperate with the army. This cooperation could help in their task, but not more than that.

Interestingly, Protasov found no reason for the failure to convert other than the cantonists attending prayer services. The report does not specify any location, from which one can assume that this was a common phenomenon. Secret gatherings are mentioned, which ostensibly had nothing to do with prayers in local synagogues. It probably refers to organizing prayers within the cantonist institution.

The report further states that "they meet with their coreligionists and hear from them all kinds of baseless promises." This document should be compared with the testimony of those who participated in the revolt of the Arkhangel'sk half-battalion, who, when questioned, testified that, when they were in St. Petersburg, elderly Jews would come and console them. It can be assumed that the Jews spoke among themselves of the hope that the cantonist institution would be abolished. If this is correct, it shows the tireless efforts to cancel the decree. Not only were such promises encouraging and instilled hope, they also brought closer the possibility of accountability to the parents and the community after release.

Whatever the case may be, it can be determined that minors left their base and had constant contact with the local community until 1845, eighteen years after the implementation of the conscription law. It is interesting to compare this document with Berel Klinger's memoirs in *Berko the Cantonist*. There we learn that the cadets would regularly go to town and walk around without supervision. Sometimes, they rained terror on the locals. Only those with complete confidence can behave in such a manner.

Even after the 1845 prohibition, we have no evidence that the tsar's order was carried out in full. As is known, not every tsarist order was executable in practice.

According to the new regulations, the minors were permitted to pray within the institution under the supervision of an older Jew. It can be assumed that they looked for adults to organize prayer services for the boys from units close to the cantonist institutions. There seems to be a contradiction: why give the cantonists a legal right to have public prayers according to the law and at the same time to let the military and Church officials exert pressure in order to get the Jewish boys to convert?

Even if we presume that the report was prepared by the priests with the provocative intention of arousing the tsar's fury and causing him to forbid the cantonists from going out to town, we must note that the Holy Synod was not authorized to issue a prohibition forbidding going to a synagogue of its own accord. It needed the tsar's special permission. From a formal point of view, the permission to go to synagogues was anchored in the regulations, but with a note that it would be granted only in the event of there being no *minyan* at the base.

The need for some kind of legislative action to cancel this clause in the regulations indicates that in principle the regulations on freedom of worship also applied to the cantonists, but for some reason Jewish lobbyists did not know how to take advantage of these clauses in the courts in order to ease the pressure on the boys.

From the time the letter was sent by the metropolitan of Astrakhan' to the Synod (November 29, 1844), it did not take long until the decree was imposed by the Minister of Defense—it was passed on March 21, 1845, after only three months. This shows that Protasov's position was strong, and that he worked with full vigor in complete agreement with the tsar.

In any case, the aforementioned report includes an acknowledgment of a reality that historians must keep in mind. It doesn't seem as though the priests would have taken it upon themselves to admit failure.

Part IV

COERCION AND CONVERSION PROCESSES

1

The Policy of Conversion: The Concept and Its Implementation

It seems that a document that was at the base of the philosophy of recruiting minors is an anonymous opinion letter found in the documents of the Tsar's Own Chancellery in the well-known Third Section.[1] After conducting an amateurish historical analysis of the Jewish people, the author of the letter comes to the conclusion that Jews in Russia had to undergo a "fundamental reform in order to free themselves from the influence of the fanatical rabbis and the Talmud." One of the methods recommended by this "expert" was conscription of minors. The author proposes confronting the children with a reality that did not allow for observance of commandments, as a result of which the Jews would abandon their religion. Indeed, we see evidence for the implementation of this rationale in practice. Therefore, it can rightly be claimed that the document was submitted as a basis for the planning of the operation.[2]

This "expert's" report on the "Jewish problem" was kept in a secret file in the bureau, from which we can understand that the authorities gave it great significance. It is quite probable that Nicholas I read it himself. The letter does not recommend exerting physical pressure on the minors. The author was obviously of the opinion that the reality of army life would suffice to break the child's spirit. It should be noted that the author does not voice any expectations of converting the cantonists to Christianity; just that they forsake their Judaism. Still, he ignores the possibility of the minors receiving freedom of worship, similar to

---

1   Rossiiskii gosudarstvennyi voenno-istoricheskii arkhiv [Russian state archive of military history], f. 405, op. 5, d. 7370, ll. 8–31.
2   This is not the only document. Gessen, *Istoriia*, 147 mentions a letter of a retired major, written in the same tone.

adult soldiers. In practice, there was a strange lack of proportion between the rights of an adult Jewish soldier and those of a minor.

Our "expert" clearly demonstrates his attitude when it comes to Jewish girls. In his opinion, these too should be taken away from their parents as early as twelve years old and brought to distant settlements, to marry local Christians. He goes into detail calculating all the circumstances, and comes to the conclusion that the girls would not put up too much resistance as, unlike the boys, the girls were not learned. Their destined husband would be Ukrainian criminals, known, as he writes, for "their Christian religiosity"!

The pragmatism and cynicism of the "expert" leave no doubt: His method of dealing with the boys, including the fact that he does not include a recommendation to use force, is not accidental but, rather, well calculated. To verify this, we turn to interrogation protocols of sailors from the Arkhangel'sk half-battalion. They pinpointed their inability to observe *mitzvot* as the reason for their conversion. The significance of this admission is that it presents a different consideration from that of physical pressure and abuse. It must be mentioned that in their interrogations only some of the soldiers could point to specific acts of force. This did not stem from lack of courage on the part of the soldiers who did not specify any such act; we see that they dared go public for the first time with the accusation of forcible conversion. Even after pressure at the time of "persuasion" more than sixty percent persisted in their refusal to convert, and yet they were unable to say how Christianity was forced on them. Thus, we see that the method of propagating conversion was sophisticated.

Michael Stanislawski regards[3] the fact that converts were offered various incentives as one of the proofs of a deliberate policy of conversion. Already in July 1829, it was decided in the ministerial committee to separate the Jews who converted while in military service from those who remained Jewish. It is interesting to note that from documents of a later period we understand that this order was not respected, and Jews remained together with the converts, a fact which was actually beneficial as a method of conversion. There was discrimination when it came to promotion, but even here there were many exceptions. We know, for example, that, without converting, the cantonist Herzl Tzam reached the rank of major in a combat unit. The story of Aaron Olshansky is well known. He served as a company sergeant major in an elite unit of the tsar's personal guards without having converted. (On his death he was given a Jewish burial

---

3   Stanislawski, *Tsar Nicholas I and the Jews*, 31–40.

with full military ceremony.) Some other examples are the discussion about the promotion of paramedics (see above) and Merimzon's story.

Shaul Ginsburg quotes a document[4] showing that the tsar issued a secret directive allowing priests in military units to perform baptisms without receiving permission from the heads of the military priesthood, in order to speed up the conversion procedures. As of 1843,[5] Nicholas personally undertook supervision of the speed of conversion, demanding monthly progress reports. On the April report, the tsar noted "too little," and in July—"miniscule progress." When in July a report of twenty-five conversions was submitted, the tsar wrote to Protasov: "I am disappointed with the lack of positive results of religious conversion of cantonists and Jewish soldiers. The matter should be presented in all seriousness. . . ." There is no doubt that the tsar's directive to speed up conversion was interpreted as permission to use all means to achieve this goal, even though this was nowhere explicitly stated.

Based on the tsar's wish, the minister of defense demanded that the number of priests attached to cantonist battalions must be increased and that guidelines of conversion methods be composed for the priests. Protasov passed the directive on to the heads of the military and naval clergy, following which the head priest of the navy, Vasilii Katovich, issued an instructional document on the matter in October 1848. This document encourages the chaplains to talk with the soldiers individually. The conversion must be conducted "with dignity and respect, without the use of coercion."

Ginsburg found evidence that, in order to promote conversion, the cantonists were forbidden to contact their parents, local Jews, and Jewish soldiers. Similarly, he states, written correspondence and talking in Yiddish were forbidden. According to Ginsburg, only adults were allowed to assemble for prayers, not cantonists. When conducting this research, we discovered in the archives of the tsar's navy (see above, 178) a directive forbidding the cantonists to leave the base for prayers, but giving them full permission to pray on the base in the presence of an authorized Jewish soldier. In addition, Merimzon testifies in his memoirs that he corresponded with his parents without any interruption. We understand that the cantonists would leave to go to town of Sundays, and that they could also leave during the week. The contradiction can be resolved by the fact that the guidelines of the higher authorities were

---

4   Shaul Ginsburg, *Historishe Verk* (New York: Cyco, 1938), vol. 3, 62.
5   Ibid.

not carried out because of the negligence of those meant to enforce them and because of real difficulties that they encountered in practice.

In any case, for the purpose of this study, it would not be correct to assume that the instructions of Father Katovich to act gently were not carried out on the ground, while the rest of the instructions were. Rather, each of the commanders probably behaved according to his personal ability and desire. It was to this that Queen Victoria basically testified when she said that the tsar was not aware of the level of corruption among his people.[6]

The cantonists had money, which they used to bribe the "educational" staff of the cantonist units in order to receive permission. In bases far from the center of the country, the staff often lived a life of debauchery, getting drunk and gambling. For that they needed Jewish money.[7]

Although we do not know what caused the tsar's change of approach to the issue of conversion, the year 1843 is marked as the end of the "calm" period and the beginning of the mass conversion campaign. Nevertheless, it is unclear to what extent the tsar was strict about the matter over the years.

The speeding up of the activity as of 1843 should be compared with the priests' efforts to point to the difficulties in converting in 1846, when the tsar demanded explanations from the chief procurator for the failure in converting. It seems that the earlier attempts to expedite the process did not lead to the expected result.

One cannot repudiate, as Stanislawski does, the guidelines for preventing forced conversion. The cantonist Moisy Spiegel, who was conscripted later, at the beginning of the fifties, served in a base in Tobol'sk, Siberia and, as mentioned above, the priest of the battalion would take him home to play with his children. Spiegel speaks of them as his friends. The priest would invite Spiegel to his room to talk to him about religion in an effort to persuade him to convert, "because they had to report that the conversion was carried out willingly"! Spiegel was successful in resisting the brainwashing, and did not agree to convert.

One of the first testimonies that refers to the conversion procedure is found in a document[8] that grants extra rights to priests operating in cantonist battalions. In 1829 the tsar issued a special order to facilitate missionary activity.

---

6 Westwood, *Endurance and Endeavour*, 89.
7 See, for example, the testimony of the soldier Nikolai Nazarov in the document of his interrogation at Kronshtadt on March 8, 1856, Central Archives for the History of the Jewish People, HMF626, copy from Gosudarstvennyi arkhiv Rossiiskoi Federatsii [State archive of the Russian Federation], f. 109, 1 eksp., op. 30, d. 340.
8 Ginzburg, "Mucheniki-deti," 55, from the archives of the Synod.

On August 1, 1829, the Synod issued a permit via Adjutant General Count Kleinmikhel', the tsar's personal assistant, according to which any priest or teacher in cantonist schools was allowed to convert the boys who expressed their wish to do so, without needing special permission from the senior priesthood. This permit was extraordinary in that it was a significant deviation from the church's regulations, which required prior approval for every act of baptism. The permit testifies to the importance of conversion for the tsar: to promote conversion of cantonists it was possible to undermine the authority of the senior clergy.

Evidently, enticement and coercion to convert were carried out fast so as to surprise the boy and baptize him when he reached breaking point, in order not to miss the opportune moment. However, there were many occasions, when after agreeing to convert, the boys went back on their decision under the influence of their peers. So, the priests were not very successful. In the Saratov battalion, which was considered most "effective," 576 boys converted in the fourteen years from 1828 until 1842; an average of 41 each year. In the least effective institution, in the area of Ural'sk, 101 Jews converted over a period of six years; about 17 each year.[9] The numbers indicate that until 1843 there had been no proactive conversion activity, and that each unit operated according to the ability and understanding of its commanders. In those six years, between 1842 and 1848, in Tomsk only three Jewish children converted.

Thus, we find, that despite the decision to distance Jews from their religion by drafting them into the army and cantonist battalions, the task was not very successful before 1843. It was then that, at the initiative of Count Sergei Uvarov, the Minister of Education, laws were passed imposing Christian state inspections of the Jewish educational system, and an attempt to establish a framework of Jewish state schools. This marked a new policy towards the Jews, called *sblizhenie* (rapprochement). Later, additional projects were planned by the ministerial committee for the complete reform of Jewish life. In an attempt to demarcate periods in the tsar's policy relating to the cantonists, we note that this was the beginning of a new era of activity initiated towards extensive conscription and religious conversion.

As written above, already at the beginning of this book, it is clear that 1843 was a year of change, but the reasons that brought this change are not so clear. One of the possibilities is the appearance of new characters in the imperial

---

9   Rossiiskii gosudarstvennyi voenno-istoricheskii arkhiv [Russian state archive of miltary history], f. 405, op. 5, d. 7370, ll. 7–60.

court. Indeed, two names start to appear frequently: the minister of defense, Chernyshev, and the chief procurator of the Holy Synod, Count Protasov. These two officials had a much more prominent status than Kiselev, Kankrin, and Uvarov, who were considered liberal. However, on further study of these two figures, it became clear that they both had already been active beforehand, and so the change of policy cannot be linked to their influence, although some particular initiatives certainly were. It is therefore necessary to continue to clarify the circumstances surrounding this drastic change.

In this study we will make do with sketching the general outlines of the change in policy towards the Jews, beginning with the establishment of the ministerial committee for reforming the lives of the Jews at the initiative of Count Kiselev. In my opinion there is a connection between proactive conversion and the activity of Minister Uvarov who intended to abolish the traditional Jewish educational frameworks.

On April 29, 1843, Chernyshev sent Tsar Nicholas's directive to Protasov:

> We must begin the conversion to Christianity of those members of the Jewish religion who are in institutions for military cantonists. The mission should be carried out by priests trained for the purpose, who will receive additional guidance when necessary from authorized sources. Count Protasov will prepare special guidelines. **Special attention should be paid to the matter, and it all should be done with great care, restraint, and without any attempt to exert pressure.** (Emphasis mine, Y.M.)[10]

This is a complex directive. On the one hand, it is made clear that the tsar has initiated a campaign of top priority had been initiated by the tsar. On the other hand, the document warns against exerting physical pressure to reach the goal of the campaign. Is there an implied double meaning, or does the document reflect the complex way in which the tsar himself viewed the issue? We have already mentioned that the British missionary Lewis Weill[11] tried to persuade the tsar that pressure should not be used when converting Jews. Moreover, had this directive really called for unrestrained coercion, it is doubtful whether there would have been a need to emphasize persuasion, and to select priests skilled in this art of persuasion.

---

10 Ginzburg, "Mucheniki-deti," 55, correspondence between Chernyshev and Protasov.
11 See above, 56.

It is interesting that this is the first time we find the minister of defense's direct involvement in the issue of the cantonists, in general, and in that of conversion, in particular. Chernyshev also details the institutions and the number of cadets in each, in a document that has great potential for research:

List of institutions with the number of Jewish cantonists already there, or supposed to arrive, March 1, 1843:[12]

Institution	No. present	No. expected	Total no. of soldiers
Carabiniers training unit #2	12	263	5000
Carabiniers training unit #3	–	293	5000
Carabiniers training unit #4	–	109	5000
Arkhangel'sk half-battalion	43	91	1000
Pskov half-battalion	103	83	1000
Kyiv battalion	6	–	1000
Novogrudok	–	195	1000
Revel' half-battalion	19	140	1000
Kazan' battalion	1762	–	2000
Perm' battalions	629	–	2000
Saratov battalions	326	–	2000
Simbirsk battalion	93	–	1000
Orenburg battalion	1071	–	2000
Troitsk half-battalion	83	–	1000
Ural'sk battalion	65	–	1000
Omsk battalion	9	250	1000
Tobol'sk half-battalion	18	100	1000
Irkutsk	10	–	1000
Tomsk	29	150	1000
Voronezh battalion	353	271	1000
Astrakhan' regiment	–	158	1000
Krasnoiarsk regiment	8	–	1000
Total		6753	36000

---

12   Ginzburg, "Mucheniki-deti," 55, Chernyshev's letter to Protasov, April 29, 1843.

This list mentions a total of twenty-two institutions, of which three are infantry training units, nine are battalions, six are half-battalions, and are two regiments. In all the units, there were 6,753 Jewish cadets between the ages of twelve and eighteen. Namely, there were seven age groups, so that, of an average of a thousand men, there were about fifteen percent Jewish conscripts out of all conscripted minors. This percentage is seven times higher than the percentage of Jews in the empire.

If we calculate the number of those expected to arrive at the different units, it appears that, according to plan, 2,222 boys were expected to arrive during the conscription year of 1843, whereas in fact only 1,300 were drafted. The difference can be explained by the fact that cantonists who transferred from one place to another were included in the total amount.

The amount of the cantonists was not equal in each unit, and it is difficult to find a criterion for placement. The Arkhangel'sk half-battalion that transferred two hundred cantonists for regular service in 1855, included only about forty in 1843, meaning that the number of cantonists in the units was not fixed. Although in the Jewish area of Kyiv we find no more than eight boys, in Voronezh, located near the Pale of Settlement, there were relatively a lot of boys, and in the areas furthest away, such as in Krasnoiarsk or Tomsk, there were very few. We hear of "success" in conversions in Saratov, but it appears that there was a relatively small number of cantonists there. In contrast, in Kazan' there were 1,1762 boys, and in Orenburg, which hardly appears in the church reports, there were 1071.

It is not clear how 1,762 cantonists served in Kazan', when a battalion consists of only 2,000 soldiers. Moreover, it is unclear why such a large number of Jews were concentrated in one location, a fact that certainly did not help the conversion efforts. Could there be a mistake in the list?

In his letter to the Holy Synod, Chernyshev notes that there were only twenty-nine priests appointed to teach religion in all units from the list, which equals one priest for every 200 cadets. This miniscule number is surprising. Can one man possibly implement the general conversion plans (and that is without calculating the other 30,000 cadets who also studied their Christian religion)?

On May 3, 1843, following the tsar's order, Protasov ordered the senior chaplains of the navy and the army "to reconsider the qualifications of the priests attached to the cantonist units. When necessary, they must be replaced or posts added in the event of a shortage. All of this must be immediately reported to the Synod." At the same time, an order was given to the Katovich to issue detailed instructions for the activities of the aforementioned priests. The speed with which he fulfilled his order shows that the issue of conversion was assigned top priority at the time. Already in October 1843, Katovich submitted a twenty-five-page booklet titled "Guidelines for the clergy of military institutions regarding bringing Jewish cadets to convert to Christianity." After studying it for two weeks, Nicholas noted that "the guidelines are very correct and well written. We express our admiration for the author." In January 1844, the booklet was printed in many copies on high-quality white paper and sent to the cantonist institutions.[13]

Among other things, Protasov wrote that, when being persuaded, "the children might claim that they want to remain Jews through loyalty to their fathers' and forefathers' religion, and that in converting they would be severely hurting their fathers' feelings, and these would curse them." Loyalty to their family, especially to their fathers, seems to have been the biggest obstacle in the missionary activity to convert the children. This is mentioned also in the Arkhangel'sk documents, where one of the interrogated sailors claims that the sailor Artemii Malamud was among the instigators of those who denied the truth of Christianity, as his father was a rabbi and had made his son swear that he would not convert. This was also the plea of mothers to their children at the time of parting, something that was deeply engraved on the children's hearts.

On January 4, 1844, Chernyshev told Protasov about the successful conversion of forty-eight cantonists in Tobol'sk:

> His Majesty was deeply impressed by the fact that the archbishop of Tobol'sk succeeded in converting forty-eight cantonists from the Tobol'sk half-battalion. The tsar said that he would be even happier if, in the rest of the church territories, the archbishops would also achieve the same success in converting Jewish children to the Orthodox religion.

In 1845, the tsar awarded badges of appreciation to the priests of the battalions in Perm' and Saratov, Danchevsky and Sofronov, for their efficiency in converting cantonists.

Among the evidence of mass baptism that Ginzburg found in the archives of the military and the Synod immediately after the 1917 Bolshevik Revolution, before they were locked away for decades, is a list of conversion "successes" in cantonist institutions:

---

13   Ginzburg, "Mucheniki-deti," 57.

1843	Arkhangel'sk	125 Jewish children and teenagers
1843	Voronezh	567
1845	Saratov	130
1844	Tobol'sk	48
1845 (July 3)	Perm'	95
1845 (July 13)	Perm'	171 (a total of 613 minors were converted in 1840–1843)
1851	Sychevka	41 cadet minors
1853	Saratov	134
1854	Saratov	223

All in all, there were 3,000 "successes" during the ten years of coercion, 1843–1854. Because of the relative rarity of "bombastic" reports, we assume that these were acts staged for reporting and display, like Potemkin's colonies,[14] and the real achievements were not so amazing. Otherwise, it is impossible to explain the tsar's constant demands to increase the efforts, and the attempts of the clergy to explain the slowness of conversion with objective reasons, such as the boys' connection with the Jewish community or with their families.

It can be assumed that between 1843 and 1846 top priority was given to religious conversion, subject to Uvarov's new project of reforming the Jews by making them "civil[ized] in the shadow of the cross,"[15] but the tsar did not busy himself with this continuously over the years. The issue had its ups and downs according to circumstances.

In most of the reports dealing with missionary activity, the names of the Chernyshev and Protasov, appear. Protasov's activity in turning the Church into a state institution similar to a government office is well known. He is also famous for persecuting Staroobriadtsy (Old Believers). In our opinion, this connection is not accidental: it shows a symbiosis of two ambitious officials who flattered the tsar. Chernyshev enjoyed a certain period of closeness to the tsar, and that is probably what stimulated him in converting the cantonists.

---

14 In the eighteenth century, Prince Potemkin would create fake buildings in order to impress Catherine the Great who travelled through the area to check how fast the colonies he had committed to building were being constructed. These fake buildings are known in literature as symbols of an impressive facade or show designed to hide an undesirable fact or condition.

15 Levanda, *Sbornik zakonov*, 233–234.

2

Punishment and Pressure as Means of Coercion

Documents testify to a deliberate and guided policy of applying targeted punishment for the sake of religious conversion. Archbishop Vladimir wrote the following to Count Protasov on November 21, 1848:

> Converts should be given extra benefits compared to those who refuse in order to influence them to change their position. For this purpose, a monetary grant should be given to a converted cantonist. Although it is not so ethical, considering the reality, such a step should be allowed.[1]

It should be noted that the Church also saw an ethical problem in monetary temptation to convert. Thus, in practice, the conversion of Jewish boys was irregular even in the eyes of the priests.

The Archbishop of Arkhangel'sk, Father Georgii, testifies in his letter to Count Protasov that converts were openly treated more leniently. There were also additional means of punishment and coercion that have not yet been highlighted: harassment and transferring those who refused from one institution to another.[2] Moisy Spiegel wrote[3] that he was given light punishments for routine transgressions in kitchen chores and duties in the commanders' homes.

Israel Leib Itzkovitz, who served in Arkhangel'sk from 1853, relates that in regiment 2 there was a Jewish apostate by the name of Evgraf Gulevich. Every evening, when Gulevich was lying on his bed, Itzkovitz would bring several children to him. Gulevich used to make the children kneel down, and he tried to

---

1   Ginzburg, "Mucheniki-deti," 75.
2   Ibid.
3   Spiegel, "Zapiski kantonista," 249.

convince them that Jesus is the "true redeemer" using biblical citations. He kept those who were not convinced next to his bed all night, continuously harassing them. Itzkovitz adds that many children agreed to convert as a result of this abuse. Children between the ages of twelve to fifteen resisted for longer and were beaten more. At the beginning of 1855, the entire half-battalion of Arkhangel'sk converted except for one seventeen- or eighteen-year-old boy. Before every midday meal they would flog him 100 times as he lay there wallowing in blood. After each flogging session, they would send him to the clinic, where he would be treated and then sent back to his unit.[4]

In that same half-battalion in Arkhangel'sk, sailors were interrogated when they were drafted into active service and complained that they had been forcibly converted. When asked about the details, Itzkovitz, who had converted in 1854 taking the name Aleksandr and was now eighteen, confessed that, when he was a cantonist, the commanders exerted heavy pressure on him that he convert. However, despite his having been coerced, he preferred to remain a Christian. The vast majority of those interrogated gave similar testimonies. However, Michael Beilin, who converted in the same year at the age of twenty-three, claimed that no one pressured them. Still, the final report of the military prosecutor to the Ministry of the Navy explicitly mentions that the commander did not only use persuasion, but also imposed the most severe penalties.[5]

Another sailor, Pavel Bocher, confessed that he was forced into converting by Podpolkovnik D'iakonov, and that he had agreed to convert when he realized he would not allowed to observe *mitzvot*. This admission is most important as it matches the forecast of the "expert" who recommended drafting the Jews, assuming that they would give in as a result of not being able to observe the precepts of their religion (see the files of the Third Section, quoted above, 34). Namely, it was not fear of punishment for not converting that caused Bocher to convert, but his inability to live a Jewish life.

All those interrogated testified that they arrived at the base with ritual articles—*tallit*, *tefillin*, and a prayer book—which were confiscated from those who were unable to hide them.

According to the document of May 20, 1856 that summarized the investigation in the Ministry of the Navy,[6] out of the 130 cantonists of the Arkhangel'sk

---

4 Itzkovitz, "Vospominaniia evreiskogo kantonista," 55–65.
5 Central Archives for the History of the Jewish People, HMF626, copy from Gosudarstvennyi arkhiv Rossiiskoi Federatsii [State archive of the Russian Federation111], f. 109, 1 eksp., op. 30, d. 340.
6 Ibid.

half-battalion who claimed that they had been forcibly converted, two testified that they had been deprived of food. One testified that a non-commissioned officer had fed him soap. Others testified that they had been flogged mercilessly. The document states that all the rest of those who complained were unable to describe specific instances of exertion of pressure.

On the other hand, Meir Merimzon relates, as cited at the beginning of this volume, that, when they arrived at a village, they were made to stand in rows for a roll call, and heaps of birch rods were placed in front of them, ready to beat them. They announced that whoever wanted to convert to Christianity should take one step forward. There were many children who, out of fright, took that step. "I said to myself, 'I'm the son of a *melamed* and the grandson of a rabbi; I will remain faithful to my father's Torah. If necessary, I will give up my life for *Kiddush Hashem*.' From then on, they began to make us suffer, but I will not go into details concerning stories of this, as these things are known."

We brought Merimzon's story in the first chapter, but here we should note that he does not tell which torture he bore as a result of his loyalty to Judaism. Merimzon here completely skips over the story of abuse. In contrast, he elaborates on the punishments he received in school, which were a result of his not knowing the Russian language, but not because of his refusal to convert. Paradoxically, Merimzon's story is quoted in many studies despite the fact that he does not go into details about his suffering.

Merimzon demonstrates literary skill in his narrative as well as an excellent memory for details and a tendency to elaborate. Therefore, the fact that he fails to describe the abuse he was victim of because of his loyalty to Torah demands explanation. Whatever the case may be, it is clear that these harassments were limited in time, otherwise how can it be explained that he was not punished at all for attacking a Christian boy, and even received support for this from his commanders? In addition, how was it that after he moved to new accommodation he "would walk to school happily," as he relates? Comparing his story with similar memoirs reveals that there were two periods in a cantonist's life—the period of acclimatization and that of routine life. The first period, although very hard, was short, and it was in this initial period that conversion attempts were usually concentrated. The second period was easier and, for some, even enjoyable.

Ginzburg[7] tells more stories of coercion. Children were forcibly baptized when they went to bathe in the river and the sergeant held their heads under water until they agreed to convert. One boy was put into a sack and thrown

---

7   Ginzburg, "Mucheniki-deti," 77, the report of the bishop of Saratov, November 9, 1853.

down a stairwell, and when he continued refusing to convert, they pulled the sack back up the stairs of the building. Cantonists told of being fed with salted fish and not being allowed to drink water until a consent to convert had been extorted from them. Evsei Greikopf wrote in his memoirs that he agreed to convert only after he was continuously beaten and forced to walk barefoot on coals. Vladimir Kaufman had needles stuck under his nails, etc.[8] There is a rumor that an entire regiment of cantonists drowned themselves when they were taken to be baptized in the river, but there are no authorized testimonies confirming it.[9] From the report of the conversion of the children in Kazan'[10] on the banks of the Volga, we understand that each child was accompanied to his baptism by at least one Christian ("godfather"), so it is difficult to imagine a simultaneous mass baptism.

---

8   Ibid.
9   Adina Ofek, "Cantonists: Jewish Children as Soldiers in Tsar Nicholas's Army," *Modern Judaism* 13, no. 3 (October 1993): 277–308.
10 Central Archives for the History of the Jewish People, HMF626, copy from Gosudarstvennyi arkhiv Rossiiskoi Federatsii [State archive of the Russian Federation], f. 109, 1 eksp., op. 30, d. 340.

3

Criminal Constitutional Law as a Means of Coercion

In our opinion, punishing those who refused to convert should be seen as a means of coercion and as a deterrent. An example is the persecution of the soldiers of the Arkhangel'sk half-battalion as an example. There is an ancient medieval Church law which forbids forcible conversion, but it also forbids reneging the conversion even if it was achieved by force. The state systems were also in need of some sort of law sanctioning punishment for refusal to convert, but no such law existed, at least regarding the Arkhangel'sk half-battalion. In an internal correspondence between the government ministries, found in the investigation files of the Arkhangel'sk cantonist revolt, there is indeed a proposal sent to the Ministry of the Navy for punishing the rebels, although its constitutional basis seems very weak.

> The amended criminal constitutional law states:
>
> ... Clause 184. Someone who condemns the Christian religion or the Orthodox Church in public, or criticizes the Holy Scriptures, will be sentenced to deprivation of civil rights and serving harsh labor for up to eight years. If there is no medical order to exempt him from flogging, he will be punished with flogging.
> And if he did not do this in public but with the purpose of harming the religious faith, the sentence is denial of civil rights and deportation to distant colonies.
> Clause 140. The soldiers of the navy and its institutions who speak heretically of the Christian religion will be sent for treatment and persuasion according to the laws of the Church.
> Clause 190. For the offense of verbal or other means of incitement to leave Christianity to become a Muslim, a Jew, or a member of any other religion,

> the sentence is denial of rights due to him by virtue of his social status and hard labor in army fortresses for a period of eight to ten years. If the offense was carried out violently, he will be sentenced to hard labor in the mines for a period of ten to fifteen years. . . .
>
> Clause 218. Whoever converted from Christianity and behaves in contradiction to the Church's instructions, but according to the customs of another religion, will be transferred to the ecclesiastical command for return to Christianity. . . .
>
> Clause 223. A person who desecrates the sacred bread or wine or abuses any sacred object will be sentenced to flogging, the negation of his rights according to his status, and harsh labor for life.

Although, ostensibly, not one of these transgressions was committed, the authorities decided to bring to trial two sailors—Faifer[1] and Alexander Vax—who were accused of spitting out the communion bread. In addition, sixty-four sailors were accused of negatively influencing others by remaining heretical regarding Christianity after "persuasion." The verdict stated: "They must be removed from the naval base at Kronshtadt [where they served after their studies in Arkhangel'sk] and dispersed among different units in remote areas. The clergy must continue trying to persuade them to return to Christianity and the commanders of the units must supervise them very closely."

The means of pressure used to achieve conversion were so varied that it seems there was not one uniform method of coercion or directed guidelines on the matter. Probably, it was often a local initiative stemming from the spirit of the imperial command to accelerate conversion. It seems that the methods of mass coercion were necessarily different from the improvisations of the uneducated junior officers.

---

1 No one saw him spit this out, but he confessed to his commander of having done so, and apparently also told his friends as proof that he did not want to convert. Thus he incriminated himself.

4

Group Dynamics

Podpolkovnik D'iakonov of the Arkhangel'sk half-battalion was creative beyond measure. He seems to have designed a method of group dynamics that included, first of all, a specific atmosphere. It was known to all, and the conscripts were told in advance, that everyone on that base would be baptized. The anticipation and the fear prepared the atmosphere for conversion. As soon as the cantonists entered the base, D'iakonov announced to the children that no one would leave there before being baptized, which broke their will to resist. This was especially noticeable in the story of the 1855 revolt. To drive his point home, he had the fresh recruits work together with apostates who had already despaired of their Judaism, and who convinced the youngsters by personal example that all resistance would be useless, and that the best thing would be to give in immediately. Artemii Malamud, who tried to commit suicide by jumping into a pit, was saved by his friends. They spoke to him saying that it was not worth his while committing suicide because of conversion (whereas every child knows that converting to Christianity is included in the precept of *yehareg ve'al ya'avor*—"Let him be killed rather than transgress," see above). We see in Terent'ev's trial[1] that the children who had converted would beat those who remained loyal to Judaism.

The non-commissioned officer Balkin (who later exerted pressure on the children) advised the boys to hide their ritual objects and take them out when they returned. Possibly, this advice misled the cantonists concerning the seriousness of their agreement to convert, which in fact was a point of no return. The cantonists hoped that it would be a passing episode and did not attribute much thought to it.

Thus, we see that a routine coercive framework was created, which used threats and beatings as part of the conversion method, but was actually well built on the basis of psychological manipulation. Its existence may explain the paradox presented above: according to the investigation files, those who resisted conversion could not name any concrete example of coercion.

---

1   See *Voskhod* 4 (1881): 45.

5

Conversion on the Way

The children were already exposed to pressure to convert at the beginning of their journey to the institution they were sent to. On the one hand, the convoy units were evidently not given the task of missionizing. One can assume that the lazy soldiers did not do more than the task to which they had been assigned—escorting the minors. On the other hand, due to the total lack of supervision of the superiors, precisely during transition the children were exposed to the brute force of the sergeants. The difficult conditions of the journey could have been used as a tool of missionary manipulation.[1] A harsh description of the dumping of the body of a boy who died from the hardships of the journey from Smolensk[2] raises the suspicion that there were also more gruesome attempts to break the boys' spirit if they showed resistance to conversion.

Indeed, in 1851 the bishop of Smolensk informed the Synod:

> I received a report from the priest of the church in the town of Sychevka, Petr Afonsky, of January this year. Before Christmas, a group of one hundred small children arrived in Sychevka on the way from Vilna to Perm' and stayed here for a rest of nine days. The escort of the assignment, the escort officer from the Vilna fortress, Loginov, who has the rank of sub-lieutenant, submitted his statement on December 23, 1850 to the effect that: Forty-one Jews freely expressed their desire to go through the conversion processes and to belong to the Orthodox world already when they were in Sychevka.... The priest Petr Afonsky baptized all forty-one in two groups, on December 27 and 30. The ceremonies were held in the church in the presence of the above officer, the mayor, civil and military officials,

---

1 See, for example, Herzen, *My Past and Thoughts*, 252–253.
2 Rossiiskii gosudarstvennyi voenno-istoricheskii arkhiv [Russian state archive of military history], f. 405, d. 8692.

> and the town residents. Father Petr adds that the enthusiastic religious zealousness of the escort officer ensured that the children already know Christian prayers, some of them on a superior level....[3]

This report raises several questions. First, how could children who did not speak Russian learn the Christian prayers on a journey of a few months (see, for example, Merimzon's memories of his efforts to learn Russian, and the difficulties he met)? Furthermore, why didn't the other fifty-eight children convert? The fact that the report tells that all one hundred children were drafted in one location, a fact which shows that the authorities were not afraid to concentrate large numbers of Jews in one unit. One might assume that there was a group of children who were raised in different circumstances and perhaps knew Russian because they belonged to a different social class.

---

3   Ginzburg, "Mucheniki-deti," 64.

6

Incentives

Aside from physically abusing those who refused to convert to Christianity, the church always used various incentives to convert. The cheapest type was granting a reduced sentence, another type was monetary.

Father Vladimir, the bishop of Tobol'sk, wrote on November 21, 1844:

> The converts should be granted benefits in contrast to those who refuse, so that the latter will learn a lesson from the benefits, and request to be converted of their own accord. Monetary grants should also be distributed. **Although it is not so ethical** (!), it is beneficial for the purpose and can be permitted. (The bold is mine, Y.M.)

This is also the opinion of the archbishop of Saratov, Iakov, who suggested that, beyond the twenty-five gold rubles given as a grant for conversion, another twenty-five rubles was to paid to the one baptizing priest (letter to Protasov, December 18, 1844).[1]

As there seem to have been different suggestions as to the amount of the grant, in his last year, Nicholas I issued a personal directive:

> **To be distributed by the Inspection Division of the Ministry of the Navy**
>
> It has already been determined by the tsar (in 1847)[2] concerning the subordinates of the infantry as follows: The Jewish subordinates who enter

---

1   Ginzburg, "Mucheniki-deti," 64.
2   Levanda, *Sbornik zakonov*, 674 (no. 566).

> Orthodox religion will be awarded seven rubles and fifteen kopecks. His Majesty is pleased to copy this regulation for the naval offices.
>
> August 1854[3]

Thus, the officially sanctioned amount was much less than suggested and used previously. However, it is likely that those who converted benefited from grants from additional sources, such as the Synod itself, or the local church which took care of funding the convert's expenses "for changing his lifestyle."

---

3 Ibid., 831 (no. 724).

7

Participation in Christian Rituals

As one of the effective ways of encouraging conversion, the army forced the Jewish boys to participate in Christian rituals even before conversion. This was done under the pretense of mandatory participation in lessons on the Christian faith, which were part of the curriculum of the cantonist school. Even morning prayers were considered part of the day's routine, and disrupting the order of the day was followed by severe punishment. This was a simple but sophisticated means, intended to get the Jewish boys used to Christian rites and to remove the fear of the unknown. Christian morning prayers are very simple and do not demand real participation. Thus, the resistance threshold was lowered.

It was common practice for the priest to preach to the boys. The sermons were based on Christian sources. In addition, there were special sermons for the Jews. During the course of the sermon, the priest tried to convince the boys, quoting the Jewish Bible, that Christianity is based on the Torah and the words of the prophets of Israel. It is unclear whether the boys, who were trained to learn Torah in Hebrew, were able to connect the priest's words with what they had absorbed at home. In addition, at first the boys were not fluent in Russian, and certainly not in Church Slavonic, which is used for Orthodox prayers and is very different from spoken Russian.

Before their conscription, the boys had been raised to keep a distance from Christianity, and to regard it as unacceptable idol worship. They had learned that it was forbidden to eat with Christians and enter their churches—it was even customary to spit when passing one. Sermons given by a priest or any other preacher unfamiliar with the Jewish methods of Torah learning would have undoubtedly aroused repulsion on the part of the Jewish cantonists. Therefore, the effect of such an attempt at persuasion was almost nil, and the main influence that came from the Jews' participation in the sermons was the fact that they were sitting together with the Christians, so that the topic of conversion became a matter of routine.

The archbishop of Tomsk, Father Afanasii, wrote to Protasov that he was trying to get the cantonists to convert "by allowing them to take part in religious ceremonies that I conduct."[1] Thus, the Jewish children had the "great privilege" of hearing the ceremonies performed by the hypocritical Afanasii, who describes his coercion as an honor.

Besides getting the children used to Christian rituals, the priests also tried to impress the cadets by showing them the splendor of the churches. The archbishop of Perm', Arkadii, wrote to Protasov in 1844 that "the cantonists from the Perm' battalion are taken to church ceremonies specific to the holidays.[2] The sacred aura of the churches, the ceremonies conducted in an atmosphere of festivity and grandeur, cannot but make a deep impression of the hearts of the cantonists."

The Perm' battalion commander instituted Christian prayers with the cadets' choir several times a day: in the morning; before studies started; after the studies; before the midday meal; after the midday meal; and in the evening:

> To preserve order,[3] Jewish cadets were also present during prayers... and similarly, for the sake of order, Jewish cadets were present together with Christians in lessons of religion. They listened to the explanations of the Christian Orthodox religion and for homework learned the tenets of the religion by heart.[4]

Rebinder, from the cantonist institution in Smolensk, reported in the same spirit. He was sent to check whether it was true that pressure was being exerted on the children. He reported that the children did not complain of this. However, he admitted that they were forced to pray according to the Greek Orthodox custom. He presented this as being legitimate, and in his opinion, this did not constitute religious coercion.[5]

---

1   Ginzburg, "Mucheniki-deti," 74.
2   Ginsburg, *Historishe Verke*, vol. 3, from the Synod documents.
3   This is a classic example of ambiguity when it came to implementing coercion.
4   Ginzburg, "Mucheniki-deti," 74; Ginsburg, *Historishe Verke*, vol. 3, 377–416.
5   Central Archives for the History of the Jewish People, HMF759, copy from Gosudarstvennyi arkhiv Rossiiskoi Federatsii [State archive of the Russian Federation], f. 109, 1 eksp, d. 330.

When a directive was received not to exert physical force, the inventive clergy looked for alternative methods, but they found nothing better than coercion. The obligation to participate in the church ceremonies was accompanied by the threat of punishment for "not adhering to order and to the timetable, lack of diligence in studies, etc."[6] Namely, at the end of every effort to persuade "gently," there were always floggings under the guise of preserving order. Klinger[7] was flogged for his refusal to participate in morning prayers, but the punishment seems to have been bearable, or maybe the torturers did not persevere with him.

There was no absolute obligation to convert. Spiegel writes[8] that he took part in the prayers in the cantonist institution in Irkutsk where he served, but he did not convert. Moreover, he stood out for his good voice when singing Christian prayers, and the local priest showed off the child's talents in front of visitors. Spiegel's internal life seems not to have been harmed, and he was capable of singing hymns for Jesus while remaining faithful to Judaism. The question is whether the majority of the children were as immune as he was, capable of withstanding such a situation of split personality.

As related above, Spiegel was even invited to the priest's home for a heart-to-heart talk. However, in the majority of cases, the clergy did not make do with an invitation. They forcibly brought the cadets to religious lessons.[9] For example, in Omsk, the priest would assemble the Jewish cadets in the church every Sunday and deliver a sermon on Christianity specially for them. The metropolitan of St. Petersburg, Kutnevich, instructed the spiritual educator of the Revel' battalion as follows:

> Because, according to the instructions of the military authorities, the Jewish cantonists are to participate in lessons on faith together with the Orthodox cadets, the teacher should not satisfy himself with giving explanations to the Christians. He must incorporate in his sermon ideas directed at the Jews, and sometimes even initiate a direct appeal to the Jewish cadets.

---

6   *Evreiskaia starina* 2 (1909): 115.
7   Grigor'ev, *Berko the Cantonist*, 26.
8   Spiegel, "Rasskaz starogo soldata," 249–259.
9   As an aside: precedents of forcing Jews to listen to Christian sermons are found in Western Europe from the Late Middle Ages.

As this was written in 1844, we can assume that Kutnevich had carefully studied all the reports of priests' progress in conversion, and had summarized their various experiences. It is interesting that he points to the military authorities as the ones who insisted on the Jewish boys being present in the lessons.

The content of such a sermon is presented in the report of archbishop of Perm', Arkadii, to Protasov. Arkadii relates that the cantonists were taken in groups each evening to the commander's home, where a priest presented to them the advantages of Christianity based on evidence of how it spread throughout the world.[10] He stressed its purity and superiority over all other religions. The priest proved to the cadets, not through hatred but through Christian love, the falsehood of Judaism, which is based on the Talmud and stems from the rabbis' lack of comprehension and from popular distorted opinions among the Jews. The influence of the talk was strengthened by the commander's active participation.[11]

We are talking here of sophisticated social religious activity. The cadets would be taken to the commander's home to create a warm family setting, away from the harsh atmosphere of the barracks. Tea and refreshments were probably also served. The lecturer prepared his sermon in advance. It had to include historical evidence of Christianity's spreading throughout the world, probably with the aim of demonstrating how Judaism has remained the religion of one nation in contrast to Christianity, as well as an analysis of the state of the Jewish people and the behavior of the rabbis. He also presented Christianity's values such as love of one's fellow man, Christian morality, preaching forgiveness, etc., and contrasted them with Jewish values. This was very difficult for the clergy because, although they had studied their Old Testament, they did not know the Jewish interpretation of, and commentaries on, the Torah. They had no idea of the Mishna and Talmud from the Jewish perspective, and so could give no adequate picture of Jewish values. The commander's participation in the discussion helped to create an ambience of trust and closeness, making it difficult for the cadet to persist in his obstinacy in the face of the friendly atmosphere in the house. Of course, the fear of opposing the commander's will also existed.

---

10   Here we penetrate their "laboratory" of persuasion. The Church's conclusive evidence of the truth of Christianity is its worldwide acceptance.
11   Ginsburg, *Historishe Verke*, vol. 3, from the Synod documents.

8

Missionary Instructional Literature

The missionizers repeatedly reported to their superiors that the Jews were more learned than they were, and therefore it was impossible to convince them. They felt helpless, and demanded that they be equipped with the relevant knowledge and written material concerning the preferability of Christianity.

As mentioned, Ginsburg writes[1] that the tsar would add personal comments on reports of the number of converts: In April 1843, he wrote "very few"; in June, "miniscule progress";[2] and in July, when only twenty-five cantonists converted, the tsar commented to Protasov that the clergy responsible had to be rebuked. At the same time, the Minister of Defense wrote to Protasov that the tsar demanded an increase in the number of priests in the cantonist battalions. He also ordered to prepare explicit guidelines for missionary work.[3] In accordance with this demand, in October 1843, Kutnevich, the head chaplain of the army, issued a document[4] from which one can deduce that the main point in the art of persuasion was to prove the superiority of Christianity based on the tenets common to both religions.

In our opinion, questions must be asked about the very need for written material: Does this testify to the beginning of a new operation, or a change from conversion through coercion to conversion through persuasion? If so, what caused the change in policy? Was it the failures of physical coercion, pressure from Jews, international pressure, or other factors?

---

1 Ibid., 68–69.
2 Ibid., 68–69; Rossiiskii gosudarstvennyi voenno-istoricheskii arkhiv [Russian state archive of military history], f. 405, op. 5, d. 7371.
3 Ginsburg, *Historishe Verke*, vol. 3, 68–69, Rossiiskii gosudarstvennyi voenno-istoricheskii arkhiv [Russian state archive of military history], f. 405, op. 5, d. 7370, ll. 8–31.
4 Ginsburg, *Historishe Verke*, vol. 3, 68–69; Ginzburg, "Mucheniki-deti," 47.

The guidelines for the missionizers provide decisive proof of a strategy of conversion, although forced conversion was not mentioned. They state that there had to be a missionizing priest in each cantonist school. We would have expected to find in the document guidelines for cooperation with the army, and the division of tasks between the army and the church. However, there is no mention of any such division, except for a statement, according to which the army can help in the conversion if the priest has reasonable relations with the army. From here we understand that if such relations did not exist, the army would not help missionizing. Instead, the document proclaims that conversion depends on divine kindness, and therefore the task should be approached with deep religious zealousness. The priest should continuously pray for blessing and success in his deeds. In addition, the priest may not interfere with matters of the local authority, may not pay attention to the commanders' lifestyle, and must avoid all conflict with the authorities. These warnings testify to the existing tension between the priests and the military authorities, showing that the relations between the priests and the officers were unstable. Evidently, the clergy repeatedly condemned the officers in the schools for acts of corruption and drunkenness. Moreover, the priests were only asked to avoid clashes with the military, but not to support them, so one cannot expect any fruitful cooperation or successful division of roles between the priests and the army commanders. This seems even more amazing because it appears from various cantonist testimonies that the army occupied a key position in all coercive activity for religious conversion. This is also the impression given by Father Afanasii's report[5] that the preaching meetings were held in the commander's home, and the commander, who had no religious training, played a significant role in exerting pressure on the youth.

---

5 Ginsburg, *Historishe Verke*, vol. 3, 74.

9

Supervision of Conversion Methods

No documents have been found indicating that Nicholas I issued a direct order, either orally or in writing, to force the Jewish boys to convert.[1] If no order for forcible conversion was given, it might mean that the tsar was cut off from reality and did not receive a reliable report. This assumption is hardly reasonable, considering the customary absolute obedience to the tsar's orders, and the fear of punishment. So, even if the order was indeed not given, the tsar could have dropped hints that would have been understood by his advisors and ministers. There might also have been an oral directive that was not written down, as it was contrary to the law.

I tend to believe the second possibility. The tsar did not need to say everything. At the same time, the tacit agreement gave the authorities the option not to give freedom of action to the officials on the ground, a freedom that also had the potential to endanger monarchical rule. It can therefore be understood why, while accelerating the conversion processes at Protasov's command, warning was repeatedly given to the senior ranks of the church to avoid physical coercion.

The archbishop of Perm', Arkadii, complained to Protasov in his letter of September 8, 1845, that, although 171 out of 179 cantonists agreed to convert within two weeks of arriving in Perm', their battalion priests were too hasty in bringing boys to convert. He wrote as follows: "From the speed with which these boys converted, it cannot be said that the converts knew enough about Christian concepts at the time of their conversion." In other words, the archbishop was doubtful as to the propriety of the baptism, although he did find a loophole for its validity in that conversion "is not only performed by man, but by

---

1   Rossiiskii gosudarstvennyi voenno-istoricheskii arkhiv [Russian state archive of military history], f. 405, op. 5, d. 7371.

the will of God, and therefore the baptism is valid."[2] Still, it is clear that in his opinion there was no true justification for this type of conversion. His reaction shows that there was tension between the Church and the military clergy. The former did not look favorably on the dizzying speed of the baptisms, and was surprised by it, even though it could not oppose it.

Since it cannot be assumed that the military clergy here used means that were out of the ordinary in the Russian army, the phenomenon of such quick agreement of the Jews requires further study. We find a similar precedent in the file of the revolt of the graduates of the Arkhangel'sk battalion, where, within a short time, young men between the ages of eighteen and twenty agreed to convert.

The authorities' opposition to unusually harsh physical coercion to convert is evident in the 1844 decision to remove Father Smirnov, a teacher in the cantonist battalion of Simbirsk, for exerting physical force. Criticism of similar activity appears in the report of the military prosecution department of the Ministry of the Navy on the activities of Podpolkovnik D'iakonov:

> ... Nevertheless, in summary of the testimonies of Jews who converted, it can be concluded that their conversion did not stem only from having been convinced with love, rather, coercive measures were used by imposing unnecessarily severe punishments. These deeds are in opposition to the government's wishes, and the results are harmful.
>
> Signed: General of the prosecution corps, Prince Golitsyn.[3]

This assessment was given after the death of Nicholas I, but similar statements are found in the directives issued by Nicholas himself; for example in the 1843 order for the mass conversion of cantonists: "... and one must act with utmost care, out of love and without applying pressure."

It is unclear whether one can see in these specific cases an expression of government policy to prevent coercion. If there had been such a policy, the government would have removed dozens of priests from their positions, not just Smirnov. In any case, the very need of a brutal officer like D'iakonov for strict methods of punishment, and the creation of mass psychological distress through sophisticated methods adopted by the priests, indicate that the government wanted to

---

2   Ginzburg, "Mucheniki-deti," 79.
3   The Central Archives for the History of the Jewish People, HMF626.

carry out the plan with full vigor and out of religious fanaticism, but with as little effort as possible and without too much noise.

It is interesting to bring here the memories of the cantonist Yaakov Hermanovitz.[4] He was conscripted in 1847, at the time of the conversion campaign, as the son of a prisoner sent to the military colonies in Siberia, and was sent to serve in the Irkutsk half-battalion that was notorious for its cruel coercion. Yaakov tells, for example, that he was fed salted fish without the possibility of drinking, that a child was "crucified" between two bunk beds, that a boy was thrown down a stairwell inside a mattress cover, and that forced baptism occurred when the unit was by the river. Therefore, it is particularly surprising to hear from him that the "obstinate" children were invited to the dean of the college for priests, Father Petukhov. The priest, who was responsible for guiding the novices of the clergy and was probably the highest spiritual authority in the city, asked them:

> "Don't you want to become Christians?"
>
> "No, no. We want to remain Jewish like our fathers and forefathers."
>
> "Then that is what you will do—you will remain Jewish, and may the God of Israel be with you." [According to Hermanovitz, he was not speaking scornfully.]

Among the institutions charged with examining this matter was the Third Section of the Tsar's Own Chancellery, headed by Count Benkendorf. It seems that the matter was important to Nicholas, and it was no coincidence that he assigned the responsibility for this to his political police force. For this purpose, Benkendorf combined the positions of the head of political intelligence and the commander of the military police, the Gendarmerie.

---

4   Published in *Evreiskaia starina* 2 (1909): 116–119.

10

The Jewish Boys' Resistance to Conversion

The obvious conclusion from the stories reviewed in the previous chapter is that the boys persevered beyond what was expected in dealing with the military system and did not convert. The tsarist plot failed, and one can understand Nicholas's anger. One of the assumptions that can be used to explain this conclusion, which is contrary to the common opinion, is that, due to the strong opposition of the boys, the conversion methods were not effective and the system was unable to implement them.

In this connection, Moisy Spiegel's testimony quoted at the beginning of this book is interesting. After many hardships, Spiegel was sent in 1853, at the age of nine, to the cantonist school in Tobol'sk, Siberia, a true wilderness. According to his narrative, despite the abuse that he experienced, he remained faithful to his Judaism. He tells how he was invited to the home of a local priest where he played with the children, who were his friends. The priest would then try to convince the stubborn Jewish boy to convert. According to Spiegel, all this was because the priest was obliged to report to his superiors that the cantonists converted from their own free will.

What is new in this story is the relationship between the clergy and the child—one of love and tolerance. Thus, we assume that conversion was the result of the boys' free will, and Spiegel freely did not agree to convert, even though he was only ten years old, completely under the control of gentiles, and far away from any inhabited area. But what is most important is Spiegel's statement that the priests had to report of voluntary conversion, and that they made an effort to ensure that their report was trustworthy. At the same time, we cannot know whether the reason Spiegel gives for his visits to the priest's home reflect his knowledge at the time, or whether it is the product of his rationalization when writing his memoirs.

Berko Klinger[1] also tell of his visits to his commander's home in his memoirs. It is true that his book does not tell of visits for the sake of persuasion—Berko had to help the commander of the city fortress, a major-general, with astronomical calculations. As in Spiegel's case, here, too, a minor refused to convert. But, in contrast to Spiegel, he also refused to participate in the Christian prayers, something that did not disturb the friendly relationship between him and the general. Klinger relates that, for every refusal to participate in the prayers, he was flogged ten times, but he did not give in. One can assume that this punishment was not meted out to him uniformly throughout the years. The additional punishment of standing guard under a heavy load ended with him fainting, but his commanders did not punish him again once he returned from the hospital.

Researchers generally pay attention to the number of converts among the cantonists. In our opinion, the number of those who refused should also be noted. It is likely that there were more of those who refused than those who converted (two-thirds vs. one-third, according to Gessen).[2]

The fate of those who did not convert is illustrated by Moisy Spiegel who progressed well from one class to the next and was presented to the other cantonists as a good example. Berko Klinger, who also remained Jewish, was later promoted to an important commanding position and served as a military topographer. During his schooling, Klinger was appointed as the class mentor in arithmetic, in what must have been a hostile environment for a stubborn child. Israel Leib Itzkovitz testifies[3] that during training for military service the children were beaten by their mentors, who were the same age as they were. The question of how long it took till a recruit acclimatized to the new conditions was not usually examined, but one can assume that it could not have taken long, just several months. After the natural period of acclimatization, the boys formed bands, which helped protect them from violence, at least of the mentors.

From correspondence at the end of 1853 between naval medical institutions and the supervisory department concerning granting privileges to combat medics from among the cantonists,[4] it appears that already in 1829, two years after the implementation of the conscription law, three cantonists from the Kyiv half-battalion (known as a harsh place), who had not converted, were sent

---

1 It seems as though the memories of adults are also not exact. People of their generation, who were familiar with the reality of the time, did not see anything unusual in this.
2 Petrovsky-Shtern, *Jews in the Russian Army*, 168.
3 Itzkovitz, "Vospominaniia evreiskogo kantonista," 55–65.
4 The Central Archives for the History of the Jewish People, HM2\8282/32, copy from Rossiiskii gosudarstvennyi arkhiv voenno-morskogo flota [Russian state archive of military sea navy], f. 223, op. 2.

for training as medics. In 1836, seven cantonists who had remained faithful to Judaism, were sent for training to the navy, considered a most prestigious corps. The same document mentions a similar phenomenon in the infantry. We mentioned above Major Herzl Tzam, who refused to convert, yet was promoted, and Aaron Olshansky, who served as a company sergeant major in an elite unit of the tsar's personal guards and was buried with a full military ceremony, escorted by officers of the guard.

Thus, we understand that the order to continuously persecute those who refused to convert was not consistent and did not exist at all times. Those who stood their ground were able to gain recognition of their status.

Chaim Merimzon relates that, on the journey to the institution, he and his friend decided that they would die rather than convert, but Merimzon was lucky and did not need special self-sacrifice. However, there is no doubt that many Jewish boys died in their persistence not to betray their people. Halperin quotes the testimony of a Russian soldier by the name of Bakhmatov concerning a cantonist who refused to convert. After the boy was endlessly flogged, the commander made him stand as a sentry, loaded with weapons and equipment much heavier than he could bear. After hours of standing, the boy fainted and was taken to the hospital. The commander became convinced that this cantonist would not convert, and ceased his efforts.[5] A similar story appears in *Berko the Cantonist*, and in Moisy Spiegel's memoirs. In *Berko the Cantonist*, Grigor'ev describes a fifteen-year-old boy who refused to participate in the Christian prayers, and was beaten each day till he bled. He did not let out a sound while being flogged, making a great impression on all those present.

The story of the Arkhangel'sk half-battalion deserves special attention in this connection. Unusually, we have testimony from both sides: from the cantonists, the memoirs of Israel Leib Itzkovitz, and from the authorities, the documents from the Ministry of the Navy concerning the "heresy" of the sailors who had converted. It must be said that this half-battalion was unusual in that it was more successful than other institutions for conversions. The reason for this was a superficial implementation of conversion there: the boys were allowed to wait a year in the base and, when leaving it, to announce their renunciation of Christianity in an organized fashion. We shall discuss the coercion methods in the half-battalion separately. It is interesting that only a few of those who complained were able to pinpoint specific methods used against them to force them to convert. Itzkovitz, who converted, tells of events that happened to others, but does not tell of the circumstances that brought him to convert.

---

5   Y. Halperin, *Sefer ha-gevura*, vol. 2 (Tel Aviv: Am Oved, 1950).

Itzkovitz tells that Podpolkovnik D'iakonov, the commander of the half-battalion, died suddenly after having been summoned to an investigation of the circumstances of the outbreak of his cadets' renunciation of Christianity. This matches Klinger's story, in which commander of the half-battalion also dies after being accused of fraud, but not connected to this treatment of the Jewish cantonists. Klinger describes that the commander was panic-stricken before his death, to the extent that he came of his own accord to apologize to the children for his corruption and cruelty. It is very likely that D'iakonov was afraid of being accused of exerting pressure on the children to convert. The conclusion of the military prosecutor's investigation was that "D'iakonov used improper methods for conversion, which are not consistent with methods of persuasion from love." The military prosecutor of the Naval Ministry did not see any justification for these actions. This happened shortly after the death of Nicholas I, but there was still no sign of any change in the tsar's policy concerning the cantonists. although the prosecution department left some recommendations for improving the process of conversion.

Parenthetically, the reasons for abolishing the cantonist decree must be examined, and the source found for the government's insistence on this matter. As no special effort on the part of any Jewish entity is mentioned, we tend to assume that one of the causes for abolishing the decree was that it created a negative image of Russia in Europe. Perhaps the Christians themselves were not happy with this coerced baptizing at the end of the nineteenth century.

Whatever the case may be, in a file summarizing the interrogations of cantonists from Arkhangel'sk, there are unequivocal instructions to remove unsuitable people from the conversion efforts, and also not to immediately agree to the convert's request to be baptized, but to give him time to reconsider his steps. The recommendations can be attributed to the hypocrisy of the tsarist government system, but nevertheless, the need of the government to give unambiguous, relevant instructions cannot be denied.

Under conditions that characterized a huge empire, incapable of close supervision, and lacking operative communications, it is difficult to assume that there is no element of truth in these documents. The very existence of a framework for clergy within military academies does not need to be interpreted as evidence of a planned policy of conversion, both because the presence of clergy was determined in the general regulations, and because most of the cantonists in these schools were Christians. Religion was taught as part of the curriculum, and it cannot be claimed that the curriculum was created just for the sake of the Jewish children. It was the routine of life in the military dormitory and religious studies that created favorable conditions for assimilation.

Documents of Missionary Activity

First, we present a Church report from 1829:[1]

> On August 21 of this year, on the eve of the tsar's coronation, the Church of the Holy Virgin held a baptism ceremony for twenty Jewish boys out of 280 boys who arrived from the district of Kiev. These boys came from the military cantonist battalion of Kazan'. After the great effort and positive treatment of the battalion's commander, Lieutenant Koltovsky, the Jews requested to adopt the Orthodox Christian religion. They therefore received instruction from the educator, the priest Simon Smirnov and, within a short time, after his explanations of the gospel, they were convinced of the truth of our religion. Since then they have been waiting with sacred enthusiasm to merit the title of Christians. All the participants in the ceremony shed tears of joy and excitement as the priest recited a prayer and words of ethics. The new members of the church, worthy of a new homeland, gestured in a sign of denigration and negation of their previous, inferior faith. They took an oath to be eternally loyal to Christianity and to His Imperial Highness. The entire congregation recited a prayer for our new brethren.
>
> The archbishop of Kazan' and Samara, the holy Filaret, the civil governor, the retired Artillery Major-General Dolgin, and the nobleman Kammerjunker Musin-Pushkin were the godfathers. On the very grand day of His Majesty's coronation, in the great church of Kazan', in the presence of citizens faithful to the tsar and the homeland, twenty cantonist converts

---

[1] Central Archives for the History of the Jewish People, RU349, copy from Gosudarstvennyi arkhiv Rossiiskoi Federatsii [State archive of the Russian Federation], f. 109, 1 eksp., d. 335.

> became worthy of partaking the holy communion from the hands of the archbishop, the holy Filaret. At the conclusion, the archbishop conducted the holy liturgy.
>
> The number of Jewish cantonists requesting to join the Church increases daily. Another forty are impatiently waiting to be called Christians.
>
> Signed: [name cannot be deciphered], August 1829

According to this document, two hundred and eighty boys from Kyiv were transferred to a provincial area on the banks of the Volga. This number constitutes about twenty percent of the conscripted Jewish boys who came from Kyiv. The authorities were obviously not interested in sending the boys to many different bases. Instead, they were kept in a large group, a fact that must have made conversion difficult. This begs the question: How did the government benefit from concentrating the Jewish boys in one location? Probably it was hoped that the converts would influence their friends.

As the draft took place in the winter, more than six months passed from the time of recruitment until conversion. We can assume that this time was needed to acclimatize to the new conditions, after which the chances of conversion gradually decreased.

Twenty boys constitute about ten percent of all the cantonists in Kazan'. An additional forty, another twenty percent. This percentage matches our hypothesis of the extent of success in converting the cantonists according to the figures of the Holy Synod and the Ministry of Defense.

The process of conversion was gradual. There was opposition and not all the boys were prepared to be baptized. Conversion took place in stages, starting with the easy cases and continuing with the more difficult ones. The Church had to invest a lot of effort in order to get to twenty boys within six months.

The organizers of the ceremony were not concerned that there might be a sudden outburst on the part of the boys, such as weeping or physical resistance, or demonstrative refusal to take part in the mass. Had they feared this, they would not have conducted such a public ceremony, especially on the anniversary of the tsar's coronation. The chosen date shows that conversion was considered a way of fulfilling the tsar's wishes. This whole ritual event was supposed to be a source of official joy and pride, to the extent that only members of the nobility were honored by being the converts' godfathers. It should be noted that Musin-Pushkin, one of those mentioned in this description, was considered to be a liberal and progressive member of Russian nobility.

As a side note, it is important to mention that we are talking here about military cantonists. It appears from the certificates in the Central Archives for the History of the Jewish People in Jerusalem that there were also cantonists of a different kind, as we detailed at the beginning of the book.

A similar document was written sixteen years later. On June 1, 1845, the secretary of the church management in Saratov wrote:[2]

> It is an exemplary sign and a special blessing of God that all the Jews in the Saratov battalions converted to Christianity. Festive prayers were held in the main church. At the end of the prayers a mass procession with crosses and icons was held on the way to the cantonist institute.

On November 9, 1845, the archbishop of Saratov, Father Afanasii, reported:

> On the day of the descent of the Holy Spirit, Jesus desired the conversion of 134 cantonist Jews to Christianity. On that day, they were baptized by the church in the Volga River with great rejoicing.[3]

Another report of a mass conversion comes from earlier that year:

> Perm', July 28, 1845
>
> ... At nine o' clock in the morning, in the Church of the Virgin, before a crowd of people, the baptism of ninety-five Jews was conducted by four bishops and five priests. For the Christian believer it was an uplifting sight to see how nine priests led the ninety-five converts, and together with them godmothers and godfathers all holding a candle in one hand and crossing themselves with the other. The entire ceremony was accompanied by joyous hymns sung by two choirs—that of the church and that of the army.[4]

---

2   Ginzburg, "Mucheniki-deti," 76–78.
3   Ibid.
4   Ibid.

From these enthusiastic descriptions we see that the Orthodox believers saw a deep meaning in the baptism of Jews—a ritualistic act of divine service. This excitement probably continued to affect the believers even after the ceremony and was instrumental in their continuous quest to capture Jewish souls.

> **Third Section of His Imperial Majesty's Own Chancellery**[5]
>
> **September 6, 1830–February 13, 1831**
>
> **File no. 1270**
>
> Admiral Breig's recommendation for an increased grant of forty rubles to a Jew who would agree to convert to Christianity is hereby accepted.
>
> **The tsar's personal directive**

Seventeen years later, a contradictory directive was issued, as though the tsar had forgotten his previous order:

> **Delivered on June 1, 1847 by the general on duty of the General Staff**[6]
>
> His Majesty ordered, on the recommendation of the commander of Infantry Division no. 1, to give soldier Putinsky, one of the Jews, the sum of fifteen silver kopecks on the occasion of accepting Christianity, and to determine a rule that Jewish soldiers who convert to Orthodox Christianity will receive a grant of this amount.[7]

---

5 Central Archives for the History of the Jewish People, HM2\8281/5, copy from from Rossiiskii gosudarstvennyi arkhiv voenno-morskogo flota [Russian state archive of military sea navy], f. 205, op. 1, d. 656.
6 Levanda, *Sbornik zakonov*, 674 (no. 566).
7 A much smaller sum than mentioned previously.

12

The Extent of Conversion

We learn of the extent of conversion from sources discovered by Ginzburg in the archives of the Holy Synod.[1] In the years 1845–1855, conversion reached such speed that there were not enough potential godfathers to be attached to each convert for the ceremony to take place. In Saratov, 134 cantonists were baptized in 1853, and 233 in 1854. According to Ginzburg, in Saratov alone, 1,304 Jewish children were baptized during the period of the cantonist decree. Within one year, 1842–1843, the number of children converted was 2,642. According to calculations based on figures quoted by Ginsburg[2] and the Ministry of Defense,[3] it can be concluded that a total of about 70,000 minors were drafted into the Russian army over a period of twenty-seven years.

On the other hand, N. Samter states[4] that, during the whole nineteenth century, 69,400 Jews converted in Russia, the majority being cantonists. It seems that even if the figures brought by Samter are somewhat relevant, we must distinguish between three periods during the nineteenth century regarding the speed of conversion. The first period was when the Jews had their first contact with the Christian population, and the rate of conversion was certainly lower than in the other periods. In contrast, during the last third of the century, the integration of the population, the country's industrialization, and the increase in the Jews' involvement in the life of the empire all increased the numbers. Therefore, it seems that we do not err if we attribute the majority of converts to the second half of the nineteenth century, and estimate that there were approximately 30,000 converts during the first half of the century.

---

1 Ginzburg, "Mucheniki-deti," 69.
2 Ginsburg, *Historishe Verke*, vol. 3, 36.
3 *Stoletie Voennogo ministerstva 1802–1902*, vol. 4: *Glavnyi shtab*, part 1, bk. 1, section 2: *Istoricheskii ocherk. Komplektovaniie voisk v tsarstvovanie Imperatora Nikolaia I*, 209, 247–249.
4 N. Samter, *Judentaufen im neunzehnten Jahrhundert* [Jewish conversion during the nineteenth century] (Berlin: M. Poppelauer, 1906), 91.

This number certainly matches the solid data of the Holy Synod regarding the years 1825–1855.⁵ During this period, 22,324 Jews converted.

These figures can be compared to the number of conscripts in that period provided by the Ministry of Defense. The only relevant numbers that can be accepted as trustworthy are the figures of cantonist conscription from 1843 till 1854.⁶

1843	1490	**1847**	1527	**1851**	3674
1844	1428	**1848**	2265	**1852**	3352
1845	1476	**1849**	2612	**1853**	3904
1846	1332	**1850**	2445	**1854**	3611

As is known, in 1843 the tsar's started to pay close attention to what was happening with the cantonists. It is probably as a result of his increased interest that the Ministry of Defense started to collect conscription data. Moreover, before this time there were neither orders nor excessive efforts to draft minors. Consequently, there should be a difference in the number of converts before 1843 and afterwards. In addition, one has to take into consideration that, by 1843, sixteen years of drafting minors had passed and, after that year, the cantonist policy only continued for twelve years.

The number of conscripts increased greatly starting from 1848. This conclusion verifies our assumption that 1848 should be seen as the beginning of a new period in the draft policy, and that there is some connection to the revolutionary wave that was sweeping over Europe at the time. In 1851 there was further escalation. The increase in conscription is not connected to the continuation of the conversion campaign, but rather to external circumstances. It is reasonable to assume that, in Russian reality, no campaign lasted for long, and the concentrated effort for conversion began to wane after 1848.

Based on these considerations, the average annual draft in the sixteen years of 1827–1843 did not exceed 1,500 cantonists. Thus, the total for those sixteen years was about 24,000 conscripted minors. As is known, there was no conscription at all in 1834. In the years reported in the chart, 31,318 additional cantonists were recruited within twelve years. If we assume that in the last year of Nicholas's

---

5 *Vestnik Imperatorskogo rossiiskogo istoricheskogo obshchestva* 98 (1890): 457–460.
6 *Stoletie Voennogo ministerstva 1802–1902*, vol. 4: *Glavnyi shtab*, part 1, bk. 1, section 2: *Istoricheskii ocherk. Komplektovaniie voisk v tsarstvovanie Imperatora Nikolaia I*, 209.

reign a similar number was recruited as in the previous year—3,600—the total number of recruited cantonists comes to about 60,000.

According to the data on the converts from the church archives quoted above, the approximate number of 23,000 converts in the researched period also included adult soldiers and civilians. Even if we assume that the adults were just a third of the number of converts, 7,000 men and women, the number of boys who converted were 15,000, a quarter of the approximately 60,000 recruited boys. Stanislawski is of the opinion that the number of converts was large, giving the number of 25,000 cantonists, but even this number is less than a half.[7]

---

7   Stanislawski, *Tsar Nicholas I and the Jews*, 44. His calculations are based on Samter's general number, not differentiated according to the years. We therefore preferred the numbers from the church archives as cited above.

Part V

THE REVOLT OF THE ARKHANGEL'SK HALF-BATTALION OF MILITARY CANTONISTS

1

The Reports

The following correspondence shows how the revolt was presented in the tsar's close environment. The texts of the reports are short and to the point.[1]

> File no. 340, started on February 11, 1855
>
> Third Section of His Imperial Majesty's Own Chancellery
>
> On the ninety-two cantonists from among the Jews of the Arkhangel'sk half-battalion, who were recruited this year for regular service for the naval cadet team and declared that they converted through coercion by the commander of the aforementioned half-battalion.
>
> From the commander of region A, Gendarmes Division, File no. 428
>
> November 1, 1855, St. Petersburg
>
> Captain... of the gendarmerie in Arkhangel'sk personally reports as follows:
>
> The military governor of Arkhangel'sk gave him the task of investigating the case of the ninety-two cantonists from the Arkhangel'sk half-battalion who were recruited this year to the naval cadet team from among the Jews who were baptized.
> These stated that they converted under coercion of the battalion's commanders. They now wish to serve God according to their previous religion. I regard it my duty to present the matter before His Majesty.
>
> Lieutenant [name illegible]

---

1 The Central Archives for the History of the Jewish People, HMF626, copy from Gosudarstvennyi arkhiv Rossiiskoi Federatsii [State archive of Russian Federation], f. 109, 1 eksp., op. 30, d. 340.

To the director of the Third Section of His Imperial Majesty's Own Chancellery, Lieutenant General Cavalier Dubel't, November 7, 1855

From the military governor of Arkhangel'sk

I received the report of Podpolkovnik Solov'ev's investigation, and I regard it my duty to present it for your study.

The personal bureau in St. Petersburg

Classified, November 11, 1855

File 826

To the director of the Third Section

Following your request of November 7, 1855, I informed the Military Governor of Arkhangel'sk concerning the reports on the investigation of the forced conversion of ninety-two cantonists in the Arkhangel'sk half-battalion, and I regard it my duty to report to His Honor.

General Adjutant Prince Dolgorukov

The Ministry of the Navy, Inspection Department

August 3, 1855

The Inspection Department conducted an inspection of the Arkhangel'sk half-battalion, which arrived in St. Petersburg under the command of Second Lieutenant Gedravich. During roll call, the cantonist Igor' Kapilovsky announced that he is a Jew and was forcibly converted to Christianity.

Following his statement, several additional people came forward with the same announcement. In addition, Nikolai Egolin announced that he too is Jewish, but that he converted of his own free will. He said that, as a result of his deed, the rest of his Jewish peers, who claim that they had been forcibly converted, abuse him.

I hereby am honored to inform you of all of the above,

Signed: Department's deputy director, Wing Adjutant Krabbe

The Ministry of the Navy, Inspection Department

Naval Cadet Staff, St. Petersburg

File no. 1640, August 27, 1855

Out of 208 cantonists who arrived from the Arkhangel'sk half-battalion, the following were found fit for military service in units as below:

> 41 for service in combat units (these were sent to the naval cadet team no. 1)
> 20 for naval cadet craftsmen team

The remaining 147 men are not fit for combat service because of their illiteracy.[2] For the same reason they are not fit for service in the educational navy team.
   I therefore request transferring them to other units (enclosed is a list).
   Please inform me of the results of your treatment.

Commander of the *leist*[3] crews

To the director of the military colonies

October 9, 1855

I hereby recommend suggesting to the Medical Department to recruit students for the paramedical school in Kronshtadt from among the above cantonists.

I hereby transfer the statements of complaints concerning coercion to convert to Christianity to the Ministry's Inspection Department, so that they may be examined and decisions made according to the summary of January 3, 1855.

The Commander, Lieutenant General . . .

---

2   This claim is surprising, as the cantonists learned to read and write.
3   Sailors in the port's auxiliary boats.

Report

Inspection Department, section 2, desk 1

[The first part of the letter repeats the description of the event, mentioning the accusation against Podpolkovnik D'iakonov for exerting violence.]

... and furthermore, the cantonists claim that, as part of their refusal to act as Christians, they prayed as Jews on the journey. It seems that the escort soldiers were aware of this. When they arrived at the Arakcheev barracks in St. Petersburg, they organized prayers according to the Jewish religion. The nine escort soldiers testified that all the cantonists on the journey to St. Petersburg organized Christian prayers, and that there is no truth in the claim of the ninety-two cantonists that they prayed as Jews on their way to, or on arrival at, the Arakcheev barracks.

The escort officer, Second Lieutenant Gedravich, confirmed the escort soldiers' statement, and added that he had not received any statement from the ninety-two cantonists.

The investigation materials and the statements were transferred to the management of the military colonies for their decision.

To the chief commander of the port, the management of the Kronshtadt Port

The port office, February 11, 1855

On behalf of the port captain

Report

103 cantonists, registered as Christians, arrived at the labor brigades nos. 4 and 5 on being transferred from the navy educational team.

During roll call, these soldiers did not respond to their Russian names and claimed that they are Jewish and have not accepted Christianity.[4]

---

4   It should be noted that, on February 6, 1850, a government directive was issued forbidding Jewish converts to change their family name. The purpose of this prohibition was obviously the need to identify the converts easily. See A. S. Pribluda, *Familii evreev v SSSR: Imia tvoe—sbornik* [Surnames of Jews in the USSR: Your name—a collection] (Jerusalem: Hebrew University, 1993).

I reported this to the headquarters of the chief inspector of the sailing and work crews, but I have not yet received any response to the matter.[5]

In addition, I regard it my duty to report to His Honor that those cantonists who call themselves Jews refuse to work on the Sabbath.

Signed: Commander of the Port, Captain ... [family name is illegible]

To the Inspection Department of the Ministry of the Navy

The office of the military governor in Arkhangel'sk

November 15, 1855

Lieutenant Sokolovsky conducted interrogations of those men (excluding those who left Arkhangel'sk) who, according to the Jews, were coerced into converting.

All those interrogated stated unanimously that the aforementioned cantonists converted of their own free will, without being forced by anyone. All the witnesses to the baptism testified that at the time of baptism they did not hear one claim of any type of force from those being converted. Some of those questioned also testified that those baptized did so of their own free will.[6]

Moreover, the military governor of Arkhangel'sk, Major-General Solov'ev, informed Lieutenant Sokolovsky that he talked personally with all the cantonists when they left Arkhangel'sk, but did not hear any complaint from them.

In my opinion, these cantonists should be punished for submitting a false complaint.

I hereby enclose an explanation from the commander of the Arkhangel'sk half-battalion from November 10, 1855 in his own words.

Similarly, it should be added that [the cantonists'] original signed statements were deposited with Lieutenant Sokolovsky stating that they had accepted Christianity of their own free will. The confirmations were taken from where they were stored, the files of the department for religious matters in Arkhangel'sk.

---

5 This testifies to total lack of control within the senior command following the event.
6 As the word "some" is used here, it is likely that some of those who performed the baptisms were unwilling to give false testimonies stating that the converts acted from free will, so they made do with a statement that they did not hear any claims of coercion.

> **To the military governor of Arkhangel'sk, Admiral ...**
>
> From the director of the bureau, Lugovsky
>
> Below please find a copy of the tsar's command of March 11, 1849[7]
>
> To the Inspection Department of the Defense Ministry
>
> When five recruits from the cantonist battalion of Perm' were placed in Gomel''s *jäger* divisions, they stated that the previous commander had forced them to convert to the Orthodox religion. I appointed Lieutenant Lovnovsky to examine the complaint. From the examination conducted by Lovnovsky in the *jäger* divisions of Gomel' and in the Perm' battalion, His Majesty found that the complaints were not justified. His Majesty therefore commanded to transfer those recruits who had submitted false complaints to forced labor in the convicts' regiments, and to determine the region of Kiev subordinate to the western area of the engineering corps as the location for serving their sentence. These prisoners should be supervised in such a way as to ensure that they will perform Christian rituals, because they accepted them of their own free will. At the same time, His Imperial Majesty warns not to bring such complaints before him. His Imperial Majesty emphasizes that, when converting cantonists and recruits, all means of exerting pressure to convert should be avoided, as these are contrary to the spirit of Christianity.
>
> Director of the bureau, Lugovsky

Thus, the sailors' refusal to remain Christian was not necessarily a result of the death of Nicholas I. There were similar cases in his lifetime, and probably more testimonies exist in the archives.

The punishment for the renunciation of conversion contradicted Russia's criminal law, which demanded punishment only in a case of public denigration of Christianity, and nothing like this is mentioned in the correspondence. It is therefore clear that the penalty was only determined according to the wish of

---

7   As a case of precedent.

the tsar, without any legal involvement. This is evidence of the tsar's personal interest in converting Jews.[8]

Below is a private letter written in unsteady handwriting, apparently to the commander of the Kronshtadt Port, Nikolai Karlovich Krabbe. It describes the prosecution's difficulty in defining the category of the sailors' crime:

> To Nikolai Karlovich!
>
> Following my letter of November 27 concerning the heresy of renouncing Christianity by Jews who converted, I hereby inform you that section 191 of the Penal and Reeducation Code states: "... a person who renounces Christianity, Orthodox or otherwise, in favor of a non-Christian religion, will be transferred to the ecclesiastical command for the purpose of persuasion and explanation and for return to the fold of Christianity. The aforementioned will no longer enjoy the rights he is entitled to by virtue of his civilian status, and all his property will be permanently entrusted to the kingdom."[9]
>
> The Commander, Captain ... [name is illegible]

> December 2, 1855
>
> Inspection Department, section 3, desk 3
>
> To the Military Prosecution Department of the Ministry
>
> Ninety-two of the 208 cantonists of the Arkhangel'sk half-battalion, who arrived in St. Petersburg in August of this year, stated that they had converted by force exerted by the Commander of the Arkhangel'sk half-battalion, Podpolkovnik D'iakonov.
>
> Following these complaints, the military governor of the Arkhangel'sk district conducted an investigation of the matter, and presented its results to the Tsar's Own Chancellery together with a personal opinion.

---

8   Perhaps it is relevant to note here that, 120 years later, the author served in a prisoners' regiment in the area of Perm'.
9   According to Russian laws, even a civilian who renounced his Christianity was brought to a court of law. See below.

Now another eleven have joined the above-mentioned ninety-two with the same claim, and therefore there are now 103 complainers. After this was presented to the tsar on behalf of general admiral, His Majesty was pleased to command to immediately disperse those 103 rejecters of Christianity, to abolish the spirit of rejection in the naval crews and units. It is probable that the continued rejection stems from the fact that they are together.

Further treatment and supervision should be transferred to the Prosecution Department of the Ministry of the Navy.

All relevant entities should be informed of His Majesty's order of March 11, 1849 on the identical case of five recruits of the Perm' battalion.

2

Investigation Documents; Sailors' Testimonies

We present here the investigation documents verbatim. It should be noted that most of the protocols were recorded according to the same formula. This indicates that this was actually a tendentious investigation. The vast majority of the interrogated did not know how to read, so the investigator was likely to invent testimonies. In many cases, a request from the prosecutor's office to release the suspect from the hospital, to which he was sent after an "attempt at persuasion," is attached to the testimony. Some of the respondents testified that they had been subjected to heavy physical pressure. We therefore have taken a critical approach when dealing with the material, without completely trusting any protocol.

> **Ministry of the Navy**
>
> **The Kronshtadt Port administration, June 30, 1856**
>
> **File no. 467**
>
> Below is a breakdown of evidence collected from the insubordinate sailors.
> Igor' Kopilovsky states that he was converted by force by Junior Officer Orin, and it was he who made him sit in the water.[1] Baptized in 1855.
> Andrei Malamud was converted by force by Junior Officers Orin and Golman in 1853.
> Eliya Zuss: "Sergeant Serivrikov forced me to convert, raining blows on me and pushing me to sit in the water." Baptized in 1854.[2]

---

1   Namely, he was pushed to sit inside the barrel or bowl that served as the baptizing pool.
2   This is the only testimony in first person given by a Jew who was forced to convert after the exertion of physical force during baptism.

Following are the testimonies of each sailor. They do not speak of coercion but of being led to the water. There are those who admit that they went to the water of their own accord.

Lieutenant D'iakonov's report on testimonies of forced conversion can help us understand the matter.

> **Report**
>
> ... To remind you that there exists an order of the Ruling Synod of Febuary 3, 1844, that conversion of the cantonists is to be undertaken by the military clergy. It will be conducted in cooperation with the commanders of the cantonist schools. Sergeants from among the Christian cantonists were appointed to implement the order under the supervision of the regiment's commander. All this under the assumption that neighborliness and friendship create good conditions for conversion.
>
> ... Any candidate for conversion may retract his decision. Thus, at present there are twelve Jewish cantonists who have already expressed their wish to convert, but are still being examined and are under trial. In addition, at the ceremony there is a large crowd in the church and high-ranking military and municipal officials. In these circumstances there is no possibility for forced baptism conducted by officers or junior officers.
>
> Junior officers and mentors are present in the church at the time of the baptism to enforce order and to help the converts[3] as they undress and dress at a mass baptism of more than thirty people. The junior officials extend help to the church staff in filling the barrels with water for baptism, and emptying them.
>
> In addition, the cantonists designated for baptism were interviewed by the commander of the Arkhangel'sk fortress and the commander of the Arkhangel'sk half-battalion. Complaints such as these have been submitted more than once by cantonists and parents of those conscripted at the time of the cantonists' conscription. According to the order of the Minister of Defense Chernyshev of December 31, 1851, these complaints were investigated and found lacking any factual basis.
>
> I request to protect myself from such conspiracies, so that in the future I will also be able to achieve shining results in bringing Jews to conversion

---

3   The Jews claimed that the commanders were present at the baptism in order to exert pressure on them.

according to His Imperial Majesty's wish[4] and according to the imperial command issued on December 4, 1843.

I hereby add that I report monthly on the achievements in conversions to the Military Colonies Department of the Ministry of Defense.

Signed: Podpolkovnik D'iakonov

N.B. I attach documents regarding the procedures of conversion that testify to the propriety in implementing the task.

To Father Petr Kremlin (chief priest of Kronshtadt): I send for your review the list of Jews who, according to their commander's notification, have expressed their wish to convert. You are hereby requested to examine the candidates' knowledge of our faith's principles. Please inform me of the results.

Officer of the Arkhangel'sk half-battalion, Podpolkovnik D'iakonov

Confirmation: I hereby reply that the sailors listed below passed the examination in the principles of our faith and prayer, and are found willing to accept Christianity.

This is additional evidence that another effort at persuading was carried out. As the priest Petr Kremlin testifies:

Statement given at conversion:[5]

I, cantonist of the Arkhangel'sk half-battalion, do hereby declare that I aspire with absolute desire to join the Eastern Orthodox Church. I undertake to forever remain faithful to the Church, without question.

If cantonists were baptized together, all of them would sign the same statement. The illiterate ones would stamp it with their thumb.

---

4   He his hinting at his multiple merits in converting Jews according to instructions from his superiors.
5   One of the documents that Dyakonov attached to his letter of self-justification.

> To Podpolkovnik D'iakonov
>
> Following the complaints of the five cantonists from Perm' who serve in the Bel'sky *Jäger* Division that they were coerced into converting, the minister of defense, at the order of His Imperial Majesty, appointed Colonel Lubinovsky [*sic*] to conduct an exhaustive investigation of the matter.
>
> All the complaints were found to be lacking factual basis. The subordinates were transferred to prisoners' regiments according to the order of the Ministry's Inspection Department. Care must be taken that they fulfill the requirements of the Christian religion.
>
> You must draw conclusions from the aforementioned order of the tsar, and conduct the cantonist unit under your command accordingly.
>
> Signed: Major-General Leiman[6]

As we see, the commander submitted lists of candidates to the priest, who was ostensibly supposed to handle the conversion procedures personally and report to the military command. In fact, it turns out that the priest only had a passive role in conducting the tests. Reversing the order of the conversion procedures testifies to the toughness of the commander who usurped the position of the priest. The commander made sure to maintain order and paperwork as stipulated (he knew "the rules of the game"). He even turned to the priest in writing and in an official style.

Here we can ask what would have happened had the candidate failed the examination. If he had been coerced, he could have demonstrated lack of knowledge. Would that have saved him? Added to that would be the imperfect Russian of the "new Russians," who did not know how to express themselves well in their new language.

As early as 1851–1852, a complaint was filed against D'iakonov's tyranny, but it was during the days of Nicholas I and Count Chernyshev, and D'iakonov emerged vindicated. This complaint was supported by the cantonists' parents. This fact, mentioned by D'iakonov, again raises the issue of how much the family was involved in the fate of the cantonist while he was serving in the institution

---

6   This is a classic example of ambiguity of the bureaucratic times of Nicholas I: "draw conclusions," conduct ... accordingly." The writer does not say explicitly according to which order it is forbidden to exert force, lest the complaint be examined. He also does not ignore all fear of complaints, as the tsar might support the complainers.

(and not only at the time of conscription, as is stated in most studies). We should mention the testimonies of some of the insurgents, who met their parents and other family members on their way from Arkhangel'sk to the regular units in Saint Petersburg. From the reports of searches of the property of the cantonists who served in the naval units, it appears that letters received from their families were confiscated. The continuous correspondence between the homes and the soldiers is also confirmed by documents discovered by Shaul Ginsburg.[7]

D'iakonov supposedly did not understand the meaning of the investigation. Chernyshev himself backed his actions in 1851. He was panicking. That is why he mentions the tsar's order from 1843, without mentioning the tsar's name, because Nicholas was no longer alive, and Alexander did not give any instructions in this regard. D'iakonov apparently did not understand that there would be changes in the policy towards the cantonists.

In passing, we receive confirmation that the tsar's order of March 1843 was the innovation that gave the green light for mass conversion. There was not a more significant order before this date.

Regarding the baptism procedure, the documents show that before being baptized, the soldier had to undress, and because of the bulkiness of his equipment and uniform he needed help. At the same time, it is clear that the soldier did not receive any help before going to bed, for example. If so, giving help in undressing served as a means of acceleration and encouragement, although speed was also of essence when there was a large number of converts at the same time. The soldiers were baptized in large barrels inside the church. From time to time the barrels would be refilled with water, as the water would spill out during the baptism. The floor around them was wet and dirty.

The conducting of examination by the priest cannot be ignored. With all the obsequiousness of the report, we have to understand why the implementers created additional obstacles for themselves. Or were they so sure of success that they did not fear any hitch? We asked the same question regarding the mass conversion in Kazan'. It is possible to claim that the soldiers were demoralized, but that is not clear, as later they dared to renounce their conversion. Perhaps from the start they tolerated the pretense as they planned on renouncing the act at a more convenient place.

Testimony of force being exerted at the time of the baptism was found. It can be assumed that the language of the testimony is defective, and the coercion was not just at the baptism.

---

7   Ginzburg, "Mucheniki-deti," 50–79; Merimzon, "Rasskaz starogo soldata," 290.

Moving to further documents:

> **October 18, 1855**
>
> **Protocol of the investigation of Junior Officer Orin. Questioned by Lieutenant Solov'ev of the Military Gendarmes Unit.**
>
> "I did not force the cantonists to convert. In the church I only helped them to undress and dress. I did not make them sit in the water. I did not receive an order from the commanders to force the cantonists to convert."
>
> **Statement of Mikhail Ososov, clerk at the Communal Imperial Bank, concerning the conversion of Shardinsky**
>
> "Pavel Shardinsky visited me before his baptism and requested that I participate in the conversion ceremony. He never mentioned that he had been forced to convert by anyone."

This is an unusual document regarding the informal contact between the baptizer and the convert.

> **To the Deputy Commander of the Inspection Department of the Naval Ships**
>
> From the Commander of the Mechanics Crew in Kronshtadt, December 3, 1855
>
> **Report**
>
> I am happy to inform you that, following my reports on those under my command who refuse to convert, some of them have returned to Christianity after repeated efforts of persuasion. During the ceremonies of the Christian festival of faith, they took the communion, and since then they have started going to church. When they are in the barracks they have no contact with Jews, neither with active Jews, nor with those who insist on their refusal.
>
> Thus, only seventeen converted Jews insist on refusing to be Christians. They stand out for their stubbornness and negative influence in their demonstrative behavior.

Pavel Bocher
Artemii Malamud
Alexander Vax

All three are in isolation, separate from each other and under guard. Unfortunately, I have no veteran soldiers under my command, and most of the soldiers are recruits and cantonists. I therefore request that these three Jews from my unit be transferred to a prison facility until further orders are received.[8] In addition, the head priest of the Chasovnia Bogoiavleniia Gospodnia [Chapel of the Epiphany] in Kronshtadt, Aleksandr Kutnevich, informed me that the Jew Alexander Vax declared before him that, at the conversion ceremony in the church in Arkhangel'sk, he did receive the holy bread and wine, but he did not taste them, but spat them out onto the floor. Father Kutnevich is of the opinion that for such a deed Vax should be brought before a military court. In addition, I attach a list marked with "A" of Jewish religious articles that were confiscated from the sailors. Among them are prayer books, phylacteries, and more. I request instructions on how to handle the situation.

Signed: **Captain of the Fleet of the First Rank . . .**

Chief Inspector of the Fleet Adjutant General . . . [the name is illegible]

December 16, 1855

According to the directive of His Imperial Highness, the Inspection Department transferred the material of the investigation conducted in Arkhangel'sk to the Prosecution Department following the statement of the cantonists of the Arkhangel'sk half-battalion that they were converted by force.

---

8   Together with demonstrating his confidence and achievements, the reporter is concerned about a fresh outbreak of the revolt.

The details of the circumstances are brought here once again:

> According to the directive of His Imperial Highness, the Inspection Department of the Navy Ministry turned to the Ministry of Defense to receive guidelines as to how to behave toward these cantonists. In addition, His Imperial Majesty ordered avoiding circumstances that would bring complaints of this sort. Thus he commanded that no means of force contrary to the spirit of Christianity should be used at the time of conversion. The conversion should be conducted under close supervision of the local military commanders. In future, cantonists should not be sent to persuasive talks to convert to the Orthodox religion in groups with young non-commissioned officers, who lack experience and are motivated in an exaggerated way. Through excessive efforts, they are likely to extort an agreement to convert not based on faith, and such conversion will, therefore, not be stable.[9]

The obvious conclusion is that the author of the document attributes the coercion to young non-commissioned officers, who lacked experience but showed excessive motivation and enthusiasm. In this way, he dismisses any blame that might lie with D'iakonov.

Further documents clarify the issue:

> To the deputy commander of the Kronshtadt Port
>
> From the commander of Regiment 4 of the Work Crews
>
> **Report**
>
> I hereby report that Abraham Pfeifer, of the first rank, declared on December 23 that at the time of his conversion, when offered the communion, he turned aside and spat out the sacred flesh and blood.
>
> December 29, 1855

---

9 The recommendation was given according to the results of the investigation, and therefore the prohibition reflects the reality.

Investigation committee of March 3, 1856

The sailor Alexander Bik hereby testifies that the following sailors of Crew 2:

1. Smulik Mil;
2. Artemii Malamud;
3. Andrei Peretz;
4. Alexander Vax;
5. Pavel Bocher from the craftsmen's unit

initiated and incited other companions to deny Christianity. Concerning Vax, he testified that Vax wanted to strangle him for not being ready to renounce his Christianity.

All the accused denied their guilt.

Decision of the Investigation Committee, March 8, 1856

To conduct an investigation and attempt at persuasion concerning the converts who are now in the hospital for health reasons, as to their declaration of renunciation of Christianity:

1. Igor' Kapilov [sic], Crew 3;
2. Gregory Kotler, Crew 3;
3. Michael Beilin, Crew 3.

List of the Investigation Committee's Findings, March 8, 1856

Peter Davidov, age: twenty-two, converted in 1854. "I have in my possession a *siddur*, *tzitzit*, and *tefillin* that I brought from home, and I refuse to be a Christian."

Hirsch Bren, called Mikhail, age: twenty-three, converted in 1854. Always has in his possession a *siddur*, *tefillin*, and *tzitzit*. "I hid them on the way to Arkhangel'sk. I took them out on the way back. I strongly refuse to be a Christian."

Wolf Israelovitz, age: twenty, converted in 1854. In possession of a *siddur*, *tzitzit*, and *tefillin*.

Smulik-Shmuel Mil, age: twenty-four, converted in 1854. "I took from home a *siddur*, *tefillin*, and *tzitzit*. I left them in a pit at the last stop before Arkhangel'sk."

> **Nikolai Nazarov**, age: nineteen. "I converted of my own free will in 1850. I testify that Dvorkin and Itzkovitz paid the non-commissioned officer money so that he would allow them to go and pray in the synagogue."

Thus, we have before us a report of the junior officers' corruption who cooperated with their subordinates in a way contradictory to military policy. The same non-commissioned officer who took the cantonist to his baptism was ready to allow him to pray in a synagogue in exchange for money. This atmosphere of hypocrisy undoubtedly existed also in other aspects of the cantonist-officer relationship. It was probably possible to moderate the severity of penalties in exchange for bribery.

We are also presented here with testimony of boys making an effort to observe *mitzvot* within the cantonist institution. It seems that they led a double life. On the one hand, they converted; on the other, at the first opportunity they went to the synagogue. Therefore, the act of conversion cannot be regarded as an unambiguous abandoning of Judaism, but as a sophisticated way of keeping *mitzvot* in secret. In our opinion, after studying these and other testimonies, we can say that the cantonists generally lived similarly to the Spanish Marranos in Spain. It seems that such a phenomenon has not yet received much scholarly attention.

Additional testimonies:

> **Dimitrii** [actually **Hirsch**] **Yosefovitz**, age: twenty-one, converted in 1854. Has in his possession a *siddur*, *tzitzit*, and *tefillin* that he brought from home.
>
> **Kupriian Rein**, age: eighteen, converted in 1854. Retracts his heresy of Christianity. He brought religious articles from home and hid them on the way to Arkhangel'sk.
>
> **Pavel Bocher**, age: twenty-one, forcibly converted in 1854, but is now prepared to remain a Christian, and cancels his statement that he was coerced. "It was the commander of the half-battalion who forced me to convert. Now I give up Judaism as I have been convinced that I will no longer be able to observe its tenets."[10]

---

10 See for example, the recommendation for converting Jewish boys, Levanda, *Sbornik zakonov*, 675 (no. 568).

It should be noticed that Bocher retracts his renunciation of Christianity but also mentions coercion in his testimony. If the Investigation Committee had any doubt, this testimony is a clear evidence of D'iakonov's activity of coercion.

> **Leizer (Petr) Katz**, age: twenty, converted in 1855. "I oppose observing the Christian religion as it was forced on me. I received *tefillin* and *tzitzit* from my home when I was in St. Petersburg."

As we see, the cantonists' conditions in St. Petersburg allowed them to inform their families of their location and to receive discrete packages from home. The Jewish community in the city was probably involved, despite its precarious status.

This is an unusual testimony of the Jewish soldiers' contact with the community in St. Petersburg. We should ask whether Leizer Katz's declaration was intended to hide another method of obtaining religious items, or whether the opposite is true, that others also did not bring their religious items with them, but received them in St. Petersburg. It is possible that they claimed to have brought them from home in order to strengthen their claim that they had never left Judaism. They acted in that way, for example, in connection to their claim that on the journey they prayed as Jews.

This indirect testimony of contact between the cantonists and the local community is strengthened by the fact that community elders visited the barracks. One's impression is that the community followed the movements of the Jewish soldiers in the city and attempted to help them. This behavior is probably typical of any Jewish community that operated charitable institutions. It is likely that, wherever there was a cantonist institution, the community attempted to have contact with the boys.

> **Continuation of investigation, March 12, 1856**
>
> **(Igor') Aharon Kapilovsky**, age: eighteen, baptized in 1854: "I deny Christianity as I was forcibly converted. I took my religious items from home. It is true that I was the first to raise the claim of coercion,[11] but I did not incite others. On the journey from Arkhangel'sk to St. Petersburg, I went with them all to the church, and there I did not declare that I was forcibly baptized. I was afraid that if it had been made known to the

---

11   At the time of the roll call at the Kronshtadt port.

> convoy commanders, they would have prevented me from declaring it before the commanders of the unit to which I was assigned. I now declare it as fact."

According to documents in the file of the investigation committee, Aharon Kapilovsky was in a military hospital at the beginning of his interrogation. The investigation committee decided to interrogate him even if he was on his deathbed. The reason for his being in the hospital was: "Medical needs after the church's effort to persuade him." One can imagine what sort of efforts these were, if he went straight to the military hospital after them.

> **Michael Beilin**, age: eighteen, converted in 1854. [Beilin was also "recuperating after the priests' persuasion." This is what he said after being "persuaded":] "No one forced my friends to convert. They informed of their decision to convert of their own free will. I am able to confirm the testimony as though the Jewish elders in St. Petersburg incited the soldiers to renounce their Christianity. I indeed heard these elders saying: 'We will think alone what to do with ... concerning this matter.'[12] I indeed testify that Kapilovsky tried to convince me to observe *mitzvot*."
>
> **Alexander Itzkovitz**, age: eighteen, converted in 1854. "In Arkhangel'sk they exerted heavy pressure on us to convert, and that is the reason why my friends are renouncing their Christianity. I personally remain a Christian, and declare this publicly."
>
> **Shmuel Rothenberg**, age: twenty, converted in 1854. "Yes, I have *tzitzit*, *tefillin*, and a *siddur*, which I brought from home but they were confiscated in St. Petersburg. I hid them in a private house on the way,[13] not far from Arkhangel'sk. I renounce my Christianity, as I was forced to convert against my will."
>
> **Wolff (Iakov) Yankelevitch**, age: twenty-three. "I converted in 1854. I believe that this conversion is valid, and therefore I wish to remain a Christian. I brought religious articles from home."
>
> **Andrei Movshovits**, age: twenty. "I purchased sacred articles in St. Petersburg." (Similar to the statement of Leizer Katz).

---

12 It is not clear in what connection this was said. Were they speaking about an expected softening of the government's stance?
13 This was probably a Jewish house.

Non-commissioned officer Ian Vitiuk, age: fifty-one. Sergeant major in the unit in which Pfeifer served, and it was he who flogged Pfeifer. When Pfeifer complained of this to the commander of the regiment, the commander told him that he [Pfeifer] is Orthodox, and therefore his being tormented was justified.[14]

Enclosed is confirmation from the military hospital from where the sailor Pfeifer was taken for interrogation.

Nikolai Olshovsky, age: nineteen. Converted in 1853. "Artemii Malamud's father serves as a rabbi, and he made his son swear that he would resist and not be baptized..."

(Andrei) Berko Oshorovitz, age: twenty-three. "They dragged me to the river bank, and there was not even a priest there. That is certainly not called conversion."

Filip Oshorovitz, age: twenty. Converted in 1854. "At first I denied my Christianity, but I suffered greatly for being Jewish, and now I have decided to remain a Christian."

(Nikolai) Hagai Fiedler. Agreed to remain Christian. "I and my friends saw how the commander was very severe and harassed anyone who remained Jewish, and was lenient with the Orthodox. We therefore stated that we were ready to convert, hoping that on leaving Arkhangel'sk we would be able to observe the tenets of our religion."

Faivish Zbrok, age: twenty-three. Denies his Christianity. "Already on the way to Arkhangel'sk, non-commissioned Officer Orin told us that in the battalion they would confiscate our religious articles. We therefore hid them in pits in the forest."

There were those who testified that they heard from local peasants of the especially harsh conditions in Arkhangel'sk, and there were others who testified that they hid their religious articles in pits on the way there. Fisher and Itzkovitz claimed that they dug pits in the forest.

---

14   The soldier was beaten as though he was Christian who had transgressed against his faith, a legitimate act according to the commander.

Stepan Kolotushkin, age: twenty-three, converted in 1854. Testifies that the cantonists met their brothers and sisters on the way from Arkhangel'sk to Kronshtadt.[15]

Grigorii Nesterov, age fifteen. Orthodox from birth. "In the Arakcheev barracks in St. Petersburg, Jews from Petersburg came and persuaded those who converted to renounce their Christianity. They had brought religious articles with them from Arkhangel'sk, and they deposited them with their coreligionists.[16] I do not know who initiated their renunciation of Christianity because I did not make contact with the Jewish converts."

---

15 This testimony is evidence of strong contact between the cantonists and their families.
16 Additional evidence of contact with local Jews.

3

Summary and the Decisions of the Investigation Committee

At the conclusion of the investigation, the committee determines that among the cantonists are:

Catholics from birth: 1;
Orthodox from birth: 4;
Willingly converted from the start: 14;
Converted, retracted, and then again converted: 15.
Among them is Pavel Bocher, who, despite his submission, strongly refuses to wear a cross.
In the process of persuasion to regret their decision: 11;
Insist on not recognizing their Christianity: 33;
Excessive resistance: 27;
Found to be initiators and inciters: 8.

The names of the latter are: **Artemii** [his name after conversion; his Jewish name is unknown] **Malamud, Peter Berko, Mikhail Itzkovitz, Aharon Kapilovsky, Alexander Vax (head of the revolt), Smulik Shmuel Mil, Andrei Peretz, Kupriian Nesvizhsky.**

The segmentation of the list shows the dynamics of the coercion and the variety of reactions of the Jews, who were apparently conscripted at the same time and under the same conditions, but each behaved in his own way.

The Navy Ministry, Prosecution Department

May 23, 1856

His Imperial Majesty's special committee conducted investigations in Kronshtadt in order to clarify the identity of the initiators and discover:

1. who convinced the others to deny Christianity;
2. where the religious books and articles that were confiscated in Kronshtadt came from.

The committee determined:

Three people—**Igor' Kapilov, Artemii Malamud, and Alexander Vax**—were incriminated in their peers' testimonies of instigating the heresy.

Similarly, **Peter Dvorkin, Shmuel Mil, Kupriian Nesvizhsky, Mikhail Itzkovitz, and Andrei Peretz** demonstrated exaggerated stubbornness in the face of the investigation committee's attempt at persuasion, and continued to strongly refuse to return to Christianity. An additional sixty men completely denied the truth of Christianity despite the efforts of the investigation committee. Another fourteen people retracted their statement of forced conversion, and admitted that they had converted willingly. In addition, Vax and Pfeifer are accused of spitting out the sacred host onto the floor of the church. Pfeifer declared that he never intended to convert, and therefore he put his life in danger by jumping into a deep pit from which he was extracted by Oshorovitz, a soldier from Work Crew 13. Pfeifer further stated that he now decided to remain Christian after having been severely punished for his faithfulness to Judaism.

A soldier of Naval Crew 17 stated that, ever since arriving at the Arkhangel'sk half-battalion, he was forced to learn the prayers of the Russian religion, and a special officer was appointed to supervise this. He said that he received heavy punishment for any deed considered a transgression. While being punished, it was explained to him more than once that if he were Christian, he would avoid punishment. According to him, many agreed to be converted, with the intention that after leaving Arkhangel'sk they would again be allowed to observe the tenets of their religion.

Matvei Sidorov, an Orthodox Christian from birth, stated that the battalion commander would tell the Jews that whoever did not convert would not be released from the cantonist institution.

. . . The Navy Ministry's Inspection Department transferred to the Prosecution Department the order of His Imperial Majesty to avoid in future drafting Jews into naval frameworks, and to transfer the Jews of the entire junior staff of the navy to the infantry.[1]

Therefore, based on the above, the Prosecution Department recommends:

1. prosecuting three Jewish insubordinates: **Kapilovsky, age eighteen; Malamud, age nineteen; Vax, age twenty-two,** who were incriminated by their peers' testimony as being the instigators of the heresy, in a military court.
2. prosecuting two sailors for spitting out the sacred host when taking the communion in a military court. They are:

Pfeifer, who serves in Crew 8
A. Vax, who serves in Crew 20.

3. Sixty-four additional men remained firm in the face of any attempt to persuade them to return to the Christian faith, and thus became agitating and negative examples. These are to be removed from the naval base in Kronshtadt, and dispersed among various units in remote locations within the empire.

According to clause 216 of the Penalty Code and clause 218 of the Naval Penal Code, volume 1, the clergy should be given the responsibility for continuing with efforts to persuade people to return to the Orthodox religion. Their commanders are to supervise them closely.

The investigation in Arkhangel'sk did not reveal that coercion was exerted in the cantonist half-battalion for conversion, but the testimonies given by the converts to explain the actions of the commander of the Arkhangel'sk half-battalion lead to the conclusion that not only innocent persuasion was used for conversion, but also means of coercion, namely, different forms of severe acts.

This is contrary to the government's wishes and might cause harm.

. . . The Ministry of Defense must be made aware of the seriousness of the actions of the commander of the cantonists' half-battalion based on the evidence collected about coercive methods of conversion.[2]

Signed: General Procurator of the Navy Prince Golitsyn

---

1 The discriminatory response shows that he was not concerned with the benefit of the Jews.
2 This confirms that the cantonists' claims were justified.

4

Analysis and Conclusions

A. Behavior on the Way to Arkhangel'sk

On the way to the half-battalion, the cantonists heard from villagers of the especially harsh conditions in Arkhangel'sk. Some said they heard of this from Junior Officer Orin (who later took them to be baptized). When comparing the names of the escort soldiers it becomes apparent that they were soldiers who served in Arkhangel'sk. This placement was seemingly intended for them to become acquainted with the cantonists already on the way, according to the guidelines of the priest Kutnevich: to study the character of every Jewish conscript and to exert pressure on their weak points. The junior officers learned their underlings' character, but the opposite was true too: the cantonists became aware of the corrupt nature of their officers. One testimony stated that the escort soldiers allowed them to pray in the local synagogue in exchange for bribes. The readiness of the soldiers to receive bribes made it easier, among other things, to keep in contact with the family, to receive letters and money, to update the family and community of what was happening, etc. Bribery is evidence of careless supervision of the conscripts.

It cannot be explained how the boys managed to hide their religious articles under the noses of their escorts, unless the officers received bribery and turned a blind eye. This consideration reinforces the picture presented in previous chapters regarding the relative freedom of action within the base. According to statements given to the investigation committee, the cantonists had with them *tefillin, tzitzit, siddurim*, and additional books, which they hid in various places: in the forest, in pits in the forest, in pots which they hid in the earth, or in private houses, probably belonging to Jews. Some testified that they deposited religious articles with coreligionists in Arkhangel'sk. This last method seems to be the most likely, as it is difficult to hide small objects in the forest and to take them out a year later, especially in an area with an extremely cold climate such as Arkhangel'sk. The soldiers ostensibly did not want to betray the Jews who had done them this favor, and therefore told other stories. Others claimed that they had purchased the religious articles in St. Petersburg, or that they had received them from their families when they were in the capital.

B. Methods of Coercion

Most of the cantonists were unable to define the method of coercion with respect to each individual. This can be explained by the fact that the principal coercion expressed itself in the number of punishments and the discriminatory and harsh treatment of anyone who refused to convert. This was the daily routine that forced the boys to decide which path they would take. At the same time, some of them were able to describe during interrogation the specific instances of abuse that caused them to give up their Judaism.

The repeated threat of the commander should be noted: "No one will leave here before he has converted." The place was well known among the Jews for being a "fiery furnace" of conversion.

C. Behavior of the Jews on the Base

Artemii Malamud testified that he was ready to commit suicide by jumping, but his friends prevented him from doing so. The main resistance (only passive) was at the time of baptism, even though there were officers who were present during the baptism ceremony in order to drag those who were hesitating to the baptism barrels. Vax and Pfeifer spat out the host. They did this secretly, and only later told their friends. The boys' behavior on spitting out the mass was calculated. They did this so as not to transgress the prohibition of drinking wine used in idolatrous rituals. Apparently, they had enough knowledge to distinguish between pretending to do certain things and doing things that fall into the halakhic category of transgressions for which one should rather be killed than transgress.

Berko Oshorovitz's testimony is interesting—that he was baptized in a river without a priest being present. The majority were baptized in a church ceremony attended by crowds of people.

Alexander Vax's consistent behavior should be noted. During the baptism he spat out the host and the wine, he declared his denial of his Christianity, and he threatened other soldiers if they do not follow in his ways. Similarly, one should note the complaint of one of the converts that his peers laughed at him for clinging to Christianity. It is true that it is not completely clear about which period of the process we are talking—whether during the cantonists' time in the institution, or after leaving Arkhangel'sk. If we assume that it was while they were in Arkhangel'sk, together with the testimony of the public display of conversion, we can imagine that the atmosphere in Arkhangel'sk was one of passive resistance even after conversion. D'iakonov was probably aware of it, but all that interested him was being able to report his successes, and not the Jews' adherence to their new religion.

The testimony of the Russian soldier Nazarov that Dvorkin and Oshorovitz gave money to a junior officer (Orin?) who allowed them to pray in a synagogue, raises an additional question: If the Jews had money and the officers were willing to receive bribery for giving benefits, perhaps it would have been possible to bribe the officers so that they would harass them less? For the use of money, see *Berko the Cantonist* and Merimzon's memoirs. It is interesting that other researchers do not discuss the use of money in cantonist units.

D. The Age of the Cantonists and the Circumstances of Conversion

The age of the cantonists of the Arkhangel'sk half-battalion when they were drafted into regular service ranged between eighteen and twenty-three; namely, they were adults. Most of them had converted a year earlier in 1854. As has been mentioned, in all locations conversion mostly took place in the first six months of the boys' arrival at the institution.

Probably, most of the Jews in Arkhangel'sk arrived at an age that does not match the young age when cantonists were conscripted, but as regular recruits. If so, why are they still called cantonists, and why were they brought to a cantonist institution in their late teens? The submission of the cantonists to conversion usually happened as a result of their young age (six to twelve years old). How did it happen that such an overwhelming number of young adults converted only because of the difficulties in their service? We must conclude that we learn here of a phenomenon not yet discovered by historical researchers. It seems that in the 1850s the initiators of conversion established institutions for conversion also for older boys.

This initiative ostensibly stemmed from several factors. One of them is the relative "success" in converting, and the experience that some of the half-battalion commanders acquired over the years in breaking the spirit of resistance in several cantonist institutions. It is clear that it was more convenient to conduct conversion operations in special, closed institutions than in regular units to where the older Jews were sent. Therefore, the percentage of the boys' conversion was much higher. This is probably what inspired the idea of sending young Jews to institutions of mass conversion, even though they had passed the cantonist age.

Further proof of the justification of this assumption can be seen in the high concentration of Jews in one location, the Arkhangel'sk base. The commanders were not worried about too much resistance, and they had also learned that, paradoxically, when the Jews were together, they had more success in converting. However, when news of the revolt became known, Tsar Alexander gave the command to disperse the sailors among various units, believing that their rebelliousness came from their being together. This hypothesis is absolutely legitimate, and it is unclear why it has not been previously raised. Previous experience had not taught the commanders to be careful about concentrating hundreds of Jews in one location.

E. How Did the Young People Come to Their Decision to Deny the Validity of Their Conversion?

During interrogation, some sailors testified that they decided to convert for show and planned to return to Judaism immediately on leaving the institution. Hiding their religious articles is evidence of the truth of this claim.

There is, as quoted above, an interesting testimony of elderly Jews visiting the barracks in St. Petersburg. According to this testimony, they spoke for a long time with the sailors, handed out treats, and finally said, "You alone decide what to do." It can be assumed that the older residents in the capital had already heard of the new trends of thought in the imperial court, and they guided the boys in this spirit. It should be noted that the very entry of local Jews into the "model barracks" built by the notorious Arakcheev is surprising. After all, for years there had been a severe warning not to allow contact between Jews and the cantonists. Nevertheless, whether with a bribe or due to the negligence of the system, it was in fact possible to enter this guarded place.

As a result of these factors, Vax, Malamud, and Kapilovsky started to convince their friends to declare that they had been converted forcibly and not of their free will. Beilin testified that Kapilovsky spoke with him about the obligation to observe *mitzvot*. The initiators tried to persuade the soldiers to return to Judaism. Those who did not agree were beaten and mocked. Their efforts were successful with 103 Jews who dared to declare that they renounced their Christianity. Later, another thirteen sailors joined. Evidently, their acts of persuasion lasted for some time. In fact, there had been advance preparation for this, as all sailors took out the religious articles that they had hidden on the way, and started wearing *tzitzit* and *tefillin*. We have here a secret organization with leaders, ideology, and methods of action.

In their testimonies these Jews mentioned various ways in which they received the religious articles. The majority claimed to have brought them from home, evidence of their readiness to observe *mitzvot* even in army conditions. Some claimed to have purchased them in St. Petersburg. They undoubtedly had permanent contact with their families, to the extent that their dear ones knew on which day they would be released from the cantonist institution, and their siblings came to see them. The admission that they had bought religious articles in St. Petersburg or received them from home is also interesting. All these efforts give a new dimension to the Jewish soldiers' freedom of action.

The conclusions of the study concerning the cantonist revolt in Arkhangel'sk can be validated from other sources published in the yearly journal *Evreiskaia starina* at the beginning of the twentieth century. One of the important publications there are the memoirs of the cantonist Itzkovitz[1] who served at that exact time in the Arkhangel'sk half-battalion. Itzkovitz's name appears in the list of agitators. He relates in his memoirs that he was young, and therefore at the time of the revolt he was still in Arkhangel'sk. As proof he brings the memoirs of Shmulik (Shmuel) Mil, who is mentioned as one of the leaders of the revolt. Itzkovitz details the methods of coercion in the Arkhangel'sk half-battalion and, concerning the event itself, he was able to relate that the initiator was Shmuel Mil, and it was he who, at the general roll call in St. Petersburg in the presence of Tsar Alexander II, declared that he was renouncing his Christianity. According to his testimony, D'iakonov was summoned to account for his deeds in St. Petersburg, but he died of a stroke. Some of the details were not verified by the documents of the Naval Ministry; for example, the tsar taking part in the roll call, Mil's role, and others.

The memoirs of the apostate Terent'ev (name after conversion) are another source. The evidence from his trial is interesting background material that sheds light on what happened in the cantonist base during the conversion process. The trial took place only in 1881 when Terent'ev was released from the army and decided to return to Judaism.[2]

---

1   See Itzkovitz, "Vospominaniia evreiskogo kantonista," 54–65.
2   Appears in the Russian Jewish journal *Rassvet* 3 (1881).

As we read in the minutes of the session of the St. Petersburg District Court, April 23, 1881,[3] Terent'ev admitted in court his guilt in renouncing the Orthodox religion and returning to Judaism. He testified as to the circumstances of the transgression.

As a boy he was taken to the cantonists and assigned to the military cantonist battalion in the city of Nizhnii Novgorod. There he was able to observe all the tenets of the Jewish religion. Later, in 1846, he was transferred to the battalion in Kazan', where he had no possibility of observing the tenets. There was not a single observant Jew there. They had converted all the Jews. The commander of the unit said that he preferred that they demote him of his ranks ("dress me in the coat of a simple soldier") rather than that there should be observant Jews in his unit. Therefore, they also forced him [Terent'ev] to convert. This declaration is identical with that of D'iakonov in Arkhangel'sk.

Indeed, until his release from service in 1870, he behaved as a Christian, obeying the laws of the church, because of his fear of the military authorities. He even conducted his wedding ceremony in an Orthodox church while still in the army because he "preferred to live a married life rather than a life of abandonment." Nevertheless, in secret he remained faithful to Judaism. In 1870 he began to outwardly observe *mitzvot*. For a long time he did not live with his wife because of her negative behavior. When he was summoned, after his return to Judaism, to the church offices, he declared in advance that he was not prepared to accept any preaching, because he desired to remain a member of the religion of his ancestors, and was ready to accept any penalty meted out to him.

> **Chairman of the legal team**: "In what way exactly was the coercion expressed?"
> **Terent'ev**: "They exerted pressure on us in various ways. For example, they sent us to back-breaking labor during the day, and then did not allow us to sleep at night, when preachers would come and read us from their religious books. As a result of continuous exhaustion many of us would fall asleep while walking; in the end there was no way out other than to convert." [See Itzkovitz's description of the behavior of the apostate, Non-Commissioned Officer Evgraf Gulevich.]

---

3   *Voskhod* 4 (1881).

The defense attorneys asked the witness Sandykov, who served in the same battalion and even in the same company with the accused (even though he arrived a week later): "How did they force him to convert?"

> **Sandykov:** "I am unable to detail the methods of coercion [even though he too converted]. Pressure increased especially after 1844. Thousands of cantonists were brought to the battalion. They were flogged and various methods used so that they would convert. Matters came to a pass that we ourselves forced each other to convert, and that was because we feared that if someone would not convert, it would be unpleasant for us converts. Therefore we exerted pressure on those who had not yet converted: 'Go and convert like we did.'"
> **Chairman:** "Did you yourself beat anyone so that he would convert?"
> **Sandykov:** "I probably did."[4]

Thus, from the testimonies of Itzkovitz, Sandykov, and Terent'ev, it becomes even clearer that the conversion process was based on psychology of the masses, with those who had already submitted as a result of their weakness exerting pressure on their stronger brethren.

All in all, the big revolt in Kronshtadt surprised the authorities with its dimensions and the participants' perseverance. This was the first time that young Jews organized themselves and operated successfully against the system. There is no doubt that this revolt provided Tsar Alexander's advisors with food for thought, and one can estimate that in the end this even led to the decision to abolish the institution of forced conversion.

F. Echoes of the Opposition to Conversion in Kronshtadt

Echoes of the revolt reverberated in all the military units where the insurgents arrived.

---

4   Brigadier General Rebinder wrote in his report that the cantonists in Smolensk explained their wish to convert as an expression of "identification with peers." Gosudarstvennyi arkhiv Rossiiskoi Federatsii [State archive of Russian Federation], f. 109, 1 eksp., d. 330, ll. 28–28 rev.

> **To the Commander of the District A of the Gendarmerie, July 1, 1857**
>
> **File no. 294**
>
> **Captain Samoilov, Officer of the Gendarmerie in Arkhangel'sk, announces:**
>
> On July 1 of this year, by the order of the military governor of Arkhangel'sk, a further examination was conducted by Lieutenant Grigor'ev and Captain Samoilov concerning complaint 38 of the cantonists of the Arkhangel'sk half-battalion, who were drafted into the Sixteenth Division of the infantry, and claimed that they had been forcibly converted from Judaism to the Orthodox religion.
> In conclusion of the examination, the complaint was not verified, and I hereby report to his honor of this.
>
> Signed: Lieutenant General Count ... [the name is illegible]
>
> Please convey this to the head of the Third Section of the Tsar's Own Chancellery.
>
> Prince Dolgorukov

Thus, the insurgents did not submit, despite all the pressure.

We do not have documents of the military trial conducted against the sailors who came from Arkhangel'sk. It must be remembered that the event occurred shortly before the abolishment of the cantonist decree. We do not know what caused the tsar's decision, but if any one of his advisors had thought about the significance of the Arkhangel'sk revolt, he would have found two contradictory trends. On the one hand, the conversion policy achieved its aim in full, with the conversion of the entire unit. On the other hand, it quickly became clear that this conversion was a sham. The Jewish soldiers learned to pretend to be Christians, and later they took their *tallit* and *tefillin* out of hiding. A group of hidden Jews was formed, like the Marranos in Spain in the Middle Ages. Were the military authorities interested in forming such a phenomenon in their midst? Similar episodes were probably discovered in other locations.[5] Whatever the case may be, the opposition of the cantonists to conversion to Christianity, such as we see with the revolt in Arkhangel'sk, may have tipped the scales in favor of the annulment of the decree.

---

5   Such as in Perm' in 1846.

Part VI

THE ABOLISHMENT OF THE CANTONIST DECREE

1

The Process of the Abolishment and Its Reasons

Only a year later, after the coronation of Alexander II, was it decided to equate the military service obligations of the Jews with those of the other segments of the population.

> **Imperial Declaration**[1]
>
> **Regarding good will and concessions on the occasion of the tsar's coronation.**
>
> **On this festive day, on which, with the Supreme Lord's blessing, the crown of our fathers has been placed on our head, we order:**
>
> ... Clause 27. To cancel any judicial proceedings for delay in reporting the birth of soldiers' children, who are to be conscripted as cantonists. ... Any cantonist who, according to these orders, was removed from the authority of the cantonist institution when he arrived to his parents' family, his relatives, or adoptive parents, will belong to the social status he had at the time of the census. Children of soldiers and sailors of other religions who converted to Christianity during their service are not to be transferred to their parents who belong to their previous religion. They can be transferred to Christians for adoption.
>
> August 26, 1856

---

1 Levanda, *Sbornik zakonov*, 769–857.

Personal order of the tsar to the Senate

His Imperial Majesty the tsar commands:

Jews are to be granted concessions in the obligations of conscription.

In our wish to ease the conscription obligations of the Jews, and to terminate their existing hardships, we command:

Soldiers should be drafted from among the Jews equally to other social classes. As a rule, soldiers should be brought from populations without permanent residences or professions. Only in the case of a lack should members of useful professions be drafted in addition.

1. Conscription of soldiers because of arrears in tax payments must be stopped.
2. The temporary laws of 1853, which permit, as an experiment, bringing, instead of a person obligated to enlist, a conscript of the same religion caught without a passport, shall be annulled.

August 26, 1856[2]

---

2   Ibid., no. 771.

2

The Process of Dismantling the Cantonist Institution

The Imperial Ministry of Defense, Promotion Department, 1871[1]

On granting rights accepted in the military to soldiers who came from what were previously cantonist regiments.

To the General Staff: We received a letter about granting rights to soldiers who came from what previously were cantonist regiments similar to those granted to every graduate of a military school according to order no. 120 of April this year.

The reply:

From the General Staff to the Ministry of Defense, January 8, 1871

In a letter from the Supreme Military Committee for granting ranks, a complaint was brought about discrimination in determining years of service between ordinary soldiers and soldiers from among the cantonists who served six, twelve, fifteen, or twenty-five years.

For an adequate discussion of the above problem, we must refer to the same instructions that guided us in determining different periods of service for soldiers among the cantonists.

Cantonist battalions were established for the purpose of education and training for active military service, and naturally they were subordinate to the Ministry of the Defense.

---

1 Central Archives for the History of the Jewish People, HM2\8280.

> In addition to sons of soldiers who served in the permanent army, orphans from the Kingdom of Poland, children of vagrants, and Jews conscripted before the age of eighteen were directed to the battalions of the cantonists according to the regulations of the time.
>
> Similarly, other people who did not belong to families of soldiers were sent there.
>
> In this way, children of noblemen belonging to the court were accepted to cantonist battalions according to their families' request, subject to the regulations of 1838. It is stated in those regulations that the time in the cantonist school is not included in the years of active military service.

On December 25, 1856, the Ministry of Defense and the Navy Ministry requested the exemption of cantonists who had not yet reached the age of conscription from military institutions. Consequently, the tsar issued an order that commanded to immediately release all the children of soldiers and cantonists, and to send them to their families, except those who had reached the age of conscription at that moment. The same declaration determined that Jewish cantonists who had converted to Christianity were not permitted to return to their families, but were to be left in independent Christian institutions.[2]

It is generally accepted that the abolishment of the decree is connected to the death of Nicholas and Alexander's coronation. The beginning of Alexander II's reign did not herald any changes, at least not in the field of conscription, and matters continued as usual. We should remember Alexander's attitude to the trial of the sailors from Arkhangel'sk, when he relied for his guidelines on Nicholas's precedential decree of 1846 regarding the events in Perm'.

---

2   Meaning that a boy who insisted on remaining Jewish *was* returned to his family.

3

Was It Alexander II Who Initiated the Reform in the Regulations on Jewish Conscription?

The reign of Alexander II was characterized by granting civil freedom, such as abolishing serfdom in 1861. Rumors of this trend among the new leadership quickly reached the Jewish community and aroused great expectations. The abolishment of the conscription decree, which sent Jewish children to cantonist institutes, is generally considered one of the first expressions of Alexander II's liberality. Without contradicting this opinion, we will bring several facts, which point that the process had begun already in the days of Nicholas I.

After studying the last conscription documents issued by Nicholas I,[1] we see, even in Nicholas's days, a trend to change the attitude concerning the recruitment of Jews. We refer to repeated cancellation of Jewish drafts—a phenomenon that has not received much attention from historians:

> **Imperial statement on conducting partial mobilization no. 11 in the eastern provinces**
>
> Taking into consideration the development of the present security circumstances, we recommend reinforcing the sea and land forces by creating additional military units. We therefore command:
>
> Clause 1. To conduct partial recruitment no. 11 according to the quota of 9 per 1000 people.

---

1   Levanda, *Sbornik zakonov*, 828–837.

> Clause 3. Among the Jews subject to the conscription obligation, conscripts must be taken based on the conscription regulations, addendum 685, according to which they are obliged to provide in each partial conscription 10 out of every 1000 men.

Just a month later the command was rescinded by the Senate:

> **July 19, 1854**
>
> **Command of the Ruling Senate by imperial order**
>
> On June 5, 1854, the Ruling Senate received a report from the minister of defense saying that His Imperial Majesty, as an expression of his mercy, has agreed to order that, when conducting partial recruitment no. 11, announced on April 18, 1854, Jews are not to be taken, because conscripts according to a quota of 10 out of every 1000 men has already been taken from them this year during recruitment no. 11 in the western provinces.
> This command is to be sent to all the systems dealing with the matter.

Indeed, on January 29, 1854 an order was issued to conduct conscription in the western provinces, with the aim defined as "the need to maintain reserve forces for the ongoing replenishment of units on the battlefield." Within a year, the army authorities again conducted mobilization in both recruitment areas, the west and the east. As was customary in times of peace, conscription each region was conducted once in two years, while the Jews had to supply conscripts every year. Therefore, there was no reason to recruit Jews twice a year. Ostensibly, this decision of the Senate stems from realistic considerations. Perhaps for the first time the authorities understood that there was a limit to the Jews' conscription capabilities. A more important detail is that the authorities did not announce a draft of Jews to complete the quota in areas where the community had not met the conscription demands, whether because the quotas had indeed been met (which does not seem likely), or because the authorities had become more flexible as a result of their disappointing experience in drafting Jews.[2] Moreover,

---

2   See, for example, the story of the conscription in Berdychiv, 106; Central Archives of the History of the Jewish People, HM2\9423/12, copy from Gosudarstvennyi arkhiv Rossiiskoi Federatsii [State archive of the Russian Federation], f. 109, 2 eksp.

when the decision was made for conscription in the west, it was known that the Jews there had already been drafted in the spring. So, why was it necessary to include mention of the Jews in the conscription order of this area? It is possible that we have here an opportunity to look closely at the decision-making "laboratory," and we can assume that, after the conscription order of April 18, 1854 was issued, the Jewish lobby started to operate in such a way that made it possible to rescind the decree within a month.

In December 1854, similar decisions were made:[3]

> **Order of the Ruling Senate**
>
> In light of the circumstances that have arisen, we are forced to operate the land and sea forces in full format. We therefore command:
>
> 1. To conduct partial conscription no. 12 among the peasants of the eastern provinces of the empire, with the quota of 10 out of every 1000 men. The recruitment will be implemented on the basis of a special order.
> 2. The recruitment should begin as of February 15, and should end on March 15, 1855.
>
> Jews subject to the obligation of conscription are drafted according to the conscription regulations, addendum 685, according to which they are obligated to supply 10 out of every 1000 men in each partial conscription.
>
> December 1, 1854

Later, a contradicting decision was made:

> **Command of the Senate by Imperial Order**
>
> According to the report of the minister of defense, until favorable circumstances are created, the Jews from the Taurida Kingdom and the province of Bessarabia are to be released from conscription. . . .
>
> December 9, 1854

---

3   Levanda, *Sbornik zakonov*, 831–835.

> **Command of the Senate by Imperial Order**
>
> According to the report of the minister of defense of December 31, 1854, the Senate commands to release the Jews from presenting conscripts for partial conscription no. 12 in the eastern provinces....
>
> This command is to be sent to all government systems dealing with the matter.
>
> January 6, 1955

It must be concluded that, after the law of conscription no. 12 was passed, new circumstances made it necessary to hastily cancel the obligation to draft Jews. At first, the cancellation applied only to specific areas, but within a month Jewish conscription within that draft was cancelled completely. The new developments refer, first of all, to the war with Turkey. In addition, Gessen assumes that the central cause for the decision was the impoverishment of the Jews and the fact that the supply of recruits had been exhausted.[4]

Concerning this hypothesis, it needs to be said that Gessen speaks of an economic and social situation that does not change in a moment. Therefore, one cannot accept his opinion as an explanation for the change in the imperial position that happened within a month, unless we assume the involvement of some influential government agents or Jewish lobbyists. It is not known who might have made the tsar change his mind, although we hear of the efforts by the Ministerial Committee on Jewish Affairs, headed by Kiselev, to temper the extremism of the previous tsar, Nicholas.

> **Concerning conducting partial conscription no. 13 in 17 western provinces of the empire**
>
> According to the present security situation, and to replenish the sea and land forces to their full format, we hereby command:
>
> 1. To conduct partial conscription no. 13 according to the quota of 12 out of every 1000 men....
> 2. The Jews should be released from submitting soldiers for that conscription.
>
> April 24, 1855

---

4   See above, in the section "Economic Motives," 38.

This order was published so close to Alexander's coronation that it was likely accepted without the tsar's direct involvement, as part of a routine. Academic honesty demands that we point to a change in Nicholas's position concerning Jewish conscription, without being able to confirm what exactly caused this change.

It is likely that, together with the central reason—that of security—there were secondary reasons, one of which was the clash between Nicholas I's compulsive and arbitrary nature and the reality in which it was very difficult to recruit Jews on a large scale.

In contrast to common opinion, which connects the changes in Jewish conscription to the coronation of Alexander II, I would suggest considering the continuity of the monarchy. Imperial government systems do not tolerate radical changes, and any new development must have a preparatory phase. For example, during the transfer of rule from Alexander I to Nicholas I in 1825, the preparations for passing the law of mandatory conscription of Jews were made by Alexander, but in practice it was Nicholas who promoted the legislation. This operational and organizational continuity was ensured by officials who were continually employed in the palace. During the transition from Nicholas I to Alexander II, first and foremost among such figures was Minister Kiselev. Kiselev, who had been very close to Nicholas, had an important role in raising the idea of the need for reform, including the abolishment of serfdom. Already in Nicholas's days, Kiselev initiated the release of imperial serfs who were the tsar's permanent "property." We should remember the Kiselev was also the chairman of the Ministerial Committee for Jewish Affairs. The committee was established after the opinion paper he prepared in 1840, at the request of Nicholas I, concerning the changes that were needed in matters concerning the Jews.

Immediately upon the death of Nicholas, Kiselev began to prepare material proving that the tsar's policy concerning the Jews had not been successful. On March 14, 1856, a year after Alexander II's succession to the throne, Kiselev submitted a report in which he determined that the activity in the "Jewish sphere" had failed.[5] Among other things, his report revealed the true goals of the committee's activity in the days of Nicholas I: "To promote the integration of Jews into the general population by weakening the Jews' religious faith and directing them to useful employment." He stated that "the laws concerning the Jews, and the government decisions, are full of contradictions and limitations that prevent

---

5   Arkhiv Ministerstva vnutrennikh del, departament politsii ispolnitel'noi [Archives of the Ministry of Internal Affairs, department of police enforcement], d. 3499 (1856), quoted in Gessen, *Istoriia*, 142.

the policy of assimilation." Therefore Kiselev suggested reviewing the entire legislation concerning the Jews in order to bring about maximum rapprochement with the general population, "taking the Jews' ethical condition into account as far as possible." One need not be a linguist in order to understand that Kiselev was talking about full assimilation of the Jews in the Russian Orthodox population by "weakening their faith." In other words, Kiselev recommended taking intentional actions against the Jewish religion, with the aim of conversion. His proposal was not written out of love for the Jews, but in order to improve the methods of assimilating them. Alexander II gave his approval to improve the means of achieving this goal.[6]

Kiselev's mention of the Jews' moral situation was doubtlessly meant to point to limitations of rapprochement. At the same time, however, we see his criticism of the existing laws, especially with respect to the limitations and discrimination regarding the Jews.

Simultaneously, some regional governors turned to the tsar with the claim that increased conscription was impoverishing the Jewish population, by removing workers from the labor market. The message was clear: Jews who worked paid taxes to the state treasury. A Jew in the army and his family were a burden on the general public. The governor general of the Baltic states, Prince Suvorov, wrote that "increased conscription does not annihilate the Jewish population,[7] as it reproduces quickly, but the conscriptions impoverish the community."[8]

On the basis of these points, the ministerial committee demanded cancelling the enlarged conscription quota, conscription of minors, and kidnapping vagrants. The order to abduct vagrants was anyway an experimental measure accepted for a period of three years as of 1853, and now the experiment had ended. Alexander II gave his approval, and these decrees were annulled. Regarding those who were sent to prisoners' regiments for transgressions in conscription, no decision was made, and it was only in 1859 that all those conscripted at any age and health condition were returned home. Celebrations were held in Jewish quarters in honor of the abolishment of the horrific decrees and in honor of the liberal tsar.

---

6   Ibid.
7   As Nicholas I had hoped.
8   Gessen, *Istoriia*, 142.

4

Legal Procedures against Those Who Returned to Judaism

We have already discussed the investigation and the trials of soldiers from the Arkhangel'sk half-battalion and Perm' who refused to convert. In the Arkhangel'sk case, the approach taken by the authorities was complex. On the one hand, soldiers were punished and sent to penal units for further "correction." On the other hand, the prosecution recognized that their conversion was carried out using improper methods. In a correspondence between the commander of the Kronshtadt port and the military prosecution, we hear a certain note of surprise as if the writers do not know under what pretext to punish the refusing soldiers. This was until the commander of the port received the legal opinion which invented a case of blasphemy of the "sacred rituals of Christianity," which only applied to a few soldiers: those who spat out Jesus's "blood and body" in the church.

It seems to us that those trials against those who returned to Judaism, which were also held long after the abolishment of the cantonist decree, and at the end of the Jewish soldiers' military service, may be able to explain the internal connotation that the tsarist authorities attributed to the conversion of Jews.

In the research literature, four such trials are mentioned. First, there is Terent'ev's trial, which was discussed above.[1] In his case, the investigation examined the evidence to verify the claim of forced conversion. The matters seem puzzling: Isn't a person's free will enough to choose any religion he wants? But even thirty years after the cantonist institution had been abolished, the Church regarded the former boy soldiers as its legitimate loot and was not

---

1   *Voskhod* 4 (1881).

ready to relinquish them, even if the conversion was conducted during a mass "campaign" under the jurisdiction of the authorities. There is no doubt that the Russians regarded the Jews' conversion with true religious enthusiasm, as can be understood from the description of the mass baptism ceremony in Kazan' (above, 215).

As we see from Terent'ev's and other trials, the jury usually acted with reasonable discretion, and after verifying the claims of the accused, he was exonerated. So it was, for example, in the trial of Ivan Katzman, which was held in 1869 in Moscow's district court.[2] Katzman made an interesting claim, declaring that, after his baptism, conducted by force, he never once performed any Christian ritual. This claim was reinforced from other sources. From the army's point of view, it seems that the act of baptism was an aim in its own right, and did not necessitate any further involvement in worship. The jury acquitted Ivan Katzman and allowed him to return to Judaism.

In 1879, the retired (!) private Moshe Eisenberg was arrested in St. Petersburg on suspicion of forging a certificate of discharge from military service. From the investigation documents it appears that Eisenberg was drafted in 1851 when he was eleven years old, and continued to serve in the army until 1874, for twenty-three years. After his conscription, Eisenberg was directed to the notorious cantonist institution in Arkhangel'sk. In his trial he gave details describing how force was exerted to achieve conversion: unreasonable physical punishment and torture, such as being held for a long time in a bath that had been heated to the highest temperatures. The jury acquitted him.

The story of Israel Leib Itzkovitz has been told above. He was also abducted at the age of eleven from the town of Polotsk in Belarus, and in 1853 was brought to the institution in Arkhangel'sk. After the abolition of the cantonist decree and the dismantling of his half-battalion, he was not released home, but sent to a vocational school for the artillery. (This is evidence of Itzkovitz's talents and the fact that the army needed him.) In 1871, eighteen years after he was conscripted, Itzkovitz dared to declare that he had been converted by force. Unlike the previous trials we mentioned, his declaration was made while he was still in the army and so the case did not arrive at the civil court. Itzkovitz was sentenced to "correction and reconvincing," demoted from his position, which he had acquired as a "good Christian," and sent to a different unit for further pressure and to bring him back to Christianity. Fifteen years after the abolition of the cantonist decree, the army and the Church were still struggling over each and

---

2   See *Den'* 4 (1871).

every converted Jew, unlike the civil authorities, who looked on the "religious deserters" with forgiveness.

It seems that the motives for abolishing the inequality in the conscription of Jews, including conscription of minors, included the difficulties in drafting Jews which began already in the time of Nicholas I, linked to the impoverishment of the Jewish population as a result of exhaustive conscriptions. There were also problems related to exerting force to convert. Finally, the cantonist institutions were abolished, destroying a traditional framework for mass Jewish conscription. All this, together with Jewish lobbying, which was successful thanks to the liberalization of the tsarist government during the time of Alexander II, finally led to the abolishment of the increased conscription quota for Jews.

Part VII

CONCLUSIONS AND MISCELLANEA

1

Important Documents

From the instruction booklet for priests in the cantonist institutions on converting Jewish cadets to the Orthodox religion:

> **According to the order of the Holy Governing Synod**[1]
>
> 1. The priest is to approach the task both as a special mission and by virtue of his position in the army: To convert to Christianity the Jewish cadets in military institutions, he must remember that true entry into Christianity occurs by virtue of divine kindness, and he is only a tool in the hand of God. Therefore, he is to approach this significant task after deep introspection. He must not rely on his knowledge or his diligence. He is not to promise himself or others, out of self-confidence, quick and shining successes. He is to pray for divine blessing to help him in his mission.
> 2. He must prepare a plan of action. He is to gather material regarding his Jewish cadets, their condition at the moment, and additional circumstances, such as: how dependent they are on their commanders, their relationship with Orthodox cadets, etc. The plan of implementation should be suited to these circumstances. Each detail should help achieve the goal.
> 3. The priest should attempt to acquire the trust of the military commanders, his superiors in the institution. The military authorities can be of great help and have influence in carrying out the task. He should therefore act so that the military authorities will see him as a humble servant of the Church, adhering to his faith and being friendly to everyone. He must try to distance himself from any negative incident.
>
> Written by the priest Kutnevich

---

1   The Central Archives for the History of the Jewish People, HM2\8281/4. See also Ginzburg, "Mucheniki-deti," 50–79.

2

The Efforts of the Jewish Communities to Ease the Cantonists' Conditions

The first document analyzed in this section is a letter concerning cantonists in the Riga battalion,¹ which was sent to Nicholas I on May 1, 1829. The authors of this letter were very familiar with the clauses of the regulations of August 26, 1827. They claimed that freedom of religion was granted to the soldiers, while the Jewish children in Riga faced unlawful discrimination. They did not receive permission either to go to the synagogue or to pray within the institution. Because they were not allowed to observe *mitzvot* or the festivals, and because they had no spiritual leader, they were becoming estranged from Judaism. However, in truth they did not want to abandon their religion. The letter writers asked to appoint rabbis for the minors, to allow them to pray together and to observe the Sabbath. The letter was signed by Meir son of Reuven Turchin, Leib son of Shalom Shasher Traeger, Yosef son of Tzvi Chibuk, and Shimon son of Shmuel Bender; all from Vilna.

A little earlier, on March 9, 1828,² the commander of the Gendarmerie, Count Benkendorf, ordered Lieutenant Colonel Merder, wing commander in the Third Brigade, to make inquiries concerning the Jews' complaint regarding the treatment of cantonists in Vitebsk. Benkendorf informed Merder that Jews came to St. Petersburg, "spreading rumors" that the Jewish children conscripted according to the regulations were "receiving treatment contrary to the regulations." They were treated very severely, not permitted to meet their relatives, and

---

1 Central Archives for the History of the Jewish People, HMF759, copy from Gosudarstvennyi arkhiv Rossiiskoi Federatsii [State archive of the Russian Federation], f. 109, 1 eksp., d. 196, ll. 36–39.
2 Ginzburg, "Mucheniki-deti," 22–27.

given food prohibited by their religion. This unsuitable treatment was, in the opinion of the Jews clearly directed towards conversion. In his letter to Merder, Benkendorf commands: "I therefore charge you to collect accurate information on this matter in a convenient way and with a reasonable pretext."

On the same day, Benkendorf sent an identical letter to Brigadier General Rebinder, the commander of Department 4 of District I of the Gendarmerie. This letter dealt with the condition of the Jewish cantonists in the institution for war orphans in Smolensk. According to Benkendorf, he had received a complaint that "they are forced to eat food forbidden by their religion, and are forced to denigrate their religion. The commanders set the Christian cadets on them to mock and curse them."

On April 17, 1828, Rebinder reported concerning the complaint:

> He admits that Jewish cantonists receive the same food as the others. They pray according to the Greek Orthodox rite, and in their reading and writing lessons, they learn Orthodox prayers by heart.
>
> The institution management forbids mocking Jews, but in their leisure time, and when there is no close supervision, the Christian cadets indeed mock them. At the moment there are 103 cadets in the institution, 28 of whom have converted without any coercion.
>
> I summoned several children who have not converted for a conversation. I asked them whether they do not want to convert, and they said that they have no wish to do so, and no one is forcing them to convert.
>
> I asked those intending to convert the same. They claimed that they are doing so to identify with their peers.

As a result of further investigation, Major-General Balahanov wrote to Benkendorf concerning on April 1, 1829:[3]

> In the first conscription there were not many Jews. Now there are already about 300 Jewish children in Smolensk. They claim that the treatment they receive is in opposition to the regulations.
>
> 1. They do not receive kosher food.

---

3   Ibid.

> 2. They are forced to read Christian prayers and are taught to recite by heart the prayer "Almighty God."
> 3. They are not allowed to wear phylacteries during their prayers.
> 4. Before the Passover festival, Jews from Belarus brought *matzot*. The cantonists' commander, Major Vinokurov, refused to deliver the packages.
>
> When he was in Pskov, Rebinder transferred all the details to the Commander of the Cantonist Division, Colonel Vachin. Vachin promised to give Vinokurov instructions accordingly. When Major Rebinder returned to Smolensk, he found no change in the matter. Therefore, all the above complaints are even more valid.

Merder also investigated the situation in Vitebsk and reported to Benkendorf on March 20, 1829:[4]

> According to your order of March 9, I examined your request no. 1024 concerning the cantonists in Vitebsk.
>
> I hereby inform you that there is no coercion that Jews convert. Immediately on the arrival of the Jews to the battalion, twelve of them declared their wish to convert.
>
> In order to receive instruction, a priest was invited, who instructed them over a period of a few days. During that time the Jews of Vitebsk, under the pretext of observing the tenets of their religion, sent secret messages in order to convince them not to take that step.
>
> In these messages, they promised that in a short time the Jews would be freed and would return to their previous situation, thanks to their intercession with the tsar. Similarly, they wrote about the close arrival of the Messiah, and sent letters with all sorts of curses.[5] They convinced the children not to eat the food cooked for the other cantonists. In short, they tried to dissuade them completely from the goal planned by the government for their benefit.

---

4   Central Archives for the History of the Jewish People, HMF759/a–b, copy from Gosudarstvennyi arkhiv Rossiiskoi Federatsii [State archive of the Russian Federation], f. 109, 1 eksp., d. 196, ll. 22–27.
5   *Shulten* in Yiddish. An accepted custom in East Europe.

As a result of this conspiracy, eight out of those who wanted to convert returned to their religion, and no one prevented them from doing so. Later, in addition to the remaining four, another six of those first ones regretted their decision and converted of their own free will, but two others have remained members of their previous religion.[6]

Because of the Jews' conspiracies, I do not expect great success in achieving the goal. This is despite the secret order of the government to persuade the Jews of our religion's superiority in a pleasant manner.

The Jews demand to allow the Jewish cantonists to cook kosher food and to manage a separate kitchen with separate utensils. This request was rejected based on order 111 of the General Staff, issued last year to the military cantonist divisions. We therefore forced the Jewish cantonists to eat the food that was prepared for everyone. Similarly, based on the above order, the request of the Jews of Vitebsk to accommodate the Jewish cantonists separately was rejected. As is known, the order demands placing Jews among the others at the proportion of one among every five non-Jews, at least.[7] In addition, the request to permit the cantonists to meet with family members was also rejected, this too according to the above order, clause 10, forbidding contact between cantonists and Jewish citizens. Furthermore, these minors were brought from the district of Minsk, and they certainly do not have relations in Vitebsk.

The Jews of Vitebsk also demand to allow the minors to bathe on fixed days, to fast on their fast days, and to release them from prayers on their Sabbath and festivals. Granting such a request will cause the cantonists superfluous trouble, and will prevent them from studying properly.

Now they are asking to allow them to eat only *matzot* on the Passover festival, and on the first two nights of the festival to drink four cups of wine prepared by a Jew. They complain that they are not allowed to go to their prayers, to eat in houses of Jews, and even to bring food into their rooms in the institution.

I have spoken about this to the commander of the Cantonist Division, Colonel Vachin. Vachin gives permission to use *matza*, but only as a treat, while participating in the regular meals of the unit. He also permitted the Jews to pray according to their custom in a separate room.

---

6   Merder's pretense is quite transparent.
7   This order was not carried out.

> I have tried hard to expose harsh treatment toward the Jewish cantonists, but in vain, except for the circumstances described above, which the Jews consider harsh treatment.
>
> With your permission, I will express my personal opinion on the matter. One cannot compare the situation of the Vitebsk cantonists to that of cantonists in any other town. In other towns there are no Jews in the surroundings, and therefore there is no Jewish influence on the minors. Under such conditions, within a short time, they can forget their burdensome religion and admit the preference of our religion. Whereas here, there is no end to their sophisticated complaints, and the authorities are busy with unlimited clarifications, instead of working to perform true kindness to the Jews according to the guidelines of the authorities.
>
> The only means to solve the problem, in my opinion, is to transfer the Jews to Smolensk,[8] or any other town, in order to spare all the complaints.

Here is the initial document from a Jewish community regarding the distribution of *matzot* to cantonists:[9]

> April 5, 1828[10]
>
> To the commander of the Smolensk Fortress, Major-General E. Kern
>
> We received the following letter from the Jews of Mogilev:
>
> **A request of the Jewish community of Mogilev, Belarus**
>
> We hereby request and plead that you approve the transfer of special products for the cantonist boys serving in the town of Smolensk. We would like to stress the importance of special products for the festival of Passover, based on the permission and order given last year to the engineering division.

---

8 As known, complaints were submitted by the Jews in Smolensk, as well.
9 Central Archives for the History of the Jewish People, HMF759/a–b, copy from Gosudarstvennyi arkhiv Rossiiskoi Federatsii [State archive of the Russian Federation], f. 109, 1 eksp., d. 196, l. 17.
10 Central Archives for the History of the Jewish People, HMF760, copy from Gosudarstvennyi arkhiv Rossiiskoi Federatsii [State archive of the Russian Federation], f. 109, 1 eksp., d. 330. The date refers to the day the letter was filed.

Signed: S. Shpungin, head cantor of the community; head of the community, Yetzke Staroslasky; the merchants Hirsch Lipschitz and Etya Frumkin.

Submitted in March 1828

The *matzot* were baked by the community, and now they request approval to distribute them among the soldiers in Smolensk. However, the cantonists in Smolensk were not granted permission to celebrate Passover, as we see from the report by Major Vinokurov, commander of the military cantonist battalion in Smolensk:[11]

To Major-General Kern, military commander of Smolensk

Report no. 407[12]

In reply to your order of April 3, 1828, together with the letter of the Jewish community of Mogilev, I hereby inform you that the request to supply *matzot* for Passover does not seem to me to be reasonable. One cannot set aside a special table for them in the dining room without an explicit order from you.

In addition, in the regulations of October 31, 1827, clause 111, it states that Jewish minors enjoy the same conditions as Christian minors and receive military and vocational education equal to that of the Christians. This being the case, if we release them from studies on their festivals, when the Christian students will be studying, the Jews will miss the possibility of studying the topics covered on those days. Then again, they will not learn on Christian holidays, thus missing studies twice. In general, such a practice will not contribute anything positive to their vocational or military studies. The General Staff will blame us for their failure in their studies, and this will have negative implications.

---

11 Central Archives for the History of the Jewish People, HMF760, copy from Gosudarstvennyi arkhiv Rossiiskoi Federatsii [State archive of the Russian Federation], f. 109, 1 eksp., d. 190, ll. 28–28 rev.
12 Central Archives for the History of the Jewish People, HMF759/a–b, copy from Gosudarstvennyi arkhiv Rossiiskoi Federatsii [State archive of the Russian Federation], f. 109, 1 eksp.

> Therefore, I recommend that you receive explicit permission from the superior command concerning exempting Jewish minors on festivals and transferring *matzot* to them.
>
> Signed: Major Vinokurov

Other soldiers were more fortunate:

> To Field Marshal General Golenishchev Kutuzov
>
> Dear Pavel Vasil'evich,
>
> His Majesty the Tsar has responded positively to the request of the Jews who are here on the occasion of their businesses. He has agreed to allow the distribution of dry bread, called *matza*, to the Jewish recruits in Kronshtadt for the Passover festival, which they celebrate between March 18 and 26, as well as additional supplies that they need for the two festive meals during Passover.
>
> In this manner, the tsar expresses his wish to allow the Jews to observe the Jewish ritual.
>
> In addition, supervision is necessary to ensure that the transfer of these supplies will not serve as an excuse to meet these Jews or the Jews of St. Petersburg.
>
> I am passing on the tsar's wish to you, for you to supervise the implementation.
>
> March 18, 1828
>
> Signed: A. Benkendorf

A similar letter was sent to Petr Mironovich Roznov on March 12, 1828, with the following addition: "The police should be required to issue [travel] permits to Jews beyond Kronshtadt, specifying the exact limits of the permit."

Here is the reaction of the Jewish community to this news:

> 28 Adar (March 2)
>
> To our esteemed friend, Rabbi Shaul Wolf, and his brother-in-law, the honorable Rabbi Michael Rabinowitz,

We received your dear letter from 26 Adar, and our heart was filled with joy, and our eyes lit up to see that God has inclined our tsar's heart to perform kindness and mercy towards our brethren who are serving in his army and to allow them to observe the *mitzva* of eating *matza*, etc.

Friends, we sigh over the children who are sent here, to the Minsk district. There are now sixty-two children in the military school. The treatment they receive is terrible. They are not allowed to leave the place, nor is any Jew allowed to enter the school. We tried everything possible that they be allowed to eat kosher food, but we were not successful. The imperial law, which forbids forcing minors to convert, has been violated, and they have already forced eleven children to convert.

Signed: Beinish son of Aharon Riess, Shmuel son of Aviezer Selig Zelich, Avraham son of Natan Herman

1. The request of the Mogilev community was discussed in the government further. During the meeting of the Jewish Committee on July 1, 1829,[13] this topic was raised for discussion, along with the answer of the cantonists' commander in Smolensk, who wrote that he needed approval from his superiors. The members of the committee also discussed the request to arrange a separate table for the Jews, which they decided violated the order of the chief of staff from October 21, 1827, and the request to release Jews, in addition to Christian holidays, also on Jewish festivals. They also talked about the request of four Jews, who presented themselves as emissaries of the Vilna community, concerning the Jewish cantonists in the Riga half-battalion. The cantonists there were prevented from gathering for public prayer or from going to prayers in the town in their free time. They were not allowed to gather for public prayer on "the Festival of Esther, in memory of the downfall of Amalek." They were also prevented from eating *matza* on Pesach. They were forced to work on the Sabbath and were prevented from approaching rabbis and mentors. In response, the members of the committee cited clauses 91, 92, 93, and 94 of the regulations, which allowed the Jews freedom of worship in their free time, and permitted them to turn to

---

13   Central Archives for the History of the Jewish People, HM2\8280/9, copy from Rossiiskii gosudarstvennyi voenno-istoricheskii arkhiv [Russian state archive of military history], St. Petersburg, f. 560, op. 10.

rabbis or to determine a place for prayer within the institution. In the draft of the cantonist regulations, the right to appoint rabbis was given also to the minors, but this clause was deleted by an order from above.[14]

The Jewish Committee's decision:

> The Chief Rabbi of Posvol', Vilna Province [now Pasvalys, Lithuania], together with his three deputies, applied last year with the request to appoint rabbis for the recruits. The director of the Department for Religious Affairs informed the chief of staff that:
>
> 1. the communities are not permitted to send rabbis to the minors;
> 2. regarding the adult soldiers, the government will make a decision concerning the appointment of rabbis;
> 3. the commanders on military bases are responsible for the decision concerning releasing the soldiers on the Sabbath and festivals;
> 4. regarding the answer of the cantonists' commander in Smolensk, the matter belongs to the authority of the management of the cantonists. They can be allowed to fulfill the commandments of their religion subject to the regulations and as the commanders see fit.

Another interesting document is this evidence of Jewish fundraising in the first years after passing the cantonist decree, when it was hoped that bribes could help to annul the new law:

> File 9590
>
> The Bureau of the commander of the Special Lithuanian Division [surname illegible, according to archival documents it could only be Cavalry General Rosen].
>
> To General Count Tolstoi
>
> June 15, 1828
>
> Classified

---

14 Important testimony, unknown till now.

We received a letter from the head of the Imperial Third Department, Benkendorf, concerning the fundraising conducted by the Jews to fund the activities of the Jewish community's emissaries. I have therefore issued an order to all the district governors under my command to collect in a most secretive and exact manner all the information on the subject, so as to expose this affair. I gave a special task to the acting governor of the Volhynia district to investigate the deeds of Rabbi Isaac of Berdichev. This rabbi went to the town of Kherson for the above purpose. Special attention should be paid to his activities and his contacts. In the event that the suspicions of fundraising against him are verified, the money should be confiscated as well as the documents likely to expose the extent of the deed in all its details.

Together with conveying this information to your honor, I see need to inform you that, as early as 1826, rumors reached me about the donations to finance the activities of the emissaries. The activity of the emissaries was aimed at maintaining the status quo and postponing the actual recruitment of Jews into the army. Under these circumstances, I ordered the governors of the provinces to gather information about the situation.

In this connection, it became clear to me that in 1818 the tsar allowed the Jews to collect lace made of silver and gold (for weddings and for burials). But now this permission has been rescinded.

The Bureau of the Second-in-Command to the Tsar, the commander of the Special Lithuanian Division

June 16, 1828

To the military commander of St. Petersburg, General Tolstoi

The Governor of the Volhynia district conducted investigation in the town of Berdichev. During the course of the investigation it became clear that, following the tsar's order of the start of Jewish conscription to the army, a decision was reached in the Jewish communities to organize a fundraising campaign of fifteen golden rubles per person. Rabbis, including Rabbi Isaac Rapaport from Berdichev, went out to conduct the campaign. I am transferring to you his letter to the Jews of Nikolaev [Mykolaiv] as well as the list of contributions received from the Jews of Nikolaev and Kherson.

The last chain of documents we quote here concerns two cantonists who died during the harsh journey after leaving Smolensk.¹⁵

> To the Commander of the Gendarmes Count Benkendorf
>
> From Major-General Balahanov
>
> June 6, 1829
>
> **Memorandum**
>
> Major General Rebinder reported last year on April 25 that, on the fifteenth of that month, sixty-seven cantonists left Smolensk. The journey was difficult and it was very cold. The cantonists marched twenty-three *versta* [24.5 km]. They came absolutely exhausted to the place where they were to stay overnight. Two of them had died on the way shortly before their stop. Their bodies were found thrown on the road. The group's commander only reported the death of one who, he said, had died suddenly. As a result of the report, I ordered Major Rebinder to supply more details. He reported that one body was found by a police officer of the Smolensk district, and the second was found by a peasant in a ditch next to the road. The police officer reported to the Smolensk district court the day after the group left the city. Regarding the second body, it was handed over to the representative of the court when he arrived at the site for the investigation. The doctor who performed the post mortem certified that the death was the result of exhaustion.
>
> Major-General Balahanov

---

15 Central Archives for the History of the Jewish People, HMF759, copy from Gosudarstvennyi arkhiv Rossiiskoi Federatsii [State archive of the Russian Federation], f. 109, 1 eksp., d. 330.

3

Conclusions

This is the first time an Israeli author has written a book about the service of Jewish boys in the Russian army in 1827–1856. Most of the research or descriptions related to this topic were published in Russian or Yiddish in the beginning of the twentieth century, and reflected to a large extent the emotional load that accompanied this chapter of Jewish history. The topic was mainly presented from a perspective of identification with the suffering of the boys, and rightly so.

Already at the beginning of this study, we believed that our approach should be based, first and foremost, on a comprehensive perspective, viewing the story of the cantonists as an integral part of the developments of that time and place. Thus, it was necessary to examine the Jewish side, particularly the involvement of the community in the conscription activity, the way decisions were made and implemented by the authorities, and the processes among the boys themselves. We approached the material in this way, looking at the sources of the early twentieth century from a critical viewpoint. Material from the Central Archives for the History of the Jewish People in the Hebrew University was an additional source, particularly the documents taken from the archives of the Russian Navy Ministry.

On the basis of this material, one must acknowledge that the policy of conscription of Jewish adults and boys into the Russian army was part of the general policy of mandatory conscription of all the country's citizens, including Muslims, Cossacks, pagans, etc. The ambition of the tsar and his statesmen was to turn Russia into a progressive country in the terms of that period. Beyond being "enemies of Jesus," an image dictated by their Orthodox views, the tsar and the authorities saw the Jews as a people different from them in their culture, their way of life, and their socio-economic structure. Nicholas I's political advisors were strongly influenced by the "political-economic" financial view, which required the active intervention of the authorities in the social and economic structure of the public. This is how the natural aspiration of the Christians for the assimilation of the Jews went hand in hand with the ideas of "improvement and advancement." Under the influence of *maskilim* who found their way into the imperial court, the ministers and the tsar came to the conclusion that it was possible to "improve" the Jewish situation by reeducating them and removing them from the "influence of the Talmud." One cannot argue that the conscription decree was only dictated by antisemitic motives, although antisemitism certainly contributed greatly to the design of the conscription policy, as well as to the physical conditions in which the Jewish soldiers in general, and the boys in particular, were held. Those meant to "educate" the Jews and attract them to Christianity were sergeants and primitive Russian soldiers.

Therefore, despite the obligation of conscription ostensibly applied to all the country's citizens, a special and different law was created for the Jews, which had a clear missionary goal. The special treatment for Jews is also evidenced by the fact that a special ministerial committee for Jews convened regularly in St. Petersburg, and that Jewish topics were also discussed by a committee of heads of government ministries. From time to time, these committees raised ideas on how to expedite the process of modernizing the Jews. One can ironically say that the Jews were the favorite toy of the tsar and his ministers. They continuously tried to categorize them, dress them in clothes that they liked, direct them, and educate them. They meddled non-stop with the Jews, without understanding that a nation deserves to live with respect, without interference.

As expressed by the best of the tsarist officials, such as Vorontsov and Frizel', and as Sir Moses Montefiore advised, the best way to modernize the Jews was to grant them equal rights, and particularly to allow them to live wherever they wished and to work in any legal occupation. But it was just these points that the tsar did not want. As he wrote in his diary: "Such a thing is not possible."

One of the novel aspects emphasized in this volume is the demarcation of periods within the recruitment policy and pointing out the connection between these periods and developments in the Russian Empire. Here, the turning point of the 1840s needs to be stressed. In 1840 Tsar Nicholas turned (we do not know under whose influence) to his closest advisor, Count Kiselev, with the request to prepare an opinion paper on "improving" the Jews. His report, which emphasizes the need for "moral reformation" of the Jews, shifted the weight from making the Jews more efficient to educating them, and led to the acceleration of opening educational institutions for Jewish secularization. Among those who implemented the new policy were the Minister of Education Uvarov, Max Lilienthal, who dealt with establishing state schools for the Jews, and, of course, the head of the Church, Count Protasov, and the Minister of Defense Chernyshev, who expedited the conversion of the cantonists. Both of the above campaigns started in 1843.

The boys' conscription began quite calmly, with less than a thousand conscripts every two years during the first stages. This number was hardly felt. The trauma of the horrors of the cantonists' conscription, which we find in popular folklore, should be attributed to the last years of Nicholas' reign, which was characterized by a significant increase in conscription quotas—up to ten conscripts per thousand taxpayers each year. Nevertheless, the peak of the conversion policy was about twelve years earlier, starting from 1843 and lasting several years. During this period we find intensive correspondence between local priests and the head of the Holy Synod, Protasov. One gets the impression that this awakening in the conversion policy came against the background of the lack of success, if not failure, of conversion activity in the previous years, from 1827 until 1843.

Detailed guidelines concerning methods of missionizing testify, without doubt, to the fact that methods of brutal coercion also did not bear fruit. Statistics teach us that less than half the cantonists converted, and if one half did not convert, we have to find the explanation for the conversion of the other half. As shown in our study, some of the Jewish conscripts were already far from religious observance before their conscription, and these were certainly easy prey for the Church. Analyzing the degree of observance of the Jewish community would, in our opinion, contribute to understanding the phenomenon of conversion. We have to acknowledge that the general Jewish public was already not religious or homogenous in the 1850s, and that this differentiation made missionizing easier.

In addition, the development of methods for conversion, such as analyzing the personality of each boy, inviting them to the home of the commanders, having them take part in the rituals as part of the school curriculum, leads to the conclusion that those who initiated the plan were interested in conversion undertaken, as much as possible, of the boys' free will.

It should be noted that the activity of the Jewish communities weakened the boys' power of resistance against the army. It is clear from the reports of the tsar's officials and the memoirs of the Jewish soldiers that the members of the *kahal* treated the children violently and with abject injustice.

The crux of the matter is that the role of the *kahal* as an autonomous Jewish institution appears here in an absolutely negative light. At the same time, we cannot regard the obligation of implementing the conscription decree placed on the *kahal* as the turning point that broke the community's trust in them, as some of the researchers believe. The breakdown of the *kahal* started already during Polish rule, when the authorities exploited this institution as a tool for extorting money from the Jewish communies. One cannot say that the *kahal* functioned unequivocally for the benefit of the authorities. We find that they often acted, as far as they understood and within the limitations of what was possible, for the benefit of the community. Bringing children for conscription instead of adults was a cruel decision, but the intention was to let the breadwinners, who were often heads of families, stay in the community.

We must also ask: Did the behavior of the *kahal* officials disrupt the recruitment processes and constitute a kind of passive resistance, or did it only serve their own interests? It seems that if the *kahal*'s support of the authorities had been significant, we would not have seen the abolishment of this institution in 1844.

After the *kahal*'s abolishment, a sort of alternative was established, the *obshchestvo*, for conscription and taxation purposes, but it was left without any authority, and was directly subject to the municipal rule and the office of the district governor. From then on, it would not be correct to regard the conscription unit as a community institution, but rather as an administrative institution of the authorities. This is implied in the memoirs of Chaim Merimzon, when the kidnappers transfer the abducted boy directly to the municipal recruiting office without the mediation of the *obshchestvo*. In short, the role of the community's administration as an autonomous body and its functioning during the period of Nicholas should, in our opinion, be a special subject of research focusing on the relationships between the spiritual leadership of the community, its administrative leadership, and the entire public.

The conscripted boys felt betrayed and abandoned by the community, handed over to the gentiles. Contributing to the feeling of alienation was the Jewish society which saw the conscripts as certain candidates for apostasy, and therefore, in many cases, cut off all contact with them. The boys received better treatment from Jewish soldiers who served in areas close to them and from local Jewish residents. In many places the soldiers established prayer houses and even appointed rabbis, observed the Sabbath, and were careful to eat kosher food. Therefore, if a boy arrived at such a location, his resistance to conversion was more stubborn and more successful, as we read in the reports of the priests on site.[1] There was often conflict between Christian army chaplains and the rabbis and Jewish leaders in the areas of the cantonist bases.

Moreover, the time of possible influence and exposure to the priests' missionizing was, as shown in this study, relatively limited—up to six months after the

---

[1] We believe that this evidence of the conscripts' living conditions within the framework of mutual relations with the environment is one of the significant discoveries made during our research for this book.

boy's arrival to the base. Jewish boys acclimatized to army conditions quickly. They found out how to make contact with veteran cantonists, with the local population, and even how to earn money to hire teachers who could help them with their studies. As soon as a boy acquired these skills, he became more immune to the attempts of conversion. The military authorities were also aware of this and therefore attempted to expedite the conversion processes, and sometimes even baptized children on the way to the army base.

With time, "conversion factories" were established, such as the military cantonist schools in Arkhangel'sk, Kazan', and Saratov. The commanders of these schools created an atmosphere of a "conveyor belt." From the day they arrived at the base, new cadets learned: "No one leaves here Jewish." The boys who converted to Christianity were a significant tool of pressure on the recruits.[2] Added to this was discriminatory and excessive punishment meted out to any trainee who did not convert to Christianity. However, as mentioned, these punishments did not last for long as the tsar's men were lazy and drunkards. The moment they came across a "hard nut," they bullied and abused him, but if the boy persisted, they would let go. Thus, in general, anyone who wanted to persist in their refusal to convert had a reasonable chance of success.[3]

During the period just before the end of the cantonist conscriptions, we discover a new phenomenon: young soldiers, who have already outgrown the official definition of cantonists, are directed to cantonist bases, as if to an organized baptism institution. Looking closer at their stories, we see a significant change in the mood of the Jewish public in the Russian Empire. The soldiers were capable of deciding to pretend to convert in order to survive, and then to renounce their Christianity when they saw fit, as we see from the investigation documents of the cantonists from the Arkhangel'sk half-battalion. This, however, was an illusion, as the chances of returning to Judaism were slim. On the one hand, the Jews' religious resistance was weakened as part of the secularization process that became noticeable at the end of the nineteenth century. On the other hand, the military authorities succeeded in creating tools for mass conversion. It was left only to copy Podpolkovnik D'iakonov's method in other military academies and to bring almost all the conscripts, including adults, to convert. Only the death of Nicholas I halted the process, although the cantonist schools remained active for a year after his death.

---

2   See, for example, the description of Terent'ev's trial above.
3   See the memoirs of Klinger, Merimzon, and Itzkovitz.

When we look for a reason for the abolishment of these schools, I doubt that it is connected to the Jews. The cantonist schools were established 150 years earlier as a shelter for orphans of soldiers. At the time of Paul I and at the beginning of Nicholas's reign they underwent certain modernization. The curricula of these schools were adapted from advanced European methods. The army viewed the schools as a tool to train military professionals, much necessary at a time when weapons and technology developed quickly.

Together with this trend of development, we witness an opposite trend: drastic reductions in the number of children who served in these frameworks. The reason is clear: economy. Maintaining cantonist schools was very costly, and it is not for naught that we find records of the calculations of how much each reduction contributed. During the course of the schools' closure, only one segment of the population retained its numbers and maintenance costs: the Jewish boys. Moreover, the number of conscripted Jewish children constantly increased, until the percentage of Jews in these schools reached fifteen percent, a total of 6,500 cadets out of 36,000.

After the abolishment of mandatory conscription of minors to the army, these schools underwent significant improvement and became prestigious educational institutions to train a younger generation of professional officers.

At a certain point, the falling numbers of students and the increasing efficiency in military schools conflicted with the schools' second role: being a tool for assimilation. We do not know whether the new tsar, Alexander II, understood that the rapprochement among various groups of populations in his state accelerated anyway, and that the need for tools to exert pressure in this regard was diminishing.

During the twenty-eight years in which minors were conscripted, more than 60,000 Jewish children passed through the gates of the military institutions. Their personal destiny was trampled by the military machine. Whoever converted to Christianity distanced himself completely from the Jewish people. It was here that the plan of Nicholas I failed. The apostates, including the cantonists, did not have any significant influence on the united Jewish community. Perhaps this consideration also contributed to "liberal" Alexander II's decision to abolish the decree that denigrated the Russians in the eyes of Europe, which was celebrating the dawn of a new era.

In 1856, Kiselev, who in 1840 had initiated the renewal of the "modernization" campaign against the Jews, turned to Alexander II with a written report admitting that the activity of the Jewish Committee had failed. He confessed that one of the aims had been to reduce the size of the Jewish population, and that it was not achieved. The Jews continued to multiply and to oppose the social and financial reforms dictated from above. In addition, conscription was not a productive tool for the government. The increased Jewish quotas of ten conscripts for every thousand taxpayers reduced the community to the brink of impoverishment. They caused a lack of manpower capable of paying the taxes so necessary for the state treasury. In addition, as mentioned above, the soldiers who converted, among them the graduates of the cantonist schools, did not return to influence the Jews. They were rejected by the community and joined the Russian nation. One of the significant causes for the failure of the conversion operation of the cantonists lies in the ministers' lack of understanding this natural process.

Admittedly aside from the considerations originating within the Jewish community, the new tsar had additional considerations for canceling the decrees of his predecessor and striving to change the structure of his regime in a liberal spirit. Thus, the decree of the conscription of minors was abolished, and the conscription methods of the Jews became equal to those of the general population.

Even after the cancellation of the cantonist decree, the cantonist period remains in the national memory as a traumatic experience of abuse of Jewish children. This book awakens in collective Jewish memory pages of heroism, resistance, and lessons learned from past mistakes.

4

Topics Raised in This Book That Merit Additional Discussion

Many topics addressed in this book would benefit from a more detailed scholarly discussion. For example, what were the decisive factors in the mandating conscription for Jews—antisemitism or pragmatic considerations of the authorities? Was the trend of the *kahal* to prefer the conscription of some people rather than postponing the conscription of others just an expression of corruption, or did pragmatic considerations for the benefit of the community also guide them? In general, what influenced the *kahal*'s policy? Did ignoring state laws and the effort to falsify conscription documents help the community or harm it? Were cantonist schools only intended for conversion, or did they also contribute to the cadets' education? Could the Jewish community have operated more energetically for the benefit of the boys? Was there any reasonable chance for the Jewish boys to resist the pressure of the commanders and priests working to convert them? Did the efforts to convert the boys lead to the results that the authorities hoped for? To what extent did the failure of the conversion policy lead to the decision to abolish the cantonist decree? And to what extent might continued family support and that of the Jewish surroundings have prevented a boy's conversion? Finally, what was the extent of the influence of the Jewish soldiers' conversion, especially that of the boys, on the adaptation of the Jewish people to Russian society in the modern era?

5

Analysis of the Material Available for the Research and the Research Methods

A. The Material at Our Disposal

The material available to us can be divided into several categories. First, there is archival material from the Central Archives for the History of the Jewish People. A significant part of it, the documents of the investigation of the cantonists of the Arkhangel'sk half-battalion, had never previously been studied, despite its historical significance. In addition, there were other, as yet unpublished, documents such as the request of the Vitebsk community to supply kosher food for Passover to the cantonists and all the documents related to appointing rabbis in the army. These documents come from the archives of the Tsar's Own Chancellery, the famous Third Section.

In addition, we have provided a comprehensive translation of the conscription law and its appendices. This material has till now only partly appeared in languages other than Russian. The extensive citations clarify the topic and will help students and researchers who wish to study this topic. Similarly, we have attempted to present the full and exact text of the documents of the cantonists' interrogations. Our translations convey in an authentic manner the atmosphere of the time and allow for study of the Russian officials' style of thought and perception.

Of course, there is much significant material in the historical literature. Many memoirs and descriptions written in Russian were published relatively close to the time. The researchers who came after the memoirs had been published did not always reread the material, but often relied on earlier summaries. Thus, we succeeded in exposing significant details in the memoirs of Merimzon, Klinger, and Itzkovitz that have not been addressed previously. We noticed that in the majority of cases the cantonists did not write about their way to Christianity or their own challenges, but generally wrote about the experience of others. Rereading their memoirs broadens the historian's view of the Jewish soldier's way of life beyond the description of the hardships he underwent in the tsar's army.

The contribution of Jewish historians who wrote on the topic at the beginning of the twentieth century, and particularly the studies of Shaul Ginsburg and Iulii Gessen, cannot be underestimated. Ginsburg presents the entire correspondence between those responsible for the conversions and the heads of the Russian Church. In my opinion, not all possible conclusions have been drawn from this amazing material. These are documents that Ginsburg studied and copied immediately after the revolution in 1917. Iulii Gessen offers a contribution of similar importance, particularly with his study of processes within the Jewish community and on the government level. He cites documents from the archives of the Ministry of the Interior, from the archives of the ministerial committee on Jewish affairs, and other such documents of invaluable historical worth. It is a pity that the originals of these important documents are not known to many Jewish historians.

We made use of several items relevant to the topic of the cantonists that are cited in most of the literature and are well known, such as the descriptions of the torture of the cantonists, chiefly taken from memoirs published in *Evreiskaia starina* in the beginning of the twentieth century, particularly those of Moisy Spiegel, Chaim Merimzon, etc., and the stories of the children's abductions, which are important for understanding the topic. Although these are not research literature, we felt it was correct to quote some of the memoirs extensively, so as to make them available to our readers.

Additional material is found in research literature that does not necessarily deal with the cantonists. Here we must emphasize the studies of Prof. Michael Stanislawski and Dr. Aryeh Morgenstern.

I must also mention Emanuel Fleishfish, a new immigrant to Israel, who authored a special book called *Cantonists* from research material that he seems to have brought from Russia. The book has a rich bibliography in Russian, unknown in the West, especially regarding the structure of cantonist schools. It encompasses all aspects of the topic, giving many details of the life of the Jewish cantonist. Unfortunately, Fleishfish wrote in a literary style, without mentioning his sources, so that it is not possible to use his book for research purposes.

B. Materials for Further Research

We consulted with Jewish historians in Russia regarding additional sources for further research. They believe that there is no point in looking for significant material in provincial towns of the former Russian Empire, as such material was transferred to the central archives in Moscow years ago. Indeed, in the catalogue of the Central Archives for the History of the Jewish People there is a list of files found in the imperial army archives in Moscow. It might be possible to receive statistical information about the conscripts and more from that collection. In addition, a lot of material must exist in the archives of the Ministry of the Interior (including the police department), in archives of the ministerial committee, the Senate, and the Synod. For now, the archive research is not complete, but we feel that one cannot expect a lot of surprises.

Professor Simon Dubnow wrote in his article on the beginning of the conscription period[1] that it would be worthwhile to look for documents on fundraising in the community archives. Unfortunately, the majority of community registers has not survived to the flames of the two world wars, the Bolshevik Revolution, and the civil war. In fact, the part dealing with the community's activity and its interrelationship with the civil authorities and with the military authorities has not yet been investigated in depth. Such a study would contribute greatly to understanding the community's role, which now seems contradictory. What was the role of the rabbis? In this study we presented the rabbis as active opposition to the cantonist decree, in contrast to the *kahal*. Nonetheless, we did not find enough halakhic responsa on the topic, and that needs to be explained. A study of community registers would contribute greatly to clarifying this question.

The State of Israel should allocate a proper budget for the discovery and copying of all the documents on Jewish matters kept in the archives of Russia and its neighboring countries. The memory of the Jewish people should be preserved in Israel.

---

1   Dubnov, "Kak vvedena byla rekrutskaia povinnost'."

6

"The Small Soldiers of the Large Empire"

Soon after I completed my research, I learned that Yohanan Petrovsky-Shtern, a native of Kyiv, now living in the United States, was working on a similar study, called "The Small Soldiers of the Large Empire."[1] In a meeting with him, arranged by Professor Shaul Stampfer, I was impressed by the extent of his knowledge and his energy. He told me about his work in the archives in Moscow[2] where he collected material on the Jewish soldiers who served in the Russian imperial army. I read his manuscript closely, and envied the many sources he obtained from the Russian army's central archive. At the same time, I was happy to discover that the results of our studies were similar, and that our conclusions overlap. I saw in this a sign that we were both going in the right direction.

Dr. Petrovsky-Shtern presents interesting data in his book regarding the dynamics of the conversion. The picture he portrays confirms the conclusions of my study. On page 119 of his book he presents a chart of the total number of converts from 1829, two years after the implementation of the decree.[3] In this chart he brings the number of converts in seven battalions. Out of a total of 1862 recruits, 125 converted—less than ten percent. Dr. Petrovsky-Shtern sees in these figures proof that religious conversion was not the main goal of the conscription of Jewish minors, whereas in fact, it could be evidence of the difficulty of achieving the goal of conversion at the first stages of the implementation of the conscription decree. All in all, this was an operation for which the army was not prepared.

---

1   The name of a chapter in Petrovsky-Shtern, *Jews in the Russian Army*.
2   In my research I also used documents from these archives which were photocopied and transferred to the Hebrew University in cooperation with the University of Moscow. This cooperation has now ended.
3   Petrovsky-Shtern, *Jews in the Russian Army*, chart 3.1 based on figures of Russian military historical archives.

Moreover, Petrovsky-Shtern quotes documents showing Nicholas I's deep personal involvement in operating the conversion program.[4] Thus, already in 1829, Nicholas issued a personal order to simplify the conversion processes: to ignore the involvement of civil municipal and clerical officials in the baptism process.[5] Ostensibly, the conversion program was already in existence, but Nicholas I was "experimenting" with it. Petrovsky-Shtern gives evidence in his book that the tsar was a man of action, not a strategist.

Working in the military archive in Moscow, Petrovsky-Shtern collected much data on the extent of conversion during the more advanced stages of the program. He verifies my conclusions according to which at the beginning of the 1840s there was a significant turning point in Nicholas's involvement in the conversion processes. In order to respond to this change in the tsar's perception, the army prepared a summary report on the success of conversion from the beginning of the recruitment of the cantonists until 1839.[6] The charts that appear in this report show that 5,000 Jews were drafted in the years 1838–1839, out of whom about 1,400 converted—less than thirty percent.[7] The extent of conversion was not uniform in the different battalions. The peak was in the Perm' battalion, where 132 minors out of 136 recruits converted, while in the Kazan' battalion only 105 out of almost 1,000 Jews converted. On estimating the relevance of the data, it must be admitted that the differences between the units were so great that it is impossible to use this data other than for more intensive research. It seems that inaccurate figures were added to this chart by the reporters themselves, or that they came from different periods.

Many factors influenced the results of conversion: the time, the location, and more.[8] Nevertheless, the sum total of the results of the conversion policy presented to Nicholas I reflects the general situation: out of 15,050 minors drafted in the years 1827–1840, only 5,328 converted. Nicholas must have been surprised by the percentage of conversions. Petrovsky-Shtern emphasizes the tsar's personal involvement in the pursuit of Jewish souls. He personally examined the extent of the conversions, as seen in the corrections he made in pencil on the commanders' reports that have been preserved to this day.[9]

---

4 Petrovsky-Shtern, *Jews in the Russian Army*, 122.
5 As shown above, according to the accepted standard for conversion, the candidate, not necessarily Jewish, was supposed to go through a preparation process organized by civil bodies.
6 Ibid., charts 3.2. and 3.3, p. 123.
7 Rossiiskii gosudarstvennyi voenno-istoricheskii arkhiv [Russian state archive of military history], f. 405, op. 5, d. 3771, ll. 3–4.
8 For a detailed list of factors see above, part IV, ch. 12.
9 Petrovsky-Shtern, *Jews in the Russian Army*, 131.

Petrovsky-Shtern notes that in 1844, after seventeen years of its existence, the conversion program was reasonably integrated in the Russian army. From then on, there is a steady stream of reports on the progress of conversion, and the number of converts increased somewhat. According to Petrovsky-Shtern's theory this serves as proof that the conscription of Jewish minors was not intended, from the outset, for purposes of conversion.[10] However, he contradicts himself: "There were objective reasons for Nicholas's policy not being implemented. On the one hand, the clumsiness of the military mechanism, and on the other hand, the passive resistance of the Jews."

Among the most significant factors that hindered the execution of the tsar's malicious idea was, as noted above,[11] the influence of Jewish soldiers who served in the areas where the cantonists were directed. According to Petrovsky-Shtern,[12] Lieutenant Colonel Videnov, commander of the Kazan' brigade where 1,500 Jewish minors were held, reported to the Military Settlement Section[13] explaining the reason for his failure:[14] "Regular Jewish soldiers [adults] insist on not converting. They thus strengthen the spirit of the Jewish boys, with whom, by virtue of their duty, they are in daily contact." Through the efforts of Lieutenant Colonel Videnov, about eighteen Jewish soldiers who had an influence on the youth were transferred to another unit. The commander of the battalion in Revel' reported similarly, that the commander, Major-General Patkul' (probably of German-Baltic origin), allowed cantonists to go to the city's central synagogue for prayers, "where the rabbis persuade them not to convert."

Additional details appear in the book that verify my assumption as to the continuous contact between the cantonists and their parents,[15] despite bureaucratic obstacles, difficulties of traveling outside the Pale of Settlement, and distances of thousands of kilometers. Among other things, the children received money from their parents and even went home on vacation.[16] The commander of the battalion in Novgorod testified: "I heard from the Jews themselves, that the

---

10 Ibid., 134.
11 Ibid., part 2, "Social Aspects."
12 Ibid., 135
13 The cantonists served, among other things, as settlers of new areas, and were therefore subject to this department.
14 Report of June 6, 1845 in Rossiiskii gosudarstvennyi voenno-istoricheskii arkhiv [Russian state archive of military history], f. 109, 1 eksp., d. 231, ll. 22–27.
15 Petrovsky-Shtern, *Jews in the Russian Army*, 135.
16 Rossiiskii gosudarstvennyi voenno-istoricheskii arkhiv [Russian state archive of military history], f. 324, op. 1, d. 1318, ll. 130–140.

moment they convert, they lose all contact with their family and do not receive any financial support. This prevents them from converting."[17]

Shortly before the abolishment of the cantonist decree and the coronation of Alexander II, the number of cases of mass refusal to observe the tenets of Christianity on the part of boys forced to convert, increased. I wrote extensively about the revolt of the Arkhangel'sk half-battalion. Petrovsky-Shtern's presents additional evidence of boys who refuted Christianity after having been forcibly converted. Thirty-seven converts who were brought to Moscow in 1858 refused to remain Christians. Forty-four converted boys brought to serve in the port of Odesa in 1858 acted similarly. In 1859, thirty-two Jewish boys who had been forcibly converted in the Kyiv battalion submitted a complaint on the matter to Count Frederiks, the commander of the military force of Kyiv. There were dozens of cases of individuals and small groups who refuted the tsarist integration methods.

Nevertheless, I must note that only when I received Petrovsky-Shtern's book I realized that there are significant differences in our points of view. His chapter on the cantonists opens with an over-decisive statement: "There is a need to take a different look at the incredible effort at integrating Jewish children in the Russian army."[18] Throughout his study, Petrovsky-Shtern attempts to prove that the conscription of Jewish minors was intended for the benefit of integrating the Jews into the Russian Empire. One understands from his words that the children's suffering had no specific antisemitic nature, and was not purposely intended to bring them to conversion.

I am unable to accept this trend of thought. One cannot erase the antisemitic nature from any plan developed by the tsarist regime from in regard to the Jewish people. It is true that the government's intention was integrating all the various population groups in the Russian Empire, but the degree of cruelty, violence, and hatred toward the Jews was a determining element in the implementation of every plan. All in all, the tsar and his ministers aspired to wipe out the Jewish people by means of conversion, either intending physical annihilation or total assimilation. In contrast to other nations that populated the empire, from the tsar's point of view, the Jews were "parasites," whom he hated intensely.

Nicholas I's activity greatly harmed the children, the families, and the whole Jewish people in general. The tsar was well-educated and was very familiar with ideas of humanitarianism and tolerance. He knew what he was going to do, and no concept, such as "progress" or "integration," can justify his cruel, inhumane deeds.

---

17 Petrovsky-Shtern, *Jews in the Russian Army*, 135.
18 Ibid., 113.

Index

Abeli, Avraham, Rabbi, 88
Abraham, 25
Abramov, 162
Abuhav, Yitzḥak, Rabbi, 79
Afanasii, Father, 203, 207, 217
Afonsky, Petr, 198
Aimes, Rabbi, 102
Akhundov, Michael, Rabbi, 132
Aldukhov, Mikhail, Rabbi, 165n14, 174–76
Alexander I, Tzar, 30–31, 33, 35, 41, 43, 53, 56, 59, 84, 168, 269
Alexander II, Tzar, 11, 19, 21, 55, 62, 109, 254, 261, 264–65, 269–70, 273, 294, 303
Amalek, 285
Amsterdam, 88
Annenkov, M.N., General, 16
Antonii, Metropolitan of Novgorod, 164
Arakcheev, A.A., Count, 23, 228, 246, 253
Arkhangel'sk, 17, 19–20, 62, 121, 124, 126, 129, 132, 141, 155–56, 160, 162, 165–66, 169, 177, 182, 187–92, 195–97, 209, 213–14, 225–27, 229–31, 234–35, 237, 239, 241–46, 248–50, 252–55, 257, 264, 271–72, 293, 297, 303
Armenia, 59
Astrakhan', 124, 132, 174–75, 178, 187
Austria, 33, 48

Baḥye, Rabbeinu, 79
Bakhmatov, Soldier, 213
Balahanov, Major-General, 279, 288

Balkin, Officer, 197
Baltic Sea, 33n9, 46, 53, 270
Beilin, Michael, 151, 192, 241, 244, 253
Bekker, Lieutenant Colonel, 101–2, 104
Bila Tserkva, 112
Belarus, 30, 56, 60, 87, 96, 171, 272, 280, 282
Benkendorf, Alexandr von, Count, 46, 56, 100, 102, 167, 210, 278–80, 284, 287–88
Berdychiv (Berdichev), 68, 86, 104, 106–7, 266n2, 287
Berlin, 90
Berliner, Shlomo Herschel, Rabbi, 89
Bershanovsky, 101
Bessarabia, 267
Black Sea, 32, 127
Bludov, D.N., Interior Minister, 45
Bocher, Pavel, 192, 239, 241–43, 247
Bogoliubsky, Priest, 15
Bohuslav, 59, 111
Bonaparte, Napoleon, 37, 50
Breig, A.S., Admiral, 218
Bren, Hirsch Mikhail, 241
Brest (Brest-Litovsk), 51, 52
Britain, 63, 80
Buger, Avraham, Rabbi of Ovruch, 68

Catherine the Great, 190n14
Chabad, 61
Chartoryski, Prince, 31
Chernihiv (Chernigov), 7, 10n11
Chornobyl (Chernobyl), 68
Chernyshev, A., Prince, 55, 61, 70, 186–90, 234, 236–37, 290

Constantin, 67
Courland, 30, 41
Crimean War, 48, 62, 109

Damascus, 88
Danchevsky, 189
Davidov, Peter, 241
Derzhavin, G.R., Senator, 30–33, 41, 58
D'iakonov, Lieutenant Colonel, 18–20, 155, 192, 197, 209, 214, 228, 231, 234–37, 240, 243, 252, 254–55, 293
Dibich, H.C., Count, 76
Dik, I.M., 90
Dillon, Leizer, 59, 83
Dolgin, Major-General, 215
Dolgorukov, Prince, 60, 226, 257
Dometti, A.K., General, 16
Druia, 16
Dubel't, Leontii, Lieutenant Gereral, 70, 226
Dubno, 112
Dubnow (Dubnov), Simon, 1, 68, 147, 299
Dubrovka, 111
Dvinsk, 49
Dvorkin, Peter, 242, 248, 252

Egolin, Nikolai, 226
Eisenberg, Moshe, 272
Elfenbein, Michael, Rabbi, 127
England, 47, 89, 157
Estonia, 124
Ettinger, Shmuel, 82
Europe, 214

Feigin, M.Y., 60
Feiner, Shmuel, 44
Fiedler, Nikolai Hagai, 245
Filaret, Archbishop, 215–16
Finland, 19
Fisher, 245

Fishman-Maimon, Y.L., Rabbi, 92
Fleishfish, Emanuel, 298
France, 33, 59, 63
Frederiks, Count, 303
Friedman, Yisrael, Rabbi, 91
Frizel', Ivan, 32–33, 290
Frumkin, Etya, 171, 283
Fuenn, S., 44

Gatchina, 121
Gazanovsky, 60
Gedravich, Lieutetant, 226, 228
Georgii, Father, 165, 191
Germany, 41
Gessen, 34, 38, 41, 147, 212, 268, 298
Ginzburg (Ginsburg), Shaul, 183, 189, 193, 206, 219, 237, 298
Goihman, Avrum, 101
Goldveiss, Benjamin, 91
Golenishchev-Kutuzov, M., General, 284
Golitsyn, D., Prince, 23, 56, 59, 209, 249
Golman, Officer, 233
Gomel', 230
Gorchakov, Alexander, Prince, 165, 176
Gottlieber, B., 44
Greenblatt, Yaakov, 5–7
Greikopf, Evsei, 194
Grigor'ev, Lieutanant, 213, 257
Grigorii, Father, 162
Grodno, 40, 90, 92, 97, 99
Gulevich, Evgraf, 18, 191, 255
Gur'ev, Minister of Finance, 38

Haim, Rabbi of Volozhin, xvii
Halperin, Y., 213
Hasidism, xix, 42, 45, 148
Haskalah, 29, 44
Ḥatam Sofer, 88, 93, 95–96
Hermanovitz, Yaakov, 23–25, 210
Herzen, Alexander, 21, 23n29, 56, 145, 170
Holland, 46, 89

Iagmanikhin, V., 138, 140
Irkutsk, 12, 23, 94, 119, 162, 187, 204, 210
Israel, 12, 16, 25, 29, 36–37, 88, 92, 104, 121, 127, 191, 202, 210, 212–13, 272, 298–99
Israelovitz, Wolf, 241
Itzkovitz, Israel, 16–17, 20–21, 100, 104, 121, 144, 156–57, 160, 170, 191–92, 212–14, 242, 244–45, 247–48, 254–56, 272, 297

Jerusalem, 88, 217
Jesus, 8, 11, 15, 18, 24, 192, 204, 217, 271, 289
Judaism, xix, 19, 37, 49–50, 59, 79, 118–19, 169, 181, 193, 197, 204–5, 211, 213, 242–43, 248, 251, 253–55, 257, 271–72, 278, 293

Kagan, Yisrael Meir, Rabbi, 157
Kamianets-Podilskyi, 90
Kankrin, Georg, Count, 39–40, 46, 53, 186
Kapilov, Igor', 241, 248
Kapilovsky, Aharon, 226, 243–44, 247, 249, 253
Karlin, 93
Katovich, Vasilii, Priest 61, 183–84, 188–89
Katovits, Priest, 162
Katz, Petr, 243–44
Katzman, Ivan, 272
Kaufman, Vladimir, 194
Kaunas (Kovno), 97, 99
Kazan', 22, 124, 187–88, 194, 215–16, 237, 255, 272, 293, 301–2
Keren (Kern), Major-General, 171–72, 282–83
Kherson, 68, 287

Kyiv (Kiev), 6–7, 11, 51, 97, 99, 101–2, 118, 148–49, 161, 187–88, 212, 215–16, 230, 300, 303
Kiselev, Pavel, Count, 46, 52, 55, 57, 60–62, 186, 268–70, 290, 294
Kleinmikhel', P.A., Count, 46, 54, 185
Klinger, Berel (Berko), 140, 144–45, 152–54, 156–60, 164, 168–69, 178, 204, 212, 214, 297
Kochubei, V.P., Count, 31, 42
Kolotushkin, Stepan, 246
Koltovsky, Lieutanant, 215
Kopilovsky, Igor', 233
Korobkov, Kh., 99, 149
Kotler, Gregory, 241
Krabbe, Nikolai, 226, 231
Krasnoiarsk, 187–88
Kronshtadt, 85, 93, 113, 124, 127, 132, 173, 196, 227–28, 231, 233, 235, 238–40, 246, 248–49, 256, 271, 284
Krynky, 41
Kutnevich, I.K., Priest, 176, 204–6, 239, 250, 277

Lansky, V.S., Minister of Interior, 70, 76
Latvia, 30
Lebensohn, Avraham Dov, 44
Lehren, Y.M., Banker, 88–89
Leiman, N.M., Major-General, 236
Leskov, Nikolai, 148
Levine, Y.L., 146–47
Levinson, Y.B., 60
Lilienthal, Max, 37, 42–43, 61, 290
Lipkin, Israel, Rabbi, 92
Lipschitz, Mordechai, Rabbi, 32, 67, 171, 283
Lithuania, 1, 6, 16, 32, 60, 83, 87, 90, 147–48, 161, 167, 286
Loginov, Officer, 198
London, 21

Lorberbaum, Yaakov, Rabbi, 93
Lovnovsky, Lieutenant, 230
Lubinovsky, Colonel, 236
Lugovsky, 230

Mahler, Raphael, 45, 146
Malamud, Artemii, 189, 197, 233, 239, 241, 245, 247–49, 251, 253
Malorossiia, 36
Markovits-Zirkevich, Ivan, 167
Medved, 164
Medzhybizh, 83
Men'shikov, A., Prince, 130
Merder, K.K., General, 168, 278–80
Merimzon, Chaim, 1, 4, 8, 11nn13–13, 21, 143–45, 147–48, 150, 154, 156, 158, 160–61, 164, 166, 169–70, 183, 193, 199, 213, 252, 292, 297–98
Metternich, K., Foreign Minister, 63
Mil, Samuel, 19–20, 241, 247–48, 254
Minsk, 83, 86, 93, 97, 99, 147, 168, 281, 285
Mirkovich, Alexandr, 51
Mogilev, 85, 87, 96–97, 111, 168, 171–72, 282–83, 285
Montefiore, Moses, 33, 61, 103, 290
Mordvinov, Admiral, 49
Morgenstern, Aryeh, 88, 298
Moscow, 11, 13, 19–20, 23, 137, 140, 145, 272, 299–301, 303
Movshovits, Andrei, 244
Mstislaw (Mstislavl), 61, 86, 104–6
Musin-Pushkin, A.I., Count, Kammerjunker, 215–16
Muslims, 289
Mykolaiv (Nikolaev), 287

Nahman of Breslov, Rabbi, xvii
Novogrudok (Navahrudak), 150, 187
Nazarov, Nikolai, 184n7, 242, 252
Nesterov, Grigorii, 246
Nesvizhsky, Kupriian, 247–48

Netherlands, 89
Netziv of Volozhin, 90
Nevachovich, Leib (Nevakhovich, Leiba), 31, 42
Nicholas I, 17, 19, 23, 33, 35, 37–38, 41–42, 44–52, 54–57, 59–63, 67, 70, 84–85, 89, 93–94, 105, 107–111, 116, 119, 121–22, 125, 127, 129, 132, 138–39, 146, 152, 176–77, 181, 183, 186, 189, 200, 208–211, 214, 220, 230, 236–37, 264–65, 268–69, 270n7, 273, 278, 289–94, 301–3
Nikolinko, N.M., Major-General, 130
Nil, Archbishop, 162, 202
Nizhnii Novgorod, 13, 255
Notkin (Shklover), Nota, 31–33, 42, 59
Nova Ushytsia, 90
Novgorod, 118, 164, 173, 302
Novorossiia, 33, 39, 55
Novosel'tsev, Senator, 40, 67, 85

Ochsman, Y., 90
Odesa (Odessa), 51, 303
Ognisty, Itzko, 83
Olshansky, Aaron, 182, 213
Olshovsky, Nikolai, 245
Omsk, 187, 204
Orenburg, 187–88
Orin, Officer, 233, 238, 245, 250, 252
Orlov, G.G., Count 122
Oshorovitz, Berko, Soldier, 245, 248, 251–52
Ososov, Mikhail, 238

Panin, V.N., Minister of Justice, 49
Paris, 53
Passover, 69, 94, 130–31, 171–72, 280–84, 297
Pasvalys, 286
Patkul', A.V., Major-General, 302
Paul I, 294
Perets, Abram, 31, 42, 59

Peretz, Andrei, 241, 247–48
Perm', 20–22, 187, 189–90, 198, 203, 205, 208, 217, 230, 231n8, 232, 236, 264, 271, 301
Persia, 59
Pesach, 285
Peseles, Rabbi Aryeh Leib, 88
Peter the Great, 137
Petrovsky-Shtern, Yohanan, 300–3
Petukhov, Father, 24, 210
Pfeifer, Abraham, 240, 245, 248–49, 251
Podelo, 42
Podillia, 31n4, 97, 99
Poland, 7, 29, 34, 58, 63, 67, 90, 104–5, 120, 264
Polotsk, 16, 272
Popov, Vasilii, Senator, 33
Potemkin, Grigory, Prince, 190, 190n14
Pototsky, G.A., Count, 31
Prohorovkin, Herzl, 91
Protasov, Nikolas, Count, 55–56, 61, 174, 176–78, 183, 186, 188–91, 200, 203, 205–6, 208, 290–91
Prussia, 46–47
Przhetslavskii, Osip (Przecławski, Józef Emanuel), 67
Pskov, 23, 164, 187, 280
Pushkin, Alexander, 56
Putinsky, Soldier, 218

Rabinowitz, Michael, Rabbi, 284
Radin, 90
Rafael', Father, 164
Rapaport, Isaac, Rabbi, 68, 287
Razumnyi, Moshko, 127
Rebinder, A.M., Brigadier General, 169, 174–76, 203, 256n4, 279–80, 288
Rein, Kupriian, 242
Riess, B.A., 285
Revel', 124, 173, 187, 204, 302
Riess, Aharon, 285
Riga, 168, 173n5, 278, 285

Rimkovitch, Captain, 102
Romanov family, 46–47
Romm, E., 93, 127
Rosen, G.A. von, Cavalry General, 286
Rosh Hashana, 13–14, 93
Rossman, Moshe, 83
Rothchild, Nathan, 89
Rothenberg, Shmuel, 244
Rotstein, 146
Roznov, Petr, 284

Sabbath, 77, 89, 94, 129, 131, 150, 157, 175, 229, 278, 281, 285–86, 292
Sadigura Rebbe – Rabbi Israel Friedman, 91
Salanter, Yisrael, Rabbi, 62, 92
Samara, 215
Samoilov, Captain, 257
Samsonkin, Yitzchak, 61, 111
Samter, N., 219
Sandberg, 42
Sandykov, 256
Saratov, 57, 163, 185, 187–90, 200, 217, 219, 293
Schneersohn, Sh.Z., Rabbi, 54, 61
Schwartzman, Sh., 90
Serivrikov, Sergeant, 233
Sevastopol (Sevastopol'), 62, 127
Shabbat, 1–6, 12, 95, 156
Shardinsky, Pavel, 238
Shargorod, 111
Shick, Eliyahu, Rabbi, 90, 92
Shimon, son of Shmuel Bender, 278
Shklov, 87, 127
Shklover, 31–32, 42
Shneershon, Sh.Z., Rabbi, 54, 61
Shpungin, S., 171, 283
Shwartzman, Sh., 90
Siberia, 12, 14, 16, 19–20, 23, 36, 144, 163, 165, 167, 184, 210–11
Sidorov, Matvei, 248
Simbirsk, 167, 187, 209

Sindikov, 141, 169
Skvira, 101
Smargard, Father, 174–75
Smerkin, Berko, 124
Smirnov, Simon, Priest, 209, 215
Smolensk, 93–94, 144, 168–69, 171–72, 198, 203, 256n4, 279–80, 282–83, 285–86, 288
Sofronov, 189
Sokolovsky, Lieutenant, 229
Solov'ev, Sergei, 54
Solov'ev, Major-General, 229, 238
Solov'ev, Lieutenant Colonel, 226
Sonnenberg, Zundel, 83
Spain, 242, 257
Speransky, Count, 31, 46
Spiegel, Moisy, 12, 17n22, 143–45, 147, 154, 158n35, 159, 162, 170, 184, 191, 204, 211–13, 298
St. Petersburg, 17, 19, 31, 41, 53, 62, 67–68, 113, 120, 130, 132, 139, 155, 165, 173, 177, 204, 225–28, 231, 237, 243–44, 246, 251, 253–55, 272, 278, 284, 287, 290
Stampfer, Shaul, 300
Stanislawski, Michael, 68, 82, 92, 97–98, 99n5, 109, 182, 184, 221, 298
Starokostiantyniv, 88, 90
Staroslasky, Yetzke, 171, 283
Stern, B., 44
Strashun, Avraham, Rabbi, 88
Sukkot, 93, 150
Suvalki, 1, 6, 147
Suvorov, A., Prince, 270
Sveaborg, Rabbi of, 127
Sychevka, 190, 198

Tallinn, 124
Talmud, 41–43, 57, 60, 90, 181, 205, 290
Taurida kingdom, 267
Tcherikover, E., 44, 90
Terent'ev, 49, 141, 169, 197, 254–56, 271, 293n2

Tolstoi, Count, 286–87
Tomsk, 20, 185, 187–188, 203
Treager, L.S., 278
Troitsk, 187
Tsaritsyn, 163
Tsiprinus, 32, 67
Turchin, M.R., 10–11, 278
Turkey, 55, 268
Tzam, Herzl, 182, 213

Ukraine, 13, 55, 68, 82–83, 104, 148
Ul'ianovsk, 167
Uman, 101
United States, 300
Ural, 143–44
Ural'sk, 144, 185, 187
Uvarov, Sergey, Count, 37, 43, 46, 52–54, 56, 60–62, 185–86, 190, 290

Vachin, Colonel, 280–81
Vax, Alexander, 196, 239, 241, 247–49, 251, 253
Velizh, 49, 60
Viatka, 145
Victoria, Queen, 47, 80, 184
Videnov, Lieutenant Colonel, 302
Vilkaviškis, 1
Vilkomir, 90
Vilkovishki, 1, 147
Vilna (Vilnius), xvii, 44, 49, 51, 85, 88–90, 97, 99, 149, 168, 198, 278, 285–86
Vinokurov, Major, 172, 280, 283–84
Vitebsk, 16, 85, 99, 111, 168, 171n2, 173n5, 175n14, 278, 280–82, 297
Vitiuk, Ian, Officer, 245
Vladimir, Father, 163–64, 174, 191, 200
Vole, 41
Volga, 13, 57, 166, 174, 194, 216–17
Volgograd, 163
Volhynia, 12, 93, 97, 99, 101–4, 112, 122, 287
Volodymyr, 112
Volozhin, xvii, 54, 61, 90, 126

Voltaire, 35
Voronezh, 187–88, 190
Vorontsov, M.S., Count, 33, 39, 55, 290

Warsaw, 51
Weill, Lewis, 56, 186
Wolf, Shaul, Rabbi, 284
Wolfovich, Marcus, Rabbi, 127

Yankelevitch, Wolff (Iakov), 244
Yosef of Pollonye, Ya'akov, Rabbi, 82
Yosefovitz, Hirsh, 242

Zalman of Liadi, Shneur, Rabbi, xvii
Zandberg, Z., Jewish Deputy, 59
Zaslavsky, 12
Zbrok, Faivish, 245
Zeidel, T., 143
Zelich, S.A., 285
Zhytomyr (Zhitomir), 13, 122
Zionism, xvii
Zuckerman, Nosson (Nathan), 119
Zuss, Eliya, 233
Zvenigorod, 101–102

www.ingramcontent.com/pod-product-compliance
Lightning Source LLC
Chambersburg PA
CBHW052057300426
44117CB00013B/2162